Robert E. Lee

AT THIRTY-ONE

ROBERT·E·LEE

A Portrait

1807–1861

". . . and they shall turn their swords into ploughshares
and their spears into sickles."
—ISAIAS 2:4

*The War Years and Reconstruction will be covered in
ROBERT E. LEE : The Complete Man, 1861 - 1871,
which is now in preparation.*

ROBERT·E·LEE

A PORTRAIT

[1807 ∗ 1861]

by Margaret Sanborn

J. B. LIPPINCOTT COMPANY

Philadelphia & New York

FOR

DAVID, CATHERINE, *and* STEPHEN

that they may always find inspiration

in the example of Robert E. Lee

Acknowledgments

I AM deeply indebted to Mrs. William Hunter deButts and her sister, the late Mrs. Hanson E. Ely, Jr., granddaughters of Robert E. Lee, for permission to study, and quote from, the microfilm of the important R. E. Lee Papers in The Library of Congress. Mrs. deButts also gave permission to read and quote from R. E. Lee's three Memoranda Books in these same archives, and to quote from Lee's letters to Andrew and Harriet Talcott, to John, Eliza, and Margaret Mackay, to Martha Custis Williams, to Margaret and Caroline Stuart, to Jefferson Davis, to James A. Seddon, to John C. Breckinridge, and to J. E. B. Stuart. I am further grateful for Mrs. deButts' ever-courteous responses to many questions.

During the five years of production, I have been frequently sustained by Burke Davis' unwavering faith in this project and his encouragement. I have profited from his critical reading of the manuscript, his perception, and his advice.

Stewart Richardson, of J. B. Lippincott, has never wavered either in his belief that Robert E. Lee the *man* existed, and has counseled and encouraged me with unfailing warmth and thoughtfulness.

Miss Carolyn Blakemore has been a most discerning and sympathetic editor, and a thoroughly delightful person to work with. The book has benefited from her sound judgment.

Over the years, Mrs. Lilla Mills Hawes, Director of the Georgia Historical Society, has been tireless in furnishing prompt and exhaustive written replies to countless questions. With remarkable resourcefulness, she discovered for me little-known and unusual references to R. E. Lee during his many stays in Savannah. I am further grateful for the time she spent in driving me to all places connected with Lee in and around Savannah, and for granting permission to quote from the important material in the Society's collection. Thanks is also due the Colonial Dames of America, Georgia Branch, for permission to quote from copies of the R. E. Lee–Mackay Family letters in their collection, housed in the Georgia Historical Society.

I am also deeply grateful to the following people:

Charles F. Mills of Atherton, California, a great-grandson of Eliza Mackay, for generously giving his time to answer questions concerning Lee's relations with his family, and for supplying copies of all R. E. Lee–Mackay Family letters in his collection, as well as permission to quote from them.

Joseph M. O'Donnell, Chief, Archives and History Section, The United States Military Academy, for painstaking answers to many questions over the years, for providing copies of Lee letters, for his resourcefulness in discovering Mrs. D'Ormieulx's charming "Recollections of West Point in 1853," and for giving permission to quote from it.

Dr. Fred C. Cole, President of Washington and Lee University, for generously giving his time to answer questions and to supply information and pictures. Gene B. Hansley, former Assistant Director of the University's Information Services, for the pains he took to find unusual information. Dr. Ollinger Crenshaw, of the History Department, for supplying much of this material and checking the remainder. Dr. Allen W. Moger, also of the History Department, for permission to quote from R. E. Lee's letters to Jerome Bonaparte and his wife; and Frank A. Parsons, Assistant to the President, for many courtesies.

Admiral Irving T. Duke, Resident Superintendent of Stratford Hall, for answering countless questions by letter; for suggesting sources, providing copies of early Lee inventories; for pictures, and for granting permission to quote from the Gen. Henry Lee Letters in the Robert E. Lee Memorial Foundation, Inc., collection.

Ralston B. Lattimore, Superintendent of Fort Pulaski National Monument, for courteously answering questions by letter; for generously supplying copies of all R. E. Lee–Mackay Family letters in the Fort's collection of originals, and for sharing his own interesting manuscript letter from R. E. Lee to John Mackay.

ACKNOWLEDGMENTS

Lucius S. Ruder of Clearwater, Florida, for also graciously sharing his important manuscript R. E. Lee letter to John Mackay.

Miss Janet Fauntleroy Taylor, of Norfolk, Virginia, a granddaughter of Col. Walter H. Taylor, for her many favors and the warmth of her responses to queries, for providing a picture of her grandfather, and for granting permission to quote from his letters and books.

David C. Mearns, Chief, Manuscript Division, The Library of Congress, for his kindness and cooperation; and Mr. de Porry and the staff of the Manuscript Reading Room, for their interest and help.

Miss Elizabeth J. Dance, Librarian, The Valentine Museum, Richmond, for her interest and help while I was at work in the library, and for patiently answering questions by letter. She also granted permission to quote from Edward V. Valentine's notebook-journal. Miss Lydia Booth Sarvay, of the Museum's staff, for her interest and many favors.

Miss Elizabeth Tindall, former Reference Librarian, Missouri Historical Society, and Mrs. Frances Stadler, Manuscript Librarian for the Society, for many courtesies, and for granting permission to quote both the manuscript and printed R. E. Lee–Henry Kayser letters.

Marshall Gray, Technical Liaison Branch, U. S. Army Engineer Corps, St. Louis, for helpful information about R. E. Lee's work on the Mississippi River.

William J. Van Schreeven, State Archivist, Virginia State Library, for valuable suggestions as to new sources, and permission to quote from the C. C. Lee Papers and from letters from R. E. Lee to Jefferson Davis. Milton C. Russell, Head, Reference and Circulation Section, for promptly and courteously answering so many questions.

Howson W. Cole, Curator of Manuscripts, Virginia Historical Society, for his courtesy and help, and for granting permission to quote from the letters of R. E. Lee to Andrew and Harriet Talcott and to Jefferson Davis.

Mrs. George Bolling Lee of San Francisco, for graciously permitting the use of seven portraits in her collection.

George R. Talcott of Richmond, for his kind permission to use the portrait of Harriet Randolph Talcott.

Dr. Ives Hendrick of Boston, for granting permission to quote from the letter of Samuel Appleton Storrow to his sister, printed in his father's outstanding work, *The Lees of Virginia*, by Burton J. Hendrick.

Mrs. Henry W. Howell, Jr., Librarian, Miss Helen Sanger, Research Librarian, and Miss Mildred Steinbach, Assistant Librarian, all of the Frick Art Reference Library, for their never-failing courtesy and help.

Mrs. Virginia R. Gray, Manuscript Department, Duke University Library, who gave such splendid service in providing copies of R. E. Lee's personal letters, and wartime dispatches and letters. B. E. Powell, Librarian, for granting permission to quote from this material.

Dr. Hugh F. Rankin and Dr. Charles P. Roland, Tulane University, for their interest and help, and Mrs. Connie G. Griffith, Director, Manuscripts Division, Tulane University Library, for her thoughtfulness and aid, and for granting permission to quote from R. E. Lee's letters to Albert Sidney Johnston in the Mrs. Mason Barret Collection.

Herbert Cahoon, Curator of Manuscripts, The Pierpont Morgan Library, New York, for his courtesy and help. Frederick B. Adams, Jr., Director of the Library, for permission to quote from the original R. E. Lee–Martha Custis Williams letters in these archives.

Dr. James J. Heslin, Director, New York Historical Society, for many courtesies.

Miss Eleanor S. Brockenbrough, Assistant Director, Confederate Literary Society, Richmond, for many favors so courteously rendered, and for permission to quote from the letters of Mrs. R. E. Lee to Mrs. Robert H. Chilton.

Mrs. Margaret Moore, Curator of the Lee House, Richmond, for her gracious hospitality.

Mrs. Virginia H. Pinkerton, Norfolk Public Library, for enduring many questions, and for the loan of valuable books.

Mrs. Nancy C. English, Huntington Library Publications, for permission to quote from *"To Markie": The Letters of*

Robert E. Lee to Martha Custis Williams, edited by Avery Craven (Harvard University Press, 1933), and from "To Molly: Five Early Letters from Robert E. Lee to his Wife," by Norma B. Cuthbert, *Huntington Library Quarterly*, May, 1952.

Robert O. Dougan, Librarian, Henry E. Huntington Library and Art Gallery, for his courtesy.

Mrs. Dorothy Thomas, Librarian, Mill Valley Public Library, and staff, for their cooperation. A special note of thanks is due Miss Constance Karla, whose task it was to order and handle the mass of interlibrary loan material; this she did with unfailing cheerfulness and admirable efficiency.

Irenaeus N. Tucker, M.D., who devoted time and thought to the case histories of the mother and wife of R. E. Lee, offering as definite an opinion as is possible to make from the scant information.

Eugene Pike, Reference Section Librarian, The California State Library, and his staff, for responding fully and promptly to all questions concerning sources, and sending countless volumes through interlibrary loan.

I am grateful to Charles Scribner's Sons for permission to quote from *Letters from Lee's Army*, edited by Charles Minor Blackford III (New York, 1947); and from *War Years with Jeb Stuart* by William W. Blackford (New York, 1945); to The Bobbs-Merrill Co. for permission to quote from a letter of Dr. May to Cassius Lee, printed in *Lee of Virginia* by William E. Brooks, copyright 1932 by The Bobbs-Merrill Co., R. 1958 by William E. Brooks, reprinted by permission of the publisher; to Putnam's & Coward-McCann for permission to quote from *Lee's Dispatches: Unpublished Letters of Gen. Robert E. Lee, C.S.A., to Jefferson Davis and the War Department of the Confederate States of America, 1861–1865*, edited by Douglas Southall Freeman (New York, 1957); to Mrs. Douglas Southall Freeman for permission to quote from "Lee and the Ladies" by Douglas Southall Freeman, *Scribner's Magazine*, October, 1925; to The University of North Carolina Press for permission to quote from Henry Kyd Douglas, *I Rode With Stonewall* (Chapel Hill, 1940); and to Houghton Mifflin for permission to quote from Mary Boykin Chesnut, *A Diary from Dixie*, edited by Ben Ames Williams (Boston, 1949).

Last, but by no means least, I want to thank my family for their enduring patience and their encouragement.

Margaret Sanborn

Mill Valley, California
June 30, 1966

Contents

ILLUSTRATIONS

(following page 178)

➤➤➤ I ◄◄◄

Beginnings

1721 ★ 1813

I. Beginnings

Toward the east, Virginia stretches out to meet the Potomac River. It is a region of grassy fields and dense woodlands where in spring and summer blue-eyed grass and cowslips carpet the meadows, and quakermaids crowd roadside and ditch. Autumn finds these meadows spangled with asters and gentians, and the forests scarlet, crimson, and yellow of every hue. In winter the countryside sparkles with hoarfrost, the wind blows cold from the east, and the ponds and small streams freeze over.

On this beautiful coastal plain, in the County of Westmoreland, a broad knoll rises above field, river, and wooded ravine. On the crest of this knoll stands a great brick house, Stratford Hall. Here, in the high-ceilinged southeast bedroom where three generations of Lees had been born, among them two signers of the Declaration of Independence, Ann Carter Lee, second wife of General Henry ("Light-Horse Harry") Lee, gave birth on January 19, 1807, to her fifth child. It was another "little black-eyed brown Boy, very healthy, good-tempered, lively . . . and sweet." She named him Robert Edward in honor of two favorite brothers.

Mrs. Lee's labor was complicated by a heavy chest cold, caught while driving in an open carriage in the midst of winter, and by depression of mind. Directly following the birth she lapsed into a coma, which gave rise to the macabre tale that she had died that bleak January day, and that Robert Edward was delivered as she was being prepared for the grave.

During the entire nine months that she had carried Robert, Ann Carter Lee was sick, grieving, and oppressed by a sense of hopelessness and gathering defeat. By then Light-Horse Harry's overwhelming debts had robbed life of its smallest comforts, and bankruptcy and debtor's prison loomed large. The big old house was bare and cheerless, its finest furnishings sold to raise cash. Only the east wing was livable. With his old

3

enemy Thomas Jefferson in the Presidency, Harry's promising political career was at an end.

During these days of increasing wretchedness, when Ann Carter Lee awaited the coming of this unwanted child, she sat huddled with her other children about a charcoal brazier in one corner of the gloomy Great Hall, teaching them verses, while Harry rode about the country trying to untangle the snarl of his finances but becoming more entangled in his efforts.

In 1770, when Harry Lee was fourteen, he entered Princeton College, where he received high honors for his outstanding scholarship. Three years later he stood "stiff in lace, gold lace" in an overcrowded church in New Jersey to receive his diploma. At the time, it was predicted that he would one day be among "the first fellows of this country," since he was "more than strict in his morality, has fine genius, and is diligent."

He had chosen law as a career, but America's differences with England, and the threat of war, kept him from studying in London's Inner Temple, under the watchful eye of his mother's brother, Beilby Porteus, Bishop of London. With the start of hostilities, he secured a captain's commission from Virginia's Governor Patrick Henry and rode off from his father's home, Leesylvania, in Prince William County, to join his cousin Theodoric Bland's company of Light Dragoons.

Lee's ingenuity and daring very shortly earned him the sobriquet of "Light-Horse Harry" and an independent command of partisan troops known as "Lee's Legion." With this body of soldiers he was responsible for some of the most brilliant strategic moves of the war and gained the reputation of having contributed more than any officer to its success. He possessed the complete confidence of General Washington and earned the privilege of sending dispatches to him personally, while General Lafayette, in admiration of his exploits, swore eternal friendship to him.

Therefore, in 1781, when Cornwallis surrendered at Yorktown, no other young officer in the Revolutionary Army had brighter prospects than twenty-five-year-old Major Harry Lee. With the surrender, the big battles were over but the fighting had to continue until the last British garrison had been driven out. And until General Washington could decide which troops to send to South Carolina, where the war would be continued for two years longer, he granted Harry leave to stay in Virginia and await further orders.

Almost seven years had passed since the day he had ridden his blooded stallion off to war, carrying in his baggage, among ruffled shirts, a silver flagon and drinking cups, to quench his thirst on the field. In the role of conquering hero he now made the rounds of the manor houses, visiting kindred and friends. The laurels were still fresh on his brow, and on his breast he wore a gold medal presented by a grateful Congress in recognition of his daring capture of the British redoubt at Paulus Hook.

When he called at Stratford Hall, the estate of his cousin, Philip Ludwell Lee, he found Philip's daughter, Matilda, no longer the pretty little girl he had last seen, but a reigning belle, distinguished as "the Divine Matilda." Harry quickly succumbed to her fascination, and before his leave was up, he had secured her promise to marry him.

Though Lee possessed an engaging charm and an impulsive warmth and generosity which, combined with his brilliance and eloquence, made him irresistible, he was also highly sensitive and proud, and given to expansive dreams wherein he saw himself the hero. When these dreams vanished, he blamed others, in his anger and bitterness often suspecting his most loyal friends of contriving against him.

In such a mood of gloom he returned to the Legion after his furlough and joined General Nathanael Greene in South Carolina. Not only was he fretting at separation from Matilda, but he was gnawed by a growing discontent with the army. As he had stood at Yorktown watching the surrender, he knew that the brightest days of his military career were behind him and felt dissatisfaction at having failed to win promotion and more honors. When he reflected upon his service to his country, he became convinced that his failure to gain higher rank was due entirely to the envy and conniving of his fellow officers, carrying this obsession so far as to suspect his devoted friend and admirer, General Greene, of slighting him.

In this humor he wrote Greene in January, 1782, asking

5

permission to resign. "Disquietude of mind & infirmity of body" were the reasons he gave.

The first arises from the indifference with which my efforts to advance the cause of my country is considered by my friends, the persecution of my foes & the consciousness that it is not in my power to efface the disagreeable impression. . . . However disgusted I am with human nature, I wish, from motives of self, to make my way easy and comfortable. This, if ever obtainable, is to be got only in some obscure retreat.

Two days later, Greene replied: "There is no inconvenience I would not submit to, to oblige you, no length I would not go to serve you in the line of truth and honour. But I wish you would not think of leaving the service. Everybody knows I have the highest opinion of you as an officer and you know I love you as a friend." He concluded his letter with an appeal to Lee's vanity: "I believe few officers in America or Europe are held in higher estimation."

Convinced by the sincerity of Greene's words that his suspicions were baseless, Harry replied humbly: "I am candid to acknowledge my imbecility of mind. I hope time & absence will alter my feelings. At present my fervent wish is for the most hidden obscurity; I want not public or private applause . . . my attachment to you will end only with my life."

Greene was reluctant to lose his valuable lieutenant, and made a final attempt to dissuade him. He thoroughly understood Lee's character, and closed his letter with prophetic words:

"You are going home and you will get married, but you cannot cease to be a soldier."

For the first year after his marriage to Matilda, Harry Lee was content with the life of a country squire in his "obscure retreat" at Stratford Hall, for that great house of eighteen rooms, with its vast acreage, its fine cattle and thoroughbreds, its mill, fisheries, and allied estates, had become his wife's inheritance on the death of her father and her mother's remarriage.

6

Thomas Lee, a brother of Harry's great-grandfather, had started building Stratford Hall around 1721, choosing for its site a broad knoll which commanded a fine view of the Potomac River, yet was far enough away to be safe from pirates and Indians, and from the fevers which attacked shore-dwellers. While in London, he had bought the land from Nathaniel Pope, a great-great-grandfather of George Washington. As was the custom, when the sale was closed, the Popes called on Lee to present him ceremoniously with a symbolic twig and handful of earth.

Thomas was interested in arboriculture, and dotted his lawn terraces with horse chestnuts, beeches, magnolias, and lindens, and edged the grove with weeping willows and Lombardy poplars, two trees he introduced to Virginia.

On the river slope he planted an orchard of pear, apple, peach, and cherry trees, for the making of "Cyder" and brandy, and a vineyard for wine. East of the house he set out a formal garden with a tall box maze.

In the woods, just below the apple trees, was a spring which supplied the house with water. This shady glen was to become a favorite summer haunt for young Robert Lee.

But with the signing of the Treaty of Paris, Harry found his interest being drawn into the political arena where the task of setting up a new government was the challenge, and he began to take an active part in politics, riding long distances to attend meetings. On November 15, 1785, by a joint ballot of both houses, he was elected a delegate to Congress, convening in New York, then the Capital.

Since Matilda was unwell, she and her baby, Philip Ludwell, did not join Harry until the following April. But almost the entire summer, at the expense of Lee's duties in Congress, was passed at the Balston Springs and other spas in search of health for Matilda, and when his term ended, he was not re-elected. In his stead, Virginia chose one of Thomas Jefferson's ever-growing band of disciples, James Madison.

Lee's old resentment was aroused at what he considered the ingratitude of his constituents, and he insisted upon renouncing public life and leaving at once for Stratford, even though it was mid-December and Matilda was expecting another child shortly. The journey was made safely, but because of storms it took three weeks to reach Georgetown, rather than the twelve days Harry had optimistically estimated.

But when the Constitution was sent to the states for ratification, Lee was no longer able to remain in his "obscure retreat," and campaigned ardently for acceptance of the document; because of his interest he was chosen a delegate to the Convention in Richmond. Virginia was sharply divided on the issue, Patrick Henry being the eloquent and fiery spokesman for the opposition. It was Harry Lee who rose from his seat in the New Academy on Shockoe Hill, where the Convention met, to reply to Henry, who pleaded his point movingly with his expressive hands and face or ridiculed the cause by provoking laughter when he pushed his frowsy wig askew or removed it to twirl it about foolishly on one long finger. Days were passed in argument, but when the vote was taken, Virginia ratified the Constitution by a slim majority—89 to 79. Harry was overjoyed, and as a delegate to Congress, hurried back to Stratford to persuade Matilda to accompany him to New York, hopeful that the change might benefit her.

Ever since the birth of Philip Ludwell, Matilda had been unwell, but after the coming of her fourth child, little Henry, her decline was marked. She was presently suffering from some ailment which caused her to be "subject to fevers," have "difficulty of breathing, and great debility of body." Lee set aside his other duties to devote his time to her care, taking her to the medicinal springs in the mountains of western Virginia. But Matilda was beyond cure. On June 12, 1790, Harry wrote despondently to George Washington: "My long afflicted Mrs. Lee is now very ill & I fear cannot be preserved." Two months later, while giving birth to her fifth child, she died. Lee was plunged into inconsolable grief and brooded for months over the loss of this girl who had completely captured his heart. Her death, at twenty-six, was a blow from which he never recovered.

When Lee took his seat in the Virginia Assembly late that fall, he found his sentiments for the first time were those of the majority. During the months following the ratification of the Constitution, he had seen the dire prophecies of its adversaries realized and had been willing to change his stand. Already the results of the Northern majority and the hostility of its people toward the South—which Patrick Henry had foreseen—were felt, planting the seeds of antipathy between sections, seeds that would grow rank until the coming of the Civil War. Now that his views were in accord with the majority, Lee became leader of the Lower House, Chairman of the Committee on Propositions and Grievances, and heard himself spoken of frequently as the logical successor to Governor Randolph.

In November, 1791, a committee from the Assembly called to notify Lee of his election to the office of "Chief Magistrate of this Commonwealth," by a majority vote. He replied briefly, expressing gratitude for the honor. From Stratford he brought his three surviving children—Philip Ludwell, Lucy Grymes (named in honor of his mother, who had been one of George Washington's early loves), and Henry—and moved into what was facetiously dubbed "The Palace," a two-story frame makeshift erected for the governor's use, just below the capitol. Its unpaneled rooms were small and few (there were supposedly just four), its furniture plain and sparse, and the grass plot in front subject to the invasion of neighborhood goats.

Harry Lee was a master of spontaneous expression, a talent that served him well in politics. It was long remembered how, seated at a convivial board when the news of Patrick Henry's death reached the party, he had called for paper and pen and "in a few moments had produced a striking and beautiful eulogium upon the 'Demosthenes of modern liberty.'"

"Mourn Virginia mourn," his pen had raced across the page, "say to rising generations—Imitate my Henry. . . ."

Unfortunately, Lee also possessed a mutability that left his public career splashed with brilliant highlights and shadowed by a dullness obviously the result of a mind preoccupied. Soon after his entry into politics he began speculating in fantastic schemes to try to make a fortune. As each bubble burst and he sank deeper into debt, he became frantic to retrieve his losses, and gambled on even more reckless ventures. It was not long

9

until these speculations began to supersede all other thoughts, ultimately becoming an obsession. In 1783, he lost £8,000 in a Mississippi land venture; and when his father died in 1787, Harry's irresponsibility in money matters was so well recognized the senior Lee named a younger son executor. Just before her death, Matilda had insisted upon a deed of trust to secure Stratford and other of her estates for their children.

Now as he undertook the office of governor, he was deeply in debt and distressed by what he described as "the mad policy which seems to direct the doings of Congress." His spirits were still depressed by his recent sorrow, and to divert his "mind in its affliction," he decided to return to the profession for which he now realized he was best fitted—the army. But in his bitterness toward his own country, he considered France, embroiled in her revolution. He wrote his old comrade and admirer, Lafayette, in command of the Northern Department of the French Army, and to Francesco de Miranda, a French War Department official, asking what rank he might expect if he resigned the governorship and offered his services to their country. He heard only from Miranda, who assured him that he would be commissioned a major general, for by the time his letter to Lafayette reached Paris, the Marquis was in disfavor and had fled to Germany.

But further sorrow was in store for Lee: his duties as governor took him into western Virginia, and upon his return to Richmond he found that his favorite child (favored because of a strong resemblance to the Divine Matilda), seven-year-old Philip Ludwell, had died suddenly. This calamity, he confessed to James Madison, stirred him "to the quick" and removed him "far from the happy enjoyment of life."

He would have left for Paris at once if he had been certain about France's ability to wage a long war. As he had always done when in a dilemma, he turned to George Washington for advice. But his old commander gave him no encouragement. He urged Harry to "ponder well . . . not only on private considerations but on public grounds . . . being first magistrate of a respectable State, much speculation would be excited by such a measure." As to France, Washington considered her affairs to be "in the highest paroxysm of disorder . . . those in whose hands the government is entrusted are ready to tear each other to pieces & will more than probably prove the worst foes the country has." Temporarily, Lee abandoned his plan to fight for France, and turned his attention to another matter that he had been considering for some time.

This was a day when neither widows nor widowers remained single for long, and Harry had begun to look for a wife to mother his two small children and, most important, bring him a dower handsome enough to satisfy his most pressing debts. He confessed to Alexander Hamilton that he was "in love with every sweet nymph" he met, "but not so far gone with anyone yet as to think of matrimony," though "the beautiful Miss Allen" of Philadelphia caused him to inquire if she were "still unpossessed."

Lee was a frequent guest at Shirley, the James River plantation of Charles Carter, Virginia's wealthiest man. Here Harry flirted and danced with the Commonwealth's most charming and richest young ladies and it was here, early in 1793, that he met Charles Carter's great-niece, the beautiful Maria Byrd Farley of Westover. Maria and the Carter's lovely twenty-year-old daughter, Ann Hill, had been inseparable companions since early childhood, and Maria was now living at Shirley. It was not long until Lee admitted to being "desperately" in love with Miss Farley, so engrossed in his affair as to confess to his friends an indifference even to the course of national politics.

But Maria had other suitors whom she favored, and Lee's impassioned words left her unmoved, while the delicate, dark-eyed Ann Carter, with her "grave humor" and her beautiful singing voice, fell unintentional victim to his fascination. She kept her love for Harry a secret, encouraging Maria to accept him, but was so tormented by the hopelessness of her own passion that she became ill. Only when Lee made his offer, and Maria vowed privately to her confidante that she would reject it, did Ann reveal her secret when she cried in agony:

11

"O stop, stop Maria! You do not know what you are throwing away!"

But Maria refused him, and Lee, rejected, turned to the girl he had previously ignored and began to court Ann. His motives were so obvious that her parents were affronted and resentful. Lee's financial irresponsibility and his debts were common knowledge; it was patent that Ann's dower and inheritance were her chief attractions.

Up to this time, Ann's parents had indulged all of her whims but Harry Lee would cause the first rift. Despite her sheltered life, where there had been few important decisions for her to make, Ann had a mind of her own and was now determined to marry Lee. She is described by a relative as "intense, loving and sweet. Although she was gentle, she was firm, very resolute, and strong." She therefore remained unmoved by her parents' warnings about Lee's finances and the uncertainty of her future; by Harry's talk of setting off for France (he had revived that topic); by the fact that he was seventeen years her senior; or that she would have to contend with two notably unruly stepchildren.

At thirty-seven, Harry looked youthful, and his ebullience and vigor made him seem even younger. As governor and one of the South's most distinguished and popular men, his future seemed assured to Ann. The possible offer of his sword to France only added more luster to the aura of romance and chivalry that, in her eyes, already surrounded him.

Finding it useless to remonstrate, and because her delicate health was being impaired by anguish, Charles Carter consented to the marriage on the condition that Lee relinquish all thoughts of bearing arms for France—a plan which he perhaps did not believe Lee would abandon readily.

On Tuesday evening, June 18, 1793, the wedding was held in the drawingroom at Shirley, the rector of Westover Parish Church performing the ceremony. Only one detail has been preserved: traditionally, Ann wore about her neck the gold locket containing a miniature of her father's intimate friend, George Washington, sent as a gift to the bride. On it was inscribed: "George Washington to his dear Ann."

2

ALTHOUGH Ann Hill Carter knew when she married Harry Lee that he did not love her, she hoped ultimately to win his heart or at least bind him to her with ties of affection. But "in the short space of a fortnight," a relative of Maria Byrd Farley confided to his sister, Ann found that "her affections were trampled on by a heartless & depraved profligate. I am right as to time. One fortnight was her dream of happiness from which she awoke to a life of misery. Her fortune was soon thrown away upon his debts contracted previous to marriage: She was despised & neglected . . ." and Harry sought his pleasure elsewhere. His intrigues with other women were soon known to the Carters, and probably became general knowledge. One of Ann's kinswomen, writing to the family at Shirley, delicately recounted the details of Harry's latest amour, adding tersely but significantly: "Poor Ann."

Ann must have soon heard of these affairs and seen the futility of winning his love, but instead of escaping from her unhappy situation, as she might so easily have done, she chose to remain with Lee, thereby revealing a remarkable capacity for self-command (a trait that would be inherited by her fourth son, Robert Edward). She held the secret of her unhappiness as successfully as she had kept from Maria Farley her love for this man. With Shirley so close, her visits home were frequent. Here she basked in the devotion of her parents and her sisters and brothers, and could indulge her highly sociable Carter nature in the delights of the season at Williamsburg, the races, or festivities at neighboring plantations, temporarily submerging her unhappiness in these diversions.

During the summer following his marriage, Lee committed a breach of etiquette which brought on him the scorn and vituperative fury of Thomas Jefferson—a malediction that dogged him for years. He made the error of reporting, in a letter to George Washington, a remark of Jefferson's which Lee considered "derogatory" to the President.

Somehow Jefferson learned of Lee's letter and, already disliking Harry because he had known of Jefferson's amorous addresses to Mrs. Charles Carter's sister after she had married John Walker of Belvoir, and had acted as conciliator between the two men, Jefferson seized this opportunity to air his aversion, hoping to influence Washington against Lee. He wrote bitterly to the President, referring to Lee as "a miserable tergiversator." But Washington's attitude of indulgent father remained unchanged. And when the Whiskey Rebellion broke out, in 1794, he commissioned Lee a major general and put him in command of fifteen thousand militia.

In September Harry rode off to join his troops, leaving both Ann and his son, Henry, ill at Shirley. He was wearing the fitted green jacket, tight lambskin breeches, and plumed leather helmet of Revolutionary days. His cavalry was also dressed in the uniform of the famed Lee's Legion.

It was reminiscent of happier days, too, when General Washington and Colonel Alexander Hamilton joined him for the ride into Pennsylvania, where a show of force was all that was needed to put down the insurrection.

While Lee was away, his term as governor expired and a new chief executive was elected. When he returned to Richmond he found that Jefferson and his followers had not been idle.

"I am," Harry wrote, "an object of the most virulent enmity of a certain political faction who affect to govern the United States & belch their venom on every citizen not subservient to their will." He was charged with having acted unconstitutionally, since his term as governor and titular head of the militia had expired before he left the field. But he had illustrious company: President Washington was accused of exceeding his constitutional powers by remaining in the field while Congress was in session, and Hamilton was charged with usurping the powers of the Secretary of War.

Lee passed the winter and spring in the capital, preparing his defense should action be taken, while Ann, still unwell, remained at Shirley. There on April 12, 1795, she bore her first child, a boy named Algernon Sidney, in honor of the grandnephew of Sir Philip Sidney, a traditional Lee forebear. It was late summer before she felt strong enough to accompany Harry to Stratford Hall, where the associations awoke poignant memories in Lee's mind. That fall when he went as a delegate to the Assembly in Richmond, Ann remained at Stratford with her baby and Matilda's two children.

Eight-year-old Henry was an affectionate boy who responded warmly to his stepmother, but Lucy Grymes was highly resentful of her presence, and watched for every chance to vex and hurt her. This was not mere childish caprice, but a deeply rooted and lasting dislike. When Lucy came of marriageable age, she wiled Ann's poet-brother, Bernard Moore Carter, into taking her as his wife, making both their lives miserable. Her motive was apparently spite since she afterward wrote of her husband: "I've been accustomed to live with my father and brother, such charming men! How could I stand Bernard Carter? He is the handsomest man I ever saw, but such a fool!"

It was at Stratford, far removed from populous centers and neighbors, that Ann Carter would be most intensely lonely. Everywhere were mute tokens of the Divine Matilda's presence, and reminders of happier and more prosperous days when the guest rooms were never empty and the Great Hall was bright with music and laughter; when ships from across the sea unloaded luxuries at Lee's Landing and filled their holds with hogsheads of Stratford tobacco. In one corner of the parlor were Matilda's closed harpsichord and shrouded harp. Harry's chessmen stood deep in dust on the mahogany table near the fireplace. In the "Blue room," Matilda's ballgowns and satin slippers were laid away carefully in the press, and her jewels in a locked casket. Outside, there were empty stalls where thoroughbreds had once champed; the horses were gone now, to satisfy debts and expenses. The fields were weed-choked, the fences fallen, the mill idle, and the wharf empty. Even the very portraits of earlier prosperous Lees in powdered wigs and official robes and brave garments of crimson and blue seemed to admonish as they stared from their gilt frames upon the growing shabbiness of their surroundings.

15

Ailing, lonely, and unhappy, Ann found her life soon settling into a dull routine. She took occasional horseback rides
through the glades and down by the river, but she found these
"fatiguing." Her chief solace lay in writing letters to her parents, her favorite sister, Mildred, and her confidante, Elizabeth
Collins Lee, the wife of Harry's brother, Richard Bland, who
lived at Sully in Loudoun County. At her desk, filling the
pages with her beautiful small hand, she was able to project
herself beyond the confines of her dreary realm. It is evident
from her surviving letters to Elizabeth Collins that she kept
her secret well: there are no complaints and no bitterness.
Significantly, there are also only three fleeting mentions of the
author of her misfortune.

The first in a series of distressing events destined to cast a
further pall over Ann's life at Stratford and crowd it with
unhappy memories took place the following August 9, when
little Algernon Sidney succumbed to some malady, and was
buried next to Matilda in the brick vault that Harry had built
for her at the end of the garden. Alone with her grief, Ann
sought comfort in the heart of her family at Shirley. But the
memory of that first little boy would always remain fresh, and
"a rich curl of his golden hair was carefully preserved among
her jewels."

Harry made no attempt to farm the plantation, but passed
the greater part of his time away from home, using his persua-
sive charm to convince his creditors that they must wait for
their pay, while he borrowed more money, sold and traded
land, and mortgaged his property like a man ridden by a
demon.

Now he was about to make a fortune once more. With John
and James Marshall, he contracted to buy 160,000 acres of the
legally tangled Lord Fairfax estate, joined another group of
men in a scheme to promote Western lands, while with George
Washington he reached an agreement to purchase a part of his
old commander's Dismal Swamp holdings in North Carolina.

Robert Morris (once America's richest man) had agreed to
advance the sum when payment on the Fairfax lands fell due.
But meanwhile, he had suffered heavy losses and was unable to

lend them anything. The outcome of this venture was that, with typical generosity, Lee loaned Morris $40,000 to help him out of his difficulties. Then when it was time to pay the first installment on the Dismal Swamp lands, Harry was without cash and had to forfeit his interest. The plan to sell frontier lands was equally unsuccessful since several of the partners defaulted, and one of them, referred to in Harry's correspondence as "poor Glassel," was jailed.

But Lee was not easily discouraged: he bought back land he had previously sold to a brother-in-law, reselling it along with other holdings to Bushrod Washington, while from George Washington he received, in exchange for five hundred acres of land in Kentucky, the blooded Arabian stallion, "Magnolio."

While he was thus happily embroiled, Ann bore her second child on November 8, 1798, at Shirley. It was another boy, and she named him for her father. To Elizabeth Collins Lee she wrote gaily:

I must beg to introduce to your acquaintance my little Charles Carter, whom, from the superlative beauty of his Father and Mother, you will conceive to be possessed of a large portion, but alas! my dear, he inherits neither the Charms of the one or the other—He is a little black-eyed brown Boy; very healthy, good tempered, lively (and his Mother thinks) very sweet.

In February she returned to Stratford. The day of her arrival, Harry set out with the backing of George Washington to campaign for a seat in Congress against the highly popular Jeffersonian candidate, Dr. Jones.

On April 12, every man in the Northern Neck who owned more than a hundred acres set out sometime during the day for the polls at Montross Court House. The contest was bitter, and neither Jones nor Lee left a trick untried. Ribbon favors were plentifully distributed, and at the hustings, booths were set up and the voters served with slices of "plumb Cake" and wine— "let it be good & plenty" were the instructions. A barrel of rum and one of whiskey, with the heads knocked in, stood under a shade tree. The majority "took it straight . . . gathering in a tumult at the voting place until the noise was perfectly deafening."

Toward midafternoon a tall commanding man rode up to the polls and made his way through the crowd to the table where the electors and contestants were seated. There were no secret ballots, so that when General Washington reached the table, he simply told the elector:

"I vote for General Lee," and his vote was tallied. Lee's constituents cheered and Harry rose and bowed, while the opposition cheered Dr. Jones. When the votes were counted that night, the clerk announced that "the electors caused Henry Lee to be chosen." His victory was celebrated by a gala public dinner and ball at the Montross ordinary.

That fall, although she was expecting another child, Ann accompanied Harry by stagecoach to Philadelphia, then the greatest city in the country and considered by many "one of the most beautiful in the World." It was lure of life in this metropolis that prompted Ann's stepdaughter, Lucy Grymes, after she had married Bernard Carter, to burn down her husband's great house, Woodstock, in Fauquier County, so that she would at no time be obliged to remain in the country but could pass all year in that wonderful city.

Ann looked forward with pleasure to their stay in Philadelphia, for, as she had written Elizabeth Collins in February:

> So confined is the sphere in which I have moved for the last six months that I am totally ignorant of every occurrence beyond the distance of fifteen or twenty miles, and, excepting friends who do and always will retain their place in my memory and in whose remembrance I hope I shall exist, I may with much truth be said to live "The World forgetting, by the World forgot."

On the morning of December 19, 1799, as Harry Lee was walking from their furnished rooms in Franklin Court to Congress Hall, he heard the news of George Washington's death. He was so overcome that he turned back to the Court, where he sat grieving and reviewing the past. As he reflected, he was seized by the fear that Washington's bitter political foes might refuse to pay proper tribute to his passing, and he sat down at the desk and wrote out a series of resolutions which he planned to read before Congress the next day. He closed with those words that would become synonymous with Washington's name: "First in war, first in peace, and first in the hearts of his countrymen."

Congress asked Lee, as a delegate from Virginia, to prepare and deliver the funeral oration before both Houses and in the German Lutheran Church.

With dramatic finesse he asked the hushed audience to go with him "to the banks of the Monongahela to see our youthful Washington supporting, in the dismal hour of Indian victory, the ill-fated Braddock, and saving, by his judgment, the remains of a defeated army, pressed by the conquering savage foe. . . . Who is there that has forgotten the vales of Brandywine, the fields of Germantown, or the plains of Monmouth?" he asked.

Passing to the years as President, he went on:

Possessing a clear and penetrating mind, a strong judgment, calmness and temper for deliberation . . . with incorruptible integrity and unvarying patriotism. . . . First in war, first in peace, and first in the hearts of his countrymen, he was second to none in the humble and endearing scenes of private life; pious, just, humane, and sincere; uniform, dignified, and commanding. . . .

The eulogy was so well received that Lee planned to have it printed and sold, to earn some much-needed cash. But along with the official thanks of Congress came a request that he permit copies to be made and circulated without charge.

Harry had no choice but to submit graciously and, as his mentor would have done, with dignity.

3

DESPITE Harry Lee's aid, Robert Morris was sent to debtor's prison. Upon his release he explained to Lee his inability to repay the $40,000: "I am without one single solitary dollar to my name." This was a blow to Harry's precarious finances; he had been counting heavily on repayment of the debt.

With Thomas Jefferson in the presidency and his constituents holding office everywhere, Lee's political star had set. His proximity to financial ruin he attributed to those policies of Jefferson which he believed had "plummeted" the country from "its fair summit of prosperity" under George Washington. Therefore, whenever Lee was not trying to collect money due him or persuading his creditors to be patient, he was easing his mind by writing page after page of biting invective against Jefferson, rapidly demolishing the two and a half quires of white paper which (along with "one fine Hatt") he had bought on credit from the merchant, Lawrence Muse.

On June 19, 1800, Ann had borne her first daughter, Ann Kinloch, a delicate child whose feeble health would become another trial to Ann. She was being relieved now of the charge of Matilda's two children—the malicious Lucy was soon to marry Bernard Carter, and Henry had enrolled in the College of William and Mary. But within a year after Ann Kinloch's birth, Ann was pregnant again, and there seemed little hope that life would be anything more than a dull and perilous existence, stripped of its smallest comforts, beset with illness, debts, and the burdens of a constantly increasing family.

During the summer of 1802, she and the children accompanied Harry on what was described as "a Northern tour." Since their finances would not have allowed such a trip for pleasure, it must have been undertaken in the hope of raising capital and collecting outstanding debts. But the journey to New York was hot and strenuous, precipitating the arrival of their fourth child. On the homeward trip, as they were passing through Camden, New Jersey, Ann went into labor and was forced to stop at the house of strangers. In gratitude for their kindness, she named this healthy dark-eyed boy Smith, in their honor, flagrantly ignoring all family tradition.

After their return to Stratford, she was once again afflicted with depression of spirits and many months of invalidism, and subject to fainting spells from which she could not be revived for hours. As soon as the warm spring days arrived, she took the children to Shirley, but even in these congenial surroundings, her heart failed to lighten.

In the strict Carter code by which she had been brought up, the discharge of one's debts was a moral obligation just as faithfulness to one's wife was a sacred one. In her present mood, she saw in Harry's derelictions the end of some of her closest friendships. When life held so little that was bright, friendship was precious to this sociable lonely woman. Harry had borrowed from his brother, Richard Bland, huge unrepayable sums which ultimately contributed to Richard's financial ruin. Foreseeing the loss of Elizabeth's friendship because of this, Ann wrote to her in a melancholy vein from Shirley:

. . . my mind often recurs to you with mingled sensations of pleasure and regret. Formerly when separated from you I constantly looked forward to the period when I should again enjoy your society; but the pleasing anticipation no longer cheers my prospects, and I consider you among the number of those dear friends whom Fate has probably forever severed me from. But while I lament its award, you will remain the cherished friend of my heart, united to it by ties too strong for time or absence to weaken. . . . Think of me always my dear friend as sincerely and [page torn] unalterably attached to you.

Ann Lee

Though some friends may have dropped Ann, Elizabeth was too intelligent and far too loyal to allow anything to mar their friendship.

In the spring of 1806, Harry embarked on his final financial venture. It was fitting that this last speculation should also be the most fantastic. With Rawleigh Colston, John Marshall's brother-in-law, he bought all claims to the Chichester Estate, which had been contested in the British Chancery Court for over sixty years. He and Colston hoped their purchases would simplify the case, although they also counted heavily on Lee's friendship with James Monroe, then Minister to England, to influence the Lord Chancellor to force a settlement.

Late that June, although Ann was with child again and little Smith was sick, she set out one morning in the family's last vehicle, a rickety open carriage, for Shirley. She planned to leave the children with her parents and journey on to Sully for a long-promised stay of several weeks with Elizabeth Collins,

21

then return to Shirley and wait for the coming of her fifth and, as she had frankly confided to Elizabeth, unwanted, child.

But when she reached Shirley, she was shocked to find her family in mourning over the sudden death of her father. On July 6 she wrote to Harry, hoping to arouse his sense of duty toward her through pity:

Before I arrived at this place, the arms which had ever received me with so much delight, were folded in death! the eyes which used to beam with so much affection on me, were veiled for ever! and the cold grave was closed on my too *dear* and ever lamented Father!

It would be vain, to attempt to describe the grief, his loss has occasioned me. . . . Oh! my dearest Mr Lee remember, that your poor afflicted *Father*less wife, can only look to you, to smooth her rugged path through life, and soften her bed of death!

My poor dear Mother is bowed down with sorrow, and in very low health: a change of scene and climate, appears to be entirely necessary to her recovery. . . . The last week in this month, is fixed on for her leaving home: I trust my dear Mr Lee you will certainly bring a conveyance for me by that time, do not disappoint me I conjure you. . . .

At the time of his death it was written of Charles Carter: "In him the poor have lost their best friend, and of him it might be truly said that he was father to the fatherless and a husband to the widow—the appeal of the wretched was always *effectually* attended to by him." But the eulogy that his daughter Ann felt was most fitting, and preserved, read: "His long and prosperous life was spent in the tranquil enjoyment of Domestic Life—where from the Mansion of hospitality his immense wealth flowed like the silent stream, enlivening and refreshing every object around. In fulfilling the duties of his station he proved himself to be an Israelite indeed, in whom there was no guile."

Charles Carter had remained a man of "immense wealth" because his sagacity and prudence had never allowed him to harken to the siren call of land speculation which lured such men as John and James Marshall and George Washington. Because of this prudence, life was to be made easier for his daughter Ann and her children. When the will was read, she

22

was relieved to hear that her inheritance had been put in trust, "free from the claim, demand, let, hindrance, or molestation of her husband, General Henry Lee or his creditors directly or indirectly."

Not until the end of September did Ann leave Shirley. She was in a mood of extreme dejection, for her favorite sister, Mildred, was seriously ill, probably with tuberculosis. Since Harry had still not sent the carriage, Ann and her children, all of whom were now sick, traveled with her mother in the splendid Carter coach with its four sleek horses, liveried postillions, and attendant servants. Mrs. Carter had delayed her "change of scene and climate" because of Mildred. Since they visited friends along the way, it was mid-October before they reached Belvoir.

Mrs. Carter planned to return to Shirley when she left her sister's, so Ann wrote Harry again, asking for the old carriage at once. She hoped there still might be time to visit Sully.

But Lee ignored her request, and when November came, and no carriage, she wrote in disappointment to Elizabeth:

"When I left Stratford, one of the most pleasing objects of my Summer excursion, was to pass a few weeks with you . . . but the want of a carriage has been the obstacle to my enjoying so great a gratification: and now when I do get one, the Season will be so far advanced that I must return by the most direct rout." If she ever had her own carriage again, which she admitted was "doubtful," she would, as an added inducement for Elizabeth to visit her, send it to convey "yourself and dear family to our poor old dwelling."

The last week in December brought the carriage from Stratford. The trip home was not pleasant. Winter had begun and the open carriage gave no protection from the icy winds and rain. Ann Carter caught a cold which settled in her chest, where she had a congenital weakness.

When she reached Stratford, there was nothing to cheer her at the "poor old dwelling." Only the east wing was habitable now; even there, the rooms were shabby and cold. Harry was at home, preoccupied with writing to James Monroe, urging him to call the Lord Chancellor's attention to a settlement of the Chichester Estate. The children continued to ail, and Ann was so feeble from the effects of her cold that she feared she would be confined to the house until late spring.

Any day she might go into labor, not anticipating with pleasure the arrival of another baby. "You have my best wishes for your success my dear," she wrote Elizabeth, who was also expecting a child shortly, "and *truest* assurances that I do not envy your *prospects* nor wish to *share in them*." Just eight days later, on January 19, 1807, the midwife was sent for.

Many weeks passed before Ann left her bed, for more trials and sorrows kept her spirits low. Not long after Robert's birth, a letter from Shirley announced the death of one of her brothers, and held out little hope for Mildred's recovery. By the end of March "the darling Sister of my heart," as Ann termed her, had followed "my ever lamented Father & Brother to the tomb!"

Harry was sick, too. He had taken cold while riding to Alexandria during the winter, and spring weather brought him no relief. The doctor advised that a move to a warmer climate would be best for both Ann and Harry. In the Bermudas, Harry had a "fast friend" who "offered his house, even his purse," but once again Thomas Jefferson stood in Lee's way. Because of his recent Embargo Act, no ship could be found to take them. Seeing his financial salvation in such an enforced sojourn, Harry appealed to James Madison, then Secretary of State. He naïvely suggested that if Madison would appoint a consul to Brazil, the President "would be authorized to give me a letter congratulating your friend on his safe arrival in that quarter of the globe, such a letter would authorize the P to send a vessel with the bearer. . . . Such is my distressed condition that I humbly expose to you such ideas as occur to me favourable to my wishes." But Madison either could or would not come to Harry's aid.

During the winter following Robert's birth, Ann's condition became so serious that even Harry was concerned and used her health as a pretext to apply to Madison again for help in leaving the country. He begged the Secretary to consider this an effort "to preserve a life, the loss of which will bear me to the grave with unceasing woe." But there was no response to this plea either. Bankruptcy was now upon Lee, and the indignation of his creditors descended simultaneously in the form of irate letters and deputies armed with writs and summonses, so that the doors at Stratford Hall had to be hung with chains to prevent entry of the sheriff's men.

In 1809, Harry borrowed $20,000 from his brother Charles, giving as collateral lands purchased years before from Patrick Henry. But this last-minute act of desperation was useless. On April 24, Lee was arrested by Sheriff Edward Herndon on a court order at the demand of Jasper & Davenport. He was taken to the jail at Montross Court House, where in 1799 General Washington had ridden down from Mount Vernon to vote for him.

But the old soldier was indomitable in defeat: within the confines of his cell he was soon reliving the glorious days of the Revolution. He asked the jailer for paper and pen, and started writing what was at first intended to be a life of General Greene, but since he was unfamiliar with details of the northern campaigns, he changed it to an account of the war in the Southern Department.

When his debt was satisfied, by what means is not of record, he gathered up his manuscript and returned to Stratford, only to be arrested on another court order a few days later. This time, he was taken to Spotsylvania Court House in Fredericksburg, where during the daytime he wrote, sitting on the court green, on his honor not to leave.

He now decided that when released he would not return to live with Ann. Unlike her husband, she did not have a life tenure in Stratford, and so made immediate plans to find another home.

The news of Harry's intention spread quickly among her relatives, and she received many offers of haven. She had not yet decided which to accept when Lee changed his mind, and asked her to stay until his return.

She granted this request, but determined that Stratford, with its storehouse of unhappy memories, should no longer be her home. She reserved the right to live at a place of her own

25

choice and at length chose Alexandria, where there were schools (for they could not afford a tutor), medical care, and, most important after the years of exile, many relatives and close friends.

Everyone retains some very early recollection from childhood. Little Robert, now three, may have wondered and asked about the heavy chains across the doors, and sensed the feeling of hopelessness that filled the atmosphere at Stratford. But one memory that remained fixed, to be recalled at the time of the Civil War, was that of his mother going into the neglected garden to plant a horse-chestnut tree.

4

HARRY Lee's debts were satisfied in the spring of 1810, probably largely through the further generosity of his brothers, and he returned to Stratford to work tirelessly on the book, holding optimistic visions of the revenue to be gained from its sales. For some reason not recorded, the move to Alexandria was deferred until winter.

Old Nat was on the driver's box and the family were about to take their seats in the carriage when they found that little Robert was missing. Carter was sent racing in one direction and Smith in another, shouting for him, while Harry fumed at the delay. But it was his sister, Ann Kinloch, or "Wanze," as Robert preferred to call her, who returned from the house, where she had gone to search, grasping the escapee firmly by the hand. She had found him in the nursery, she explained, squatted before the fireplace, saying good-by to the two cherubs embossed on the metal fireback.

Following the carriage was a cart with Ann Carter's maid, Nancy, the cook, and two other house servants; the trunks, Harry's clock, his books and box of manuscript, and Robert's swinging, canopied cradle, to be in use again with the coming of another baby in February. Beside the carriage loped "Killbuck," Harry's mastiff.

In Alexandria, the little cavalcade drew up before the door

26

of the North Washington Street home of Harry's brother, Edmund Jennings Lee, an eminent lawyer, where the Stratford Lees would stay until Ann had selected a suitable house (which she later found at 611 Cameron Street). Cousin Edmund's daughter, Sally, was greatly impressed by her boy cousins' gentlemanly deportment. They were "remarkably well-behaved and obedient," she recalled. She remembered that whenever Robert went into the yard to play, his mother always put a bonnet over his long dark ringlets.

At present, the income from the trust fund set up by Ann's father (chiefly in Bank of Virginia stock) and the proceeds from her sister's investments which Mildred had left, all but sixty pounds, "to my sister Lee during her life free from the controul of her husband General Lee" were just enough to keep her and the children in modest comfort. Harry was almost wholly dependent on this income, too, for he had managed to salvage only a little land from the shambles of his financial ruin—some acreage at Hardy, Virginia, and some at Harpers Ferry which he rented for a small sum to the federal government. But he was consoled by the belief that once his book was published the money would come pouring in.

"It will have a great run!" he predicted.

By the fall of 1811, the work was finished. He had at first intended to issue it anonymously, since he had not hesitated to express his opinions of persons he did not like, and had no wish, as he said, "to spend the remainder of my life fighting duels." However, the old lust for fame overcame his caution, and he contracted with Bradford & Inskeep of Philadelphia to publish it the following spring under his name.

Though Ann bore another baby—a girl she named for her sister, Mildred—not too long after they were settled in their own house, life was considerably easier and certainly more interesting for her. There was little money to spend for a seat at the Alexandria Theatre, which brought stage favorites from Europe to its footlights, or for gowns to wear to the weekly assemblies at the fashionable City Hotel. But she was content with simpler diversions, finding most pleasure in the nearness of so many relatives and close friends.

The kinfolk with whom she and her children were destined to be on the most intimate lifelong terms were William Henry Fitzhugh and the beautiful girl he married in 1814, Anna Maria Goldsborough, who, it was said, "was fit to grace a throne." The Fitzhughs divided their time between their country estate, Ravensworth, in nearby Fairfax County, and a town house on the east side of Washington Street, near Queen. They admired Ann for managing so well in adversity, and for keeping her dignity and cheerfulness.

"One of the finest women the State of Virginia ever produced," Mr. Fitzhugh wrote of her.

Since he and his wife would remain childless, for each of Ann's progeny there was an interest and love matched only by their mother's devotion.

The first recorded incident in Robert Lee's life took place during those early months in Alexandria when he and his mother went one afternoon to call on a cousin, Mrs. Hodgson. On the way to her house on Oronoco Street, Ann told Robert about little Portia Hopkins, Mrs. Hodgson's niece, who was staying with her. But when the Lees arrived, Robert was disappointed to learn that the little girl he had counted on playing with was asleep. The only pleasant interlude for him during the long afternoon was the cake served with tea. At length, "after vainly pulling at his mother to get her to leave," the bored and weary boy tiptoed out of the parlor and ran hopefully into Portia's room. Finding her still napping, he crawled under her crib. When his mother was ready to go, she discovered him there, sound asleep.

"Something always happens to mar my happiness," Harry Lee once wrote. No statement could have better epitomized his whole ironic life pattern. On Sunday morning, July 26, 1812, as he took the stagecoach for Baltimore determined to help a friend in his stand for those civil liberties guaranteed by the Constitution, fate had in store the opening of the final act in the tragic drama of his life.

Alexander Hanson, a young Baltimore editor, was bitterly opposed to another war with England and expressed his feelings fearlessly in his newspaper, *The Federal Republican.* When President Madison approved Congress' declaration of war, Hanson summed up America's position:

"Without funds, without taxes, without an army, navy or adequate fortifications, with one hundred and fifty millions of our property in the hands of the declared enemy, without any of his in our power . . . our rulers have promulgated a war, against the clear and decided sentiments of a vast majority of the nation. . . ."

Harry Lee was as ardently opposed to the war as Hanson and joined the ranks of his supporters.

The Democrats were afraid of the editor's growing influence, and after instigating a mob to destroy his presses and the house on Gay Street where he had his office, they threatened his life "with such picturesque venom that he hurriedly decamped." When he decided to return to Baltimore, he had his paper printed in Georgetown; and on July 26, just as Lee rode into Baltimore, Hanson walked unobserved up Charles Street to the house of his partner.

By the time Lee reached the house, it was crowded with Hanson's friends, among whom were John Howard Paine, remembered as the author of "Home, Sweet Home," and General James Maccubin Lingan of Revolutionary War fame. In a corner of the parlor was a stack of muskets and dirks.

The next day the paper was distributed, and toward dusk when Lee returned to the house, he noticed knots of angry men clustered about it. He ordered the door barred and prepared for a siege. With darkness came a mob armed with brickbats and rocks. Soon all the windows were smashed and the front door battered in, and Lee, Hanson, and his friends had to use muskets to keep the crowd at bay. The militia turned out, but being sympathetic with the mob, did nothing. A parley was called, and Hanson and Lee were persuaded that jail would be the safest place. But once they were locked up, the militia left and no guard was sent to replace them.

The following night, the mob gathered about the jail. This time, most of them were well along in drink. The sympathetic turnkey gave up the keys and the rioters stormed in. Lee and

29

Hanson attempted to slip past, but were struck down at the outer door by a giant of a man named Mumma who beat them into insensibility.

Eight men thought to be dead were thrown down the steps into the street, and Lee, one of the eight, was roused to consciousness some hours later when a drunken ruffian attempted to cut off his nose. Missing his aim, he slashed the blade along the cheekbone. A three-hour orgy of torture was ended by the arrival of Dr. John Hall and several colleagues who persuaded the brutes to leave the bodies in their care until morning.

A quick examination revealed life in all of the men but one —the aged General Lingan. Carriages were ordered and the wounded taken to the hospital. As soon as Lee's hurts were dressed, he was driven secretly to the home of friends in Little York, Pennsylvania.

By the beginning of autumn, Harry was able to return to Alexandria. The family clustered in the open doorway was shocked to see the pathetic figure, crippled and bent, ease his way painfully out of the carriage and hobble up the steps. Robert, who would throughout life have a horror of the maimed and ugly, doubtless drew back into the shelter of his mother's skirts as he saw his father's face, swollen, fiery red, and scarred almost beyond recognition.

The ensuing days must have been trying ones for them all. With his passionate temper and imperious ways, Harry was difficult to please at any time. Now that he was in constant pain from his external, and more serious internal, injuries, he was impossible to satisfy.

Aware that there was no longer any hope for material success and that his health was shattered, he yearned to leave the country, hoping to find solace for an anguished mind and tortured body amid new scenes and a gentler climate. He wrote pathetically to James Monroe: "Barbadoes or the Havannah would either suit, but as I cannot speak the french or spanish language I prefer a British island. No American vessel can be got to land me unless you permit them to do so."

Both Madison and Monroe now came to his aid. It has been

suggested that they were anxious to have him gone because of his knowledge of the responsibility for the Baltimore Riot. He had recently supplied the information for an account of the violence, which was to be published shortly under his name. He had not minced words. The mob, he said, was "of governmental origin and had its foundation in executive authority." This had been a cowardly attempt "to prostrate the principles of civil liberty, and to render the laws subservient to the ambitious views and dastardly operations of a factious party. . . ." Arrangements were made for him to pass through the wartime blockade and settle on a British island.

On a summer's day in 1813, General Light-Horse Harry Lee, old beyond his years, penniless, broken in body and humbled in spirit, shuffled his way painfully up the gangway of a vessel moored at the wharf. As the tide turned to ebb, the anchor was weighed and the ship nosed gently past other craft out into the open sea, her orders taking her to Barbadoes.

At the brick house on Cameron Street, Ann Carter and the children had watched dry-eyed as the carriage drove away. It was with a sense of mingled sadness and relief that they saw the testy old man depart. They were freed of a weight that had fettered their spirits during those trying months when his groans filled the house and his temper knew no restraint, "his exhibitions of commingled rage and anguish often terrible."

Ann Carter's heart held more pity than resentment. She cherished the gold and black enameled brooch containing a lock of his blond hair that Harry gave her as a parting gift, and traditionally wore it every day for the remainder of her life.

As for the children, Harry Lee had been hardly more than a stranger to them for years, away from them in quixotic pursuit of happiness more than he was with them. At home, his thoughts and interests were far off, rambling in an illusory world where fortune could be built upon quicksand, and love and happiness grew as rank weeds by the wayside and could be had for the picking. They would never see him again. Even as his ship passed over the horizon, he was little more than a strange sad memory.

⇛ II ⇚

The Pursuit of Happiness

1813 ★ 1846

II. The Pursuit of Happiness

ALTHOUGH the grounds in the rear of the house on Cameron Street could not offer all the opportunities for adventure that Stratford did, the fact that there was room to keep a cow, two horses, and a dog suggests that there was enough space for Robert's play when the family first moved there. As he grew older and was allowed to leave the yard, experiences of another sort awaited him in the streets and alleys, at the markets and wharves, in the marshy meadows and nearby woods, and in and on the river that flowed beside this bustling town of seventy-five hundred persons.

Just a short way from where Robert lived were the Friendship and Sun Fire Companies, perennial delight of all boys. George Washington had presented the Friendship Company with a dazzling French engine which, on such festal occasions as the Glorious Fourth, was decked with garlands of paper flowers and hauled in the parade by firemen in glazed hats and shirts of scarlet and blue.

Down at the end of Cameron Street were the wharves where ships from the West Indies docked. Here Robert and his companions—most often his favorite brother, Smith, whom he had nicknamed "Rose," and his cousins Edmund and Cassius Lee—watched cargoes of rum and wine, sugar and molasses, and spice and tropical fruit exchanged for hogsheads of Virginia tobacco. When returning from the docks, they often stopped at the jailyard to stare in awe at the pillory and whipping post, where culprits still occasionally felt the lash wielded expertly by a character known as "Bobtail Bowie."

As they threaded their way through the crowded street that led to Fishtown—always a scene of bustle, billingsgate, and strong smells, the boys slackened their pace so as not to miss the Punch and Judy shows, the fakers, and the organ-grinders who performed in booths or on the street corners to large audiences of swarthy sailors. If Robert and his comrades had

35

12½ cents in their pockets they might climb the stairs to Colonel Mountford's Museum on a Saturday morning, and there gaze in wonder at his collection of marvels: live caged eagles, stuffed animals of many kinds, thundereggs, Indian relics, and mementoes of George Washington.

Robert's love of horses drew him often to that market on the south side of town. It was here that he learned early how to judge the points of a good horse—something he delighted in all his life. The woods and fields were very close to Alexandria, then, and abounded in ducks and small game while the river offered a variety of fish—a paradise for boy anglers and nimrods. Every pleasant day there was boating and swimming, and in the winter there was skating.

But life in Alexandria did not hold only joy and adventure for young Robert. He had inherited the passionate Lee temper, quick to rouse, and could not escape involvement in the quarrels and battles common to all boys, though his usually amiable disposition allowed no grudges to linger. There must have been times when he preferred, before submitting to his mother's scrutiny, to try to remedy a swollen eye or bruised lip with applications of cold water.

While his daily experiences in Alexandria were contributing to the growth of mind and body, Robert was also unconsciously partaking nourishment of a deeper nature which remained a lasting influence: the strongly felt presence of George Washington. Although he had been dead eleven years when the Lees came to Alexandria, reminders of him were everywhere. Directly across the street from Robert's home was Washington's town house. In the market square, where now the flower vendors sat in the shade of the paper mulberry trees, Washington had drilled his Virginia Rangers before he joined Braddock. At the City Tavern (later Gadsby's), he made his headquarters, and was present with Mrs. Washington at the grand ball and supper in celebration of his last birthday.

There was the post office where he had called for his mail, and the postmaster, Colonel Gilpin, who had served with him; and Stabler-Leadbeater's Apothecary on Fairfax Street where he had his medicines compounded. It was seldom that Robert

36

did not meet someone on the streets who had known Washington personally. A few of his lifelong friends, like Dr. James Craik, who had been with him in every battle from Great Meadows to Yorktown, were still living.

Arch Hall on Franklin Street was the winter home of the beautiful and talented Eleanor Parke Custis, or "Nelly" as she was generally called, though she considered the nickname "homely." She was Mrs. Washington's granddaughter, and the General's foster daughter, who had married his favorite nephew, Lawrence Lewis, in 1799. Ann Carter Lee and her children went often to Arch Hall for tea or a musical evening, when Ann sang to Nelly's accompaniment on the harpsichord and Nelly's gifted daughters played the guitar and harp.

At nearby Arlington House lived Nelly's younger brother, the General's adopted son and namesake, George Washington Parke Custis, who was known to his intimates as "the Major," a complimentary title for his part in the Battle of Bladensburg. Custis' wife was Mary Lee Fitzhugh, a sister of Ann Carter's staunch admirer, William Henry Fitzhugh.

Robert often visited at Arlington with his mother and the other children. They would play quiet games with the Custis' only surviving child, the delicate Mary Anne, or Molly. Together they would explore the woods to gather hickory nuts in season and crack them on the big mossy stone which served as a seat beneath the arbor in the grove. In spring they picked armfuls of bluebells of Scotland and lilies of the valley, Mrs. Custis' favorite flower, which she planted under each evergreen. At other times they made swings of the wild grape vines that hung from the forest trees, or visited the "quarters" to talk with those servants who had come from Mount Vernon. Their favorite was the loquacious "Mammy" who liked nothing better than to talk about the "beauty and splendid management" of Martha Washington. A favorite story was Nelly Custis' wedding, when "Ole Mistis" invited the servants in to watch the ceremony, and gave them all kinds of delicious things to eat. When the girls asked her to tell them how Aunt Nelly was dressed, the answer was invariably a vague, "Oh, all in something white," because it was Mrs. Washington, "dressed so splendid in a light flowered satin gown," who had completely captured Mammy's eye. On the way back to the house, the children often stopped to inspect the Washington coach, which was still in daily use and would remain the Custis' best carriage for many years.

On the cool portico or in the parlor, the young people listened attentively when Mr. Custis began to talk on his favorite subject, George Washington, and his own happy childhood at Mount Vernon; he usually had some new story to relate. They would follow him around when, warming to his subject, he took them on a tour of what he called his "Washington Treasury," a collection that contained his grandmother's china, the set selected by Light-Horse Harry Lee and presented to the General by the Society of the Cincinnati, several of Washington's swords, pistols, battle flags, his campgear and tent, his clothing and books and—perhaps most impressive of all to the children—the great bed in which he died.

In Robert's home there were also mementoes of George Washington, and stories that the children liked to hear about their father's intimacy with him, allowing Harry the liberty even of joking at the great man's expense. The tale Robert liked best concerned the time when Washington mentioned, at his dinner table, his need for carriage horses, and asked Harry if he knew where he could find a pair.

"I have a fine pair, General," Lee told him, "but you cannot get them."

"Why not?"

"Because you will never pay more than half the price for anything; and I must have full price for my horses."

This bantering reply set Mrs. Washington to laughing, and her parrot, perched in back of her chair, joined her. The General took the affront to his dignity in good part.

"Ah, Lee, you are a funny fellow," he retorted. "See, that bird is laughing at you."

Frequently Ann Carter recalled for the children her impressions of Washington when he came to see her father at Shirley, and they heard many of the details an observant girl notes. She minutely described his looks, his size, the tone of his voice, the sound of his laugh, and told how talkative—even eloquent—he became after a glass or two of Madeira; how well he danced, and how he liked to dance with the fashionable and pretty young women whom he admired extravagantly. Then Robert could envision him, not as he had seen him so often in Charles Willson Peale's portrait that hung in the dining room at Shirley, but as a man of flesh and blood, thoroughly warm and human.

Life in Alexandria proceeded pleasantly, with a temporary ease in finances which allowed Ann Carter to have a new carriage made by Mr. Ogle of Philadelphia. Frequent trips were then made in comfort to Shirley and other country homes. One of the excursions Robert especially enjoyed was to Woodlands, the home of William Hamilton, who introduced the Lombardy poplar and ginkgo to America, and planted his estate near Philadelphia with an extraordinary collection of exotic trees. There the impressionable boy, wandering through the beautiful grove admiring the rare trees, found pleasure so lasting that he was to remember it to the end of his life.

Far removed from these scenes, Harry Lee, as his letters attested, was roving restlessly from island to island. From Barbadoes he had gone to Santo Domingo, thence to Turk's Island and Caicos, and finally to Nassau. But Ann Carter, who spoke of herself as a "widow," did not reply often, so Harry turned to his favorite child, Carter, now at Harvard College, for information concerning them all:

"Tell me about dear Smith and Robert. Tell me of Ann; has she grown tall? And how is my last in looks and understanding? Robert was always good, and will be confirmed in his happy turn of mind by his ever-watchful and affectionate mother. Does he strengthen his native tendency?" But Carter was also dilatory in his replies, allowing six months to pass before acknowledging receipt of a gun.

But as remiss as the son was in answering them, he carefully preserved all his father's letters, certainly not for the sententious advice Harry now felt called upon to administer, since Carter was being exposed to the temptations of the world for the first time, but out of outspoken affection for their au-

39

thor, and an intuitive sense of their literary value. Of all the children, Carter had been closest to his father, who once said of him: "He has been since his birth unchangeably my delight." Carter could remember a time when his father had not been too obsessed with other matters to teach him to play chess, and to ride and shoot, or to discuss literature with him as an equal.

Apart from the admonitions to avoid the snares and pitfalls that had been his own tragic undoing, these letters were literary dissertations of a high order. In them, Harry spoke intimately and profoundly of the masters of all ages—Homer, Vergil, Hafiz the Persian, Shakespeare, Caesar, Voltaire, St. Pierre, and "the inimitable Cervantes," to list a few. He wrote of atheism, the soul, truth, and virtue. He cautioned against the reading of novels—"the narration of imaginary action. . . . Adhere to history and ethical authors. . . . Read and emulate Marcus Aurelius, the great and good emperor." Nor did he ignore physical attainments: "Dancing, fencing, swimming, riding, shooting and pugilistic adroitness are all in their place worthy of due attention. The first two are easily acquired and serve to give the body its best posture which from habit becomes fixt—pleases the fair sex, to please whom is among our secondary dutys and teaches us to defend ourselves. . . . Riding gives grace to the body. . . ."

Of Harry Lee's five children, Robert was the least like him in many ways and most like him in others. Robert taught his own children to ride, shoot, swim, row, and ice-skate, and saw to it that they learned to dance—an accomplishment in which he excelled. He set them a lofty example of truth and virtue. In their reading, he urged them to avoid novels: "They paint beauty more charming than nature, & describe happiness that never exists." His own reading was nearly as wide and varied as his father's, and the works he reread most often were among Harry Lee's favorites—Homer, Caesar, Hafiz the Persian, Shakespeare, and Cervantes.

In later life his reading was almost exclusively in the Bible, but his favorite philosopher remained Marcus Aurelius, whose character and fundamental reasoning strongly resembled his own.

Harry Lee found exile bitter. His physical suffering had tempered him, and he became suddenly aware that the lives of his wife and children had never been a part of his own. After that, his thoughts reverted to them more and more for the comfort and happiness he was always vainly seeking. On June 18, 1817, in a letter to Carter, he even recalled sentimentally that it was his wedding anniversary, and characterized Ann Carter by some lines from Pope:

> So unaffected, so composed a mind,
> So firm, yet soft, so strong, yet so refined,
> Heaven as its purest gold, by tortures try'd.

He begged again for news of "our dear Ann, Smith, Robert, and my unknown. You ought to have said something of them all, their growth, their health, their amusements, their occupations, their progress in literature, their tempers as they open." Still, as he reviewed his life, he believed he "saw nothing to regret."

In February, 1818, no longer able to control his desire to return to his family, Lee took passage on the *Betsy* bound for Savannah; with him went his battered leather trunk and a cask of choice Madeira. But off the coast of Georgia, he became so sick it was evident that he could not travel farther. Around four o'clock in the afternoon the *Betsy* threw out an anchor, lowered a boat, and the captain and mate accompanied Harry Lee into the landing at Cumberland Island, where the widow of General Nathanael Greene lived at Dungeness.

Young Philip Nightingale, the General's grandson, ran down to the landing when he saw the boat approaching, and stared in wonder at the groaning man the sailors carried gently ashore, and at the old trunk and cask of wine. Summoning the boy, Lee asked who he was, and when he heard, embraced him "with marked emotion." Philip offered his arm, but Lee was able to walk only a few steps before he sank exhausted to a log. But even while he suffered, his eloquence and sense of the dramatic did not desert him. He turned to Philip and asked him to fetch a carriage, and as the youth started off at a run, Harry called after him to take a message to his mother:

41

"Tell her I am come purposely to die in the house and in the arms of the daughter of my old friend and compatriot!"

Light-Horse Harry Lee was welcomed like an honored guest at the tall white mansion set in a grove of magnolias and live oaks. He was put to bed in the best guest chamber, and nursed with care by the ladies of the house, while Mrs. Greene's favorite maid, "the esteemed and privileged family servant" Mom Sarah, waited on him. He was frequently a trying patient, indulging his temper during paroxysms of acute pain. The first time Mom Sarah came into his room, he hurled his boot at her and ordered her out; but being a woman of spirit, and unused to such treatment, she hurled it back at him. Despite his agony, Harry smiled, and insisted that no other servant should ever attend him.

Officers of the United States fleet, which was waiting to take possession of Florida as soon as cession was made by Spain, called frequently to see Lee, as did General E. P. Gaines and other officers from nearby Fort Fernadina. Harry enjoyed the company, and for a time rallied sufficiently to walk about the garden. But then he suffered a relapse and Mrs. Greene sent for a naval surgeon. To save Lee's life, the doctor said, he would have to perform a bladder operation, for this organ had been seriously injured at the time of the Riot. But Harry protested:

"My dear sir, were the great Washington alive and here, joining you in advocating it, I would resist."

Late in the afternoon of March 25, 1818, death came for this pain-wracked and shattered man as he lay mumbling a message to his son, Carter. That night, Commodore John D. Henly, senior officer of the fleet, and General Gaines arranged the military funeral which took place the following day. Marines from the flagship *John Adams* and the brig *Saranac* formed the guard, while officers from the army and navy carried the coffin. Minute guns boomed, and military bands played the "Dead March" from *Saul* as the casket was lowered into a grave dug in the Greene family cemetery.

It was in keeping with Harry Lee's tragic life pattern that

his country paid him due homage only at his passing. Conscious of this, Mrs. Greene wrote bitterly to a friend that she had just "witnessed the Interment of another of those Patriots that our country 'in Congress assembled' so frequently speak of and so little assist."

For fifteen years, the grave of this gallant soldier whom Washington had extolled, of this statesman on whom Virginia had bestowed her highest honor, remained unmarked. Then a plain marble slab, with his name, age, and date of his death, was provided by the Divine Matilda's son, Henry, from his own exile in Paris.

2

THE Carter family was so large that it maintained its own schools for kinfolk. Classes for the girls were held at Shirley, and those for the boys at Eastern View, the Fauquier County home of Ann Lee's sister, Elizabeth, married to Robert Randolph.

When Robert Lee had exhausted the range of his mother's tutoring, he was sent to this family school. It was his first prolonged absence from home, and when he returned for a holiday, his mother noticed some evidence of the headstrong traits she had been careful to curb while he was under her vigilant eye. She mentioned her observation in a letter to her sister, and asked if Elizabeth had found Robert difficult to manage. Mrs. Randolph replied that, on the contrary, she had found him "a most engaging child," but if Ann felt he needed discipline, she would suggest the method used successfully on her own sons, namely:

"Whip and pray; pray and whip."

When Robert finished his schooling at Eastern View, he was enrolled in the Alexandria Academy. During his absence, his mother moved into the Fitzhughs' handsome Georgian house on Oronoco Street, directly across from their town house.

It was more spacious than the Cameron Street dwelling,

43

being two and a half stories, and had a garden that took in the entire length of the block planted to lilacs, viburnum, honeysuckle, jasmine, lemon trees, and magnolias.

It is probable that Fitzhugh would not accept rent, because Mrs. Lee's expenses were very high at this time. Her daughter, Ann Kinloch, had been "attacked with a dreadful complaint of the hand," requiring a two-year stay in Philadelphia for special medical treatment, and the eventual amputation of her arm to prevent the spread of what was doubtless tuberculosis of the bone. Carter, now nineteen, was in his second year at Harvard, planning on a law career. But in one year, he spent over a thousand dollars, thus using the entire sum set aside for his education and forcing his mother to end his college career. On February 2, 1817, she wrote taking him to task for his extravagance. Since only two of her letters to Smith have been preserved, and apparently none to Robert, this heretofore unpublished letter is of special interest:

My dear Carter,

I hope you will relinquish the chimerical, pernicious, and absurd idea of its being incumbent on you to enter into the amusements, and expenses of your associates. . . . Be assured you have been governed by a fatal delusion in preferring to emulate for a season what you may have thought a generous, genteel mode of conduct in your companions, to the lasting advantage which would have resulted to you, from adopting such a system, as would have enabled me to have given you a liberal education. That system tho' it would not have allowed profusion, would not have prescribed parsamony. . . . I am really astonished, confounded at your supposing that I could afford your entering into expenses at Cambridge, which I would not allow you at home. At what period could I have ever permitted you, or myself, to have hired a carriage whenever we wished to ride, or to have partaken of such amusements as required money to obtain? I am now sick, confined to my room, exercise is necessary to me, but the ground is covered with snow, and I cannot walk; and certainly it is not in my power to hire a hack for two or three days successively. I would not prevent you from going to the theatre four or five times in a season provided the actors were so good as to convey instruction. . . . And how can you expect to indulge yourself in the purchases of fruit, confectionary, & other luxuries, & in going to parties . . . when you could not afford to do so here? Nor could I ever incur those expenses, but in a very limited degree, in my more prosperous days, and now, not at all. Did you not stipulate when you left home, that no unnecessary expense was to be incurred? Was it not a doubtful question, whether I could, out of my annuity, give a college education to my sons, even if they pursued the most economical plan? . . . You even engaged to live for $400 if it would allow you to go to the College you unfortunately selected [Harry had made the selection]. . . . Any person of understanding knows, that a Boy cannot properly attend to his studies, who engages in pursuits which require the expenditure of $1000 per annum, & you have exceeded that sum. And do you think it will be remembered ten years hence by these same youths, that Carter Lee spent so much more money than his Mother could afford, that she was obliged to take him away from school before he finished his education, without subjecting you to their censure? . . . *To you*, I had looked, for the restoration of that happiness, *in part*, which my widowed lot had deprived me of. I had hoped you would be a highly educated, discreet, judicious man. That you would have been an example for your Brothers imitation—a dignified protector for your Sisters, and the pride, & solace of your Mother's declining years. But you are not pursuing the Course to fulfill such expectations. He who prefers the gratification of sensual pleasures, to the cultivation of mental endowments, will never be qualified for the performance of such duties. . . . Oh! may the God of mercy guide your steps into the paths of wisdom!

A. Lee

This letter accomplished its purpose. A very contrite young man returned home that June. He was so genuinely penitent that a means was found—perhaps through the generosity of the Fitzhughs—to pay for his remaining years at Harvard. He graduated in 1819, and opened a law office in Washington.

When Smith finished his studies at the Alexandria Academy, he decided on a naval career. His choice was influenced by his mother's lack of money. Since no naval academy existed at the time, in 1820 he obtained a midshipman's commission from President Monroe, and went to sea.

It was only natural that, with two sons away from home

and Ann Kinloch still under medical care in Philadelphia, Robert's mother should turn to him for companionship and ask him to shoulder some of the responsibilities her declining health prevented her from continuing. Paradoxically, unwanted children often prove the most amiable and winning ones. Ann soon found her chief source of comfort and pleasure in the company of this affectionate and accomplished boy, making him easily her favorite child.

Robert learned to keep house under the direction of his mother, who was considered "one of the most methodical and beautiful managers." He did the marketing, looked after the horses and, when he was older, took over the duties of nurse, and attended to his mother's business affairs.

His cousins Cassius and Sally Lee were both deeply impressed by his "exemplary behavior" and his devotion to his mother. When along in years, each wrote a recollection of Robert during his Alexandria days, speaking of his "uniform correct conduct at school and elsewhere"; of the tenderness with which he nursed his mother when she was ill; of how he took her for daily rides and cheered her by his gay talk, and provoked her to laughter by his antics. These remembrances were used by the first biographers of Robert E. Lee, with so much embroidery as to have it appear that even as a little boy their subject ignored the importunings of his playmates to join them in their games, or for a swim in the river, and hurried home to mix his mother's medicines, take her for a drive, or attend to his tasks about the house. They ascribed these nice attentions not to the great love he bore her, so natural in an affectionate child, but solely to his sense of duty.

In reading the letters of Cassius and Sally Lee, in which these recollections appear, it is of great interest (and relief) to discover that they were remembering *not* the earliest years in Alexandria, but the time when Robert was approaching eighteen and was preparing to enter West Point.

It is evident from other recollections that after Robert's return from Eastern View he undertook his studies and his new importance in the household with great seriousness and pride, and with an efficiency and industry that was natural to him. It was only normal for him to grow closer to his mother after she became so dependent on him, and, with the insight of approaching maturity, to perceive in her all the fine and endearing qualities he had formerly taken, childlike, for granted.

But there is nothing to suggest that Ann Carter was so unreasonable as to demand that Robert abandon all the joys of boyhood. Nor did he. He became an expert swimmer, horseman, oarsman, and skater, all accomplishments impossible to attain in the parlor or in attendance by the sickbed. Robert is himself the source for memories of swimming in the Potomac, of hunting in King George's Meadows for ducks, and in the nearby woods for partridges. His cousin Edmund remembered the many happy hours he and Robert spent together in such diversions, in feeding their pet English rabbits, and making their "daily visits to the markets . . . to procure meat and vegetables for our mothers, each carrying his own basket," indicating by his tone that even marketing was a pleasure excursion.

During school holidays, there were trips to Shirley, where Robert raced with his Carter cousins and astonished them with his ability to run two miles without stopping for breath. He also visited his half brother Henry at Stratford. Here Robert indulged his love of riding, and often galloped his horse all the way to Wakefield, George Washington's birthplace, without once breaking the gait. Sometimes he would follow the hounds all day on foot, and recalled years later the satisfaction he got from coming in at the kill before the mounted hunters did, because of his intimate knowledge of all paths and shortcuts.

Robert matured early into an extremely handsome and winning young man whose looks and manner attracted the notice of his elders. He was frequently commended for his devotion to his mother and sisters, and was considered a "youth of great promise."

By 1823, he had finished his studies at the Alexandria Academy. His teacher, William B. Leary, was a man of remarkable ability and pleasing personality who, in the three years that Robert went to his school, gave him a lifelong grounding in Latin and Greek, and implanted a strong and lasting affection for the schoolmaster. Nearly fifty years later Robert wrote to Mr. Leary:

I beg to express the gratitude I have felt all my life for the affectionate fidelity which characterized your teaching & conduct towards me. . . . Should any of my friends, wherever your lot may cast you, desire to know of your qualifications as a teacher, I hope you will refer them to me; for of them I can speak knowingly & from experience. . . .

The selection of a career now faced Robert. Since he was skilled in nursing, medicine was probably his first choice. But his mother's investments, which fluctuated with the economy and had now reduced her income to one-half, did not allow for the expense of study in European medical schools—a necessity at this time. Her finances were so precarious that she could often afford only veal for dinner—that was the cheapest—and almost never fowl, because she could buy only one, and after the ladies had been served, only the back was left for Robert.

With one boy at sea, Mrs. Lee probably did not encourage Robert to consider the navy. The only other career then that did not involve any expense was the army, and it was decided that Robert should try to get an appointment to the United States Military Academy. Aside from the economic aspect it was not an unreasonable choice, since his latent talent for soldiering must have stirred him. Too, this was the profession in which George Washington first achieved fame, as did Lafayette and Light-Horse Harry Lee, though at this time it is doubtful that Robert would have been greatly influenced by his father.

Robert must have often thought about the author of their misfortunes, and youth, quick to resent, may have let the blame fall where it was due. Although Ann Carter's pride kept her from speaking to her children of their father's other failings, she probably stressed his financial irresponsibility as an object lesson to her sons. But others, like the brusque old family friend who said in their presence: "Light-Horse Harry a fool was born, a fool he lived, and a fool he died!" would not have spared Robert, who must have learned the details of his father's shortcomings rather early.

48

Not until he gained the wisdom that comes through living could Robert forgive his father for the suffering his mother had borne. How completely he was able to forgive remains his secret. He named none of his sons for Harry and was entirely silent about him in surviving correspondence until the last decade of his life when, being in the vicinity of Cumberland Island twice, he visited the grave, describing the visits briefly in letters to his wife. In contrast, he was often heard to say that he "owed everything" to his mother. Until that time when he could forgive, he gave her the full portion of the love he might normally have shared with his father.

He now looked forward with pleasure to his chosen profession (though later he was to consider his choice the greatest mistake of his life), and immediate appointment was desirable. With a letter of introduction from William Henry Fitzhugh, he called on the Secretary of War, John Caldwell Calhoun. When Robert entered his office, Calhoun must have been well impressed with the handsome open countenance and the intelligent brown eyes of this sturdily built youth who stood so erect he seemed much taller than five feet eleven inches in his shoes; with the dignity of his bearing, and the absence of youthful awkwardness or arrogance. He asked Robert to be seated, broke the seal on the letter, and read:

Ravensworth Feb 7th 1824

My dear Sir,

I cannot permit the young gentleman, who will hand you this letter, to make his intended application, without carrying with him, such testimony in his behalf, as a long & an intimate acquaintance both with himself and his family, justify me in giving. He is the son of Genl Henry Lee, with whose history, you are, of course acquainted; and who, (whatever may have been the misfortune of his later years) had certainly established by his revolutionary services, a strong claim to the gratitude of his country. He is the son also of one of the finest women, the State of Virginia has ever produced. Possessed, in a very eminent degree, of all those qualities which peculiarly belong to the female character of the South, she is rendered doubly interesting by her meritorious & successful

49

exertions to support, in comfort, a large family, and to give all her children excellent educations.

The young gentleman, whom I now have the pleasure of introducing to you, as a candidate for West-Point, is her youngest son. An intimate acquaintance, & a constant intercourse with him, almost from his infancy, authorize me to speak in the most unqualified terms of his amiable disposition, & his correct & gentlemanly habits. . . . His own age (eighteen I believe) and the situation of his mother require that he should lose no time in selecting the employment to which his future life is to be devoted. . . .

Although Calhoun could promise nothing, he probably suggested that more recommendations like Mr. Fitzhugh's would help in making the final selection.

William B. Leary then wrote to vouch for his former pupil's "correct and gentlemanly deportment," and to state that "in the various branches to which his attention has been applied, I flatter myself that his information will be found adequate to the most sanguine expectations of his friends. With me he has read all the minor classics in addition to Homer & Longinus, Tacitus & Cicero. He is well-versed in arithmetic, Algebra & Euclid. . . ."

Carter Lee wrote a letter to supplement Robert's application, to state "what it would have been unbecoming in him to averred . . . viz: that his intellect seems to be a good one, that he appears to be sufficiently inclined to study, that his disposition is amiable, & his morals irreproachable."

His half brother, Henry, based his appeal chiefly on their father's Revolutionary War services.

Traditionally, the beautiful Nelly Custis Lewis introduced Robert to General Andrew Jackson, then Senator from Tennessee, who presumably used his influence to advantage. These concerted efforts were fruitful. On March 11, 1824, Robert received his appointment from President Monroe, on John Calhoun's recommendation. But because there were so many names ahead of his, he could not be admitted to West Point until July 1 of the following year.

50

That October, Alexandria prepared feverishly for the arrival of General Lafayette and his party on a triumphal tour of the United States. They had come at the invitation of President Monroe and had crossed the ocean on a United States man-of-war. Now that they were due in Alexandria, the citizens donned "La Fayette hats" and "La Fayette watch chains," and cockades of red, white, and blue, as they erected triumphal arches over Washington Street, down which the Marquis would ride. At every street corner, knots of old soldiers stood watching the excited preparations, eager to relate at the drop of a cocked hat their recollections of the General.

At the Thomas Lawrison house on St. Asaph Street, last-minute touches were being given to the rooms Lafayette and his party would occupy. At Arlington House, George Washington Parke Custis was going over the welcoming speech that the Mayor had asked him to deliver, while his wife directed plans for the private reception they were holding. General Washington's war tent had already been set up on the lawn so that Lafayette could stand under it and receive the homage of the throngs who would flock there to take his hand. Ann Carter Lee and her daughters readied the house on Oronoco Street for the General's expected call, while Robert, as a marshal in the parade, was in his uniform, practicing with the band.

On the morning of October 14, Lafayette called on Mrs. Lee. Though he was sixty-seven, he was youthful-appearing. The tall figure was still erect and commanding, the movements graceful in spite of a limp and dependence on a cane (the result of an accident some years before). But his face was unwrinkled, the red hair without gray, the hazel eyes clear. It was most fitting that while on this sentimental journey to pay his respects to Washington's tomb, to call at Woodlawn (Nelly Custis' country seat), and at Arlington, he would also come to see the widow and children of the man Washington came to regard as a son.

After he had gone, Ann Carter doubtless showed the children the letter Lafayette had written to Harry Lee, pledging eternal friendship.

51

As Lafayette passed the large Georgian house adjoining the Lees', he removed his hat and bowed to a young couple standing in the open doorway. The young man was Benjamin Hallowell, a Quaker dominie who had recently opened a boys' school in his house, and the young woman was Margaret, his bride of one day whom he jocularly styled his "La Fayette wife." Robert's cousin Cassius was attending the Hallowell School, which in a very short time achieved an excellent reputation for scholarship, and that winter Robert, perhaps apprehensive over the approaching entrance examinations at West Point, enrolled to study mathematics.

Mr. Hallowell found him to be

a most exemplary scholar in every respect. He was never behind-time at his studies; never failed a single recitation, was perfectly observant of all rules and regulations of the institution; was gentlemanly, unobtrusive, and respectful in all his deportment to teachers and his fellow-students. His specialty was finishing-up. He imparted a finish and neatness as he proceeded, to everything he undertook. One of the branches of mathematics he studied with me was conic sections, in which some of the diagrams were very complicated. He drew the diagram on a slate; and although he well knew that the one he was drawing would have to be removed to make room for another, he drew each one with as much accuracy and finish, lettering and all, as if it were to be engraved.

This letter of Mr. Hallowell's has been frequently quoted by Lee's biographers as an example of his diligence and exemplary conduct throughout all his school years, forgetting that while attending this school Robert turned eighteen, and that Hallowell was therefore describing a mature and serious young man and not a stripling.

Robert attended class only in the mornings, and it was in the free afternoons that he took his mother for drives. Cousin Sally Lee, who often accompanied them, recalled how at noon Robert would have the carriage taken out, and how, as soon as they got out into the country, he would commence "doing and saying every thing to amuse" his mother. On one of these excursions, when Mrs. Lee complained of draughts in the carriage, Robert took out his jack-knife and cut curtains out of paper, provoking much laughter when he insisted on hanging them up.

The months passed quickly, and soon it was June, time for Robert to start out on the long journey to West Point. He looked forward to the experiences ahead, though parting with his mother and sisters was hard. Ann Carter had become so dependent on him she could not imagine life without him. But trials were nothing new to her, and with characteristic fortitude she faced this one, reserving her tears until Robert was gone. Then with a sob she turned to Sally Lee standing beside her and said:

"You know what I have lost. He is son, daughter, and everything to me!"

3

JUST at West Point, the Hudson River breaks through the highlands and picturesquely floods a valley. Wooded slopes rise from the surface of the water, and every gorge and ravine holds a hidden cove. But it is doubtful whether the candidate-cadets lining the rail of the little side-wheeler that brought them up from New York had eyes for anything but the Military Academy rising on a plain 160 feet above them. They were too busy looking for the flag the helmsman said would soon be visible to notice the beauty of the landscape. After the steamer had nosed past old Fort Clinton, some of whose hand-hewn rocks might still be seen below the brow of the cliff, they saw the flag and gave several lusty cheers that startled the marsh hens to noisy flight, and attracted the gaze of a solitary sentinel guarding the landing.

As the boys filed down the wharf, the guard escorted them to a nearby cabin, and asked them to write their names and home addresses on a slate. When they were through, he loftily indicated that these lowly creatures, these would-be "Plebes," should go on up the hot steep road as far as Gridley's Hotel, just south of the reservation boundary, where they would be quartered until after their examinations. They toted their own hand luggage, but trunks were left to the manipulations of the Academy's sole porter, a veteran of the War of 1812, who wore an iron hook in place of the hand he had lost in battle.

Like others whose record of their first impressions have survived in letters and diaries, Robert was doubtless surprised to find that instead of a few old wooden buildings set in a wilderness, a neat village of brick and stone rose from the bare plain.

The next morning, Robert reported to Superintendent Sylvanus Thayer, the "Father of the Military Academy," who received him in the basement office of his handsome house. Thayer's manservant, Patrick Murphy, an ex-soldier who ruled the domestic domain with Molly, the Irish cook, made such a ceremony of ushering cadets into Thayer's presence that by the time they faced the handsome man behind the big desk they were duly awed. This desk of Thayer's contained many deep pigeonholes where he kept at his fingertips the record of each cadet. At a moment's notice, he could be thoroughly conversant with the weekly abstracts of grades, demerits, and debts, often to the chagrin of cadets who, ignorant of the pigeonholes, attributed omniscience to the superintendent.

Long years of practice had made Thayer an expert in evaluating cadet material. He knew after a few minutes' talk with a lad whether or not he would turn out to be what was termed in the slang of the day, one of Uncle Sam's bad bargains. He must have been interested in this son of Light-Horse Harry Lee, and pleased to find him better grounded academically than most southern appointees whose poor educational facilities sometimes presented a serious handicap.

After the interview, Robert went out to drill, an exercise for which he found himself totally unprepared. To his mother Lee probably wrote in much the same way as did another candidate who said: "You never saw a more awkward creature in your life than I was or appeared to be." The orders, the boy told his mother, were barked fiercely, without punctuation: "Heels-together-and-on-the-same-line—toes-equally-turned-out —little-fingers-on-the-seams-of-your-pantaloons—button-your-coat—draw-in-your-chin—throw-out-your-chest—cast-your-eyes-fifteen-paces-to-the-front," and made him despair of ever becoming a soldier.

The beating of the drums at ten o'clock was the signal to report to the parade ground for dinner roll call.

We were formed by dint of much pushing and pulling on the part of our instructors, into two ranks at *parade rest,* [another candidate remembered], and having received a short lesson, enunciated without commas, on the subject of springing like a flash of lightning from this position to that of attention at the command 'tion,' the roll was called and we started for the mess hall. We were marched in close order, in squads of fifteen or twenty each, losing step of course, and tumbling over each other all the way. . . . We were as unfortunate in the mess hall as out of it; for we were sure to take seats before the command was given, to be too slow in obeying when it came, to move our seats without permission, or to err with regard to the command *rise*, as we had done in sitting down.

"Fourth section candid-a-ates, turn out!" came ringing down the halls of Gridley's, and as Robert and the other new boys turned out, they found this was an order to form in rank and march to the post surgeon for their physical examination. When this was finished, they marched to the room where they would take the academic test.

On blackboards set up on easels, a few boys at a time nervously worked problems in arithmetic, and wrote sentences from dictation, to test penmanship and spelling; then they each in turn read aloud from a book. As proof of their distracted state, none of them afterward was in agreement whether this had been a history of the United States, Aesop's Fables, or the Old Testament!

They did not learn the results of their tests until the next morning, June 28, when they were ordered to drill before the barracks. Then the adjutant read aloud from an alphabetical list the names of those who had passed, ordering them to step forward three paces—this simple expedient entitling the boys to be styled "Cadet" officially—though they would most often hear themselves addressed as "Plebe," "Animal," or "Thing," by upperclassmen. The oath of allegiance was not signed until

September, nor did the cadet receive an official warrant or appointment until he had successfully completed a six-month probationary period and passed an oral examination at that time. Though Robert was well prepared for the academic test, it was still a relief to hear his name called and take the three paces to the front.

Knapsacks were next distributed to the new cadets, who then returned to Gridley's, packed up their clothes, and marched into Camp Adams, where third-classmen, not yet entitled to summer furlough, were under canvas until the fall semester, their activities supervised by the Commandant of Cadets, Major William J. Worth, known to the Corps as "Haughty Bill" or "Old Hant."

Each boy was issued two blankets, one canvas bedcover, four shirts, two pairs of shoes (in Robert's case these would be an unbelievable size 4½-C), four pairs of socks, two silk stocks, one pair of white gloves, one blue fatigue suit, and a bandbox in which to keep that glorious article, the cylindrical leather hat, seven inches high and shaped like a pot. It was admirably suited, so cadets had found, for smuggling food from the mess hall to quarters.

As quickly as they could be made, uniforms were issued, so that boys could exchange their conspicuous civilian dress for the enviable fitted gray jacket with collar that just cleared the ear lobes, and the braid-trimmed gray pantaloons, or white duck for summer wear.

Muskets were issued as soon as cadets learned to march and execute facings without falling over each other's heels; then the manual of arms was taught. By the middle of July, some were proficient enough to be posted as sentinels. During encampment, there were no studies except infantry tactics, which were recited to an officer. There was seldom any artillery drill, since guns and caissons had to be hauled by hand because the Point could boast only two horses, both the property of the widow of the recently deceased Post Surgeon, Dr. Cutbush, known to cadets as "Split Me." His two equines had inspired the cadet doggerel:

> And Split Me, he had horses two,
> The one was gray, the other blue.

56

In addition to drill there were dancing lessons, a compulsory course for third- and fourth-classmen, under the direction of a French dancing master. For the Plebes who were not allowed to attend Post parties, this dancing without ladies proved to be a "dry business." "Baying at the moon" was the diversion started just before Robert arrived, and had already become a traditional part of the summer encampment. It began as group singing on moonlit evenings, before the call to quarters, but had come to include stories, skits, and charades.

At eleven o'clock on July 4, 1825, the drums rolled and Robert and the other cadets marched to the chapel. For four hours, they sat on hard narrow benches, listening to Cadet Allen read the Declaration of Independence, and Cadet Henderson deliver an "eloquent" (if long) oration. One boy reported to his mother that all this time he was "squeesed up among a parcel of Cadets and squeesed up more with my belts, as we have all to wear our side arms." At three o'clock they were released from the "squeesing," and marched to the mess hall, where William Cozzens, the steward, served up an "excellent" dinner, a welcome change from his usual frugal, and often unpalatable, fare. During the meal, many patriotic toasts were drunk in champagne—for regulations concerning drinking were waived on the Fourth and at Christmas—and many more would have been proposed had not Robert's class become uproarious. The upperclassmen retired in disgust.

Through the medium of the drillmaster's rebukes: "Close up, Mr. Johnston, to thirteen inches; close up I tell you, Sir! Point your toes, Mr. Kennedy; chin in, eyes front, Mr. Mackay!", the new boys soon learned each other's names, and Robert shortly had a wide circle of acquaintance; two were to become close and remain lifelong friends. One was a fellow Virginian, Joseph Eggleston Johnston, whose father, Peter, had served in Lee's Legion; the other was John Mackay of Savannah, Georgia. Johnston, who early earned the nickname of "the Colonel," was a short wiry lad and though fun-loving, a bit fussy, peppery, and quick to take offense. Jack, on the other hand, was handsome, tall, witty, and easygoing, and soon became the favorite. He was a Shakespearean scholar.

When they had liberty on Saturday afternoons, rain or

shine the three would explore everything from "the lofty Crow's Nest to the muddiest marsh along the Hudson." They inspected old Fort Putnam, where Major André's ghost was supposed to make his nightly rounds, and examined with interest the few remaining links of the Great Chain which had been stretched between the Point and Constitution Island to prevent the passage of enemy ships during the Revolution. They visited the house where George Washington had made his headquarters in 1778, and the cottage of his aide, the Polish patriot, Count Tadeusz Kosciusko. Walking down the narrow path overgrown with shrubbery, they found the terrace where Kosciusko had in his leisure built an Old World grotto and rock garden around a bubbling spring.

When classes commenced in September, Robert and the other cadets moved into barracks and set up their equipment in strict accordance with the regulations posted on every door. The rooms were too small to admit bedsteads, so most cadets were supplied with narrow mattresses, though some letters and journals tell of the boys rolling themselves in their two blankets and sleeping on the bare floor.

At four-thirty came the morning gun, and half an hour later, the roll of drums and the cry: "Fall in there!" when it was necessary to be in the ranks or be "reported." After roll call, cadets returned to quarters, with fifteen minutes to roll up bedding, sweep (or scrub) the floor, and put everything in its place for inspection. They then studied mathematics until seven o'clock, when the drums summoned them to breakfast— frequently the remains of the previous day's dinner—usually meat cut up with potatoes, gravy, and chunks of bread, "indifferent" butter, and coffee. This was passable if there had been enough to go around; but there almost never was, so that many cadets had only bread and coffee. As a result, a good number fainted during drill.

At seven-thirty came guard mount, and half an hour later, class parade, another roll call, and then the march to classes in the Academy building. As with all members of the Fourth Class, Robert's subject was mathematics, a course embracing algebra, geometry, trigonometry, and the mensuration of planes and solids.

At eleven o'clock the fourth-classmen returned to quarters to review the day's mathematics and prepare for the afternoon class in French, taught because it was an essential tool. All important writings on military subjects were in that language, while in mathematics the methods and texts were either of French origin or in French. The course included reading and translation of Voltaire's *Histoire de Charles XII*, and Volume I of the picaresque *Gil Blas*.

Dinner came at one o'clock, and the end of classes for the day at four. The remaining time before supper was consumed by drill, sunset parade, roll call, and prayers. After supper, most often only bread and milk, cadets studied in their quarters until nine-thirty, when another roll call and inspection ended the long day. Only on Saturday half holidays were cadets permitted to receive visitors. During this free time, they were also allowed to ramble over the hills within proscribed limits; to hunt small game in season; to fish; and in winter to skate on the river. The especially studious cadet could pass two hours of his precious holiday in the school library, the only time during the week when it was open.

There was naturally a great temptation, especially during the winter, to pass these half holidays, and nights after taps, at Gridley's or Benny Havens', though both places were off limits since neither "Old Grid" nor Benny was averse to selling liquor to cadets. Although Benny Havens' public house was about two miles distant, his was the favored resort, for Benny was a most cordial and attractive character—"the only congenial soul in this God-forsaken place," Cadet Edgar Allan Poe had said of him. He was noted for his hot flip, a mixture of beaten eggs, spices, and ale or cider; and his wife, a jolly woman of Dutch origin, was equally known for her turkey and buckwheat cakes. Many who did not drink courted arrest simply for the sake of the good food and the camaraderie.

If Robert Lee "ran it" to Havens' for a filling meal, a mug of hot flip, and the bountiful *Gemütlichkeit*, he was one of the many fortunate ones who went and came back undetected. But it is unlikely that his natural frugality would have sanctioned many visits. In view of Carter's capers at Harvard, Robert had determined to apply himself with diligence to his studies and obey regulations, out of consideration for his mother and at the dictates of his own pride. He knew that his entire future rested upon his success at the Academy.

By nature, Robert was conscientious and studious, so he must have had few battles with himself to keep to his books or respect the rules; yet he was no pedant. He was noted among his friends for his love of fun, his ebullience, and his fondness for joking and teasing. He would have been no more averse to knocking at doors and stealing off before they could be answered, slipping anonymous comic notes and verses under doors, or ogling a pretty girl through a telescope, than Harry Lee and his companions had been at Princeton. He was not, however, a party to the "uproar" on Christmas night, 1826, when the consumption of overly potent eggnog prompted a number of cadets to fire pistols in the North Barracks and halloo through the halls: "Turn out the Corps! The Bombardiers are coming!" Though Robert was careful to keep his pranks within the pale of Academy regulations, he was not always able to confine his temper. Classmates have left recollections of occasional outbursts of this youthful Hotspur and his struggles to control his anger.

In January, Robert was awarded his warrant for having successfully completed his probationary period. The results of the oral examination placed him third in a class of eighty-seven. First place was held by Charles Mason of New York; and second, by William Harford of Georgia. But Robert's standing brought him the honor of being listed among the distinguished cadets in the army register of that year. From these ranks, the Corps officers were selected. Because of his proficiency in drill, Robert was made staff sergeant.

Since no cadet, except in the case of serious illness, could leave the Academy until the end of his second year, Robert joined the annual encampment on the plain. It was passed in the same way the previous summer had been, though dancing lessons were no longer considered "dry business" since Robert and his classmates were now allowed to attend the parties that occasionally enlivened the post. Then they were able to choose partners from among the Point's belles—the three Thompson girls, the Kinsley sisters, Mary Ann Mansfield, and Mary Picton.

But for boys who were passing their second summer away from home, the most welcome diversion was the arrival of relatives and friends. Though it is certain Ann Carter Lee did not take the long journey, it is not unlikely that Carter did, at her instance.

The end of encampment that year was marked by a fancy-dress ball. All cadets who wished to don costumes were welcome. Robert, who enjoyed participation in amateur theatricals, probably attended.

With the second or "yearling" year, the Third Class was introduced to advanced mathematics. French was continued with further reading and translation in the works studied the previous term. But there was an additional course in which Robert took more than usual interest, since he possessed some skill. This was drawing of the human figure from casts and models, taught by an eccentric French miniaturist, Thomas Gimbrede, known to cadets as "Jim." His admirable logic could not fail to reassure the most skeptical student. "There are only two lines in drawing," he told his class. "The straight line and the curve line. Every one can draw a straight line and every one can draw a curve line—therefore every one can draw!"

Classes were divided into sections of about twelve men each, counted off from the roll of merit. The first section, consisting of the most proficient cadets, was conducted by the professor while the other sections were delegated to assistants. Each semester, Colonel Thayer selected a qualified cadet as an assistant professor in every subject. That fall, Robert was chosen to be the assistant in mathematics, a post which brought a welcome addition of ten dollars to his monthly pay of sixteen dollars and his subsistence pay of twelve dollars (from which all expenses were deducted).

It was an honor that was highly gratifying to Ann Carter Lee, who wrote of it to Smith, then headed for a cruise in the Mediterranean. She added proudly that Robert "was advancing rapidly, never having received a mark or demerit." That June, Robert stood second in his class in what cadets termed the "immortal section," and was granted his first furlough.

At this time his mother was living in Georgetown with Mildred and Carter, who had recently been admitted to the bar of the Supreme Court, causing his mother to hope that this would place him "in a more prosperous situation." Carter had a distinct distaste for the law, preferring to pass his time "un-profitably" in literary pursuits. He is described by a contemporary as "a most intellectual, learned, and entertaining man. His social qualities were of the highest order, his humor inimitable; his classic wit flowed . . . from a well-stored mind. . . . Every subject received its best treatment from his genius. . . ."

In Alexandria he helped found the Periclean Society, a literary club whose meetings were devoted to the reading of original works by members. In its minutes are countless notations of songs, speeches, stories, and love sonnets from Carter's pen.

When Robert reached home, he found his mother a semi-invalid. He was not shocked, for he knew from her letters that she considered her disease "an unconquerable one," and felt that her hold on life was tenuous. Her frequent letters had kept him well posted on all family news for the past two years. In this way, he had learned of Ann Kinloch's marriage the previous June to the Kentucky clergyman William Louis Marshall (kinsman of Chief Justice John Marshall), who would soon make a successful shift from the ministry to law; learned also of the death of their infant daughter, and of his uncle Richard Bland Lee's passing; knew of Smith's ports of call; of Carter's love affairs, and Mildred's accomplishments in literature and music, and her promise of becoming a belle.

The presence of both her "dear boys," for Smith obtained leave also, proved stimulating to Ann Carter, and she felt strong enough to travel with all three sons and Mildred to Kinloch, the Fauquier County home of her cousin, Edward Carter Turner, whose daughter, Marietta, was Mildred's closest friend.

Wherever the Lees went, Carter was a center of attraction. "Peals of laughter" resounded from his vicinity, for he was "a boon companion and the first guest invited to a banquet." Robert and Smith, however, had admirers of another sort. Both were extremely handsome, and soon found themselves in the enviable position of having all the young ladies vying for their attention. During Smith's last cruise, his mother wrote him that a girl had come to the house to ask for his profile, "and Carter insists on being allowed to carry her one this evening which he will sell for a high price. He wishes he had thought of it before you went, he says, and he would have made Master Ranks cut many and would have sold them to your favourites, by way of getting a little money." Marietta Turner was greatly impressed by Robert's "manly beauty and fine manners," and his handsome appearance in his uniform with its "white bullet buttons," while another cousin, the "modest and affectionate" Mary Custis, also staying at Kinloch, confided to her intimates that she had lost her heart to him.

With riding parties, picnics, and boating by day; tableaux, wagon rides, and moonlight dances in the long evenings, the summer furlough passed unbelievably quickly, and it was soon mid-August, time for Robert to part again from his family. At the stage depot, he kissed the bevy of admiring cousins come to see him off, and left for New York.

When he reached the Point, he was welcomed warmly by Jack Mackay, Joe Johnston, Jack Kennedy, Hugh Mercer, and other friends who had come back from furlough. Summer for most of these boys had been passed very much like Robert's. Jack Mackay had received so much flattering attention from his five sisters' numerous and charming friends that he had compromised his heart with several of the prettiest ones. But there was little time for recounting summer conquests among the fair sex, for on September 1, frivolous talk and recollections of tender words and sparkling eyes were replaced by military life in earnest.

Robert resumed his post as assistant professor of mathematics, while his own course in that subject was supplemented by natural philosophy, a broad field that included physics, chemistry, mechanics, electricity, optics, and astronomy. Astronomy, Robert once wrote, afforded him "more pleasure than any other branch of study." He continued drawing, along with additional work in topography and landscape. A high standing in natural philosophy was important to a student whose ambition was to become an engineer, and Robert, who had decided on that field, applied himself industriously. His reward came after the semiannual examinations when he placed second in physics, and third in chemistry.

The June finals gave Charles Mason the lead again, with Robert second on the roll of general merit. His standing, together with his popularity, won him the most prized of Academy honors: Adjutant of the Corps. That summer Robert passed most of his time with his mother, for her health was noticeably worse, and he probably sensed this might be their last opportunity to be together.

September 1 brought the start of the final year. Because Robert stood high on the merit roll, he received his instruction in engineering from David B. Douglass, the head of the department. It was a course that included civil and military architecture, field and permanent fortifications, grand tactics, and the science of artillery. He had courses also in chemistry, geology, ethics, rhetoric, political economy, and constitutional law, with Professor Thomas Warren.

In the January examinations, Robert placed second in geology, chemistry, rhetoric, and moral philosophy and tied for first place in engineering with a young man by the name of Catharinus P. Buckingham, from Ohio. For the first time, Robert had surpassed the invincible Charles Mason. In April, he received permission to stay at Gridley's Hotel in order to prepare himself, without the distractions of affable roommates, for the final examinations. This was a time when, as another cadet wrote home, he would lift his eyes from his books only to eat and sleep.

The first day of June, the Board of Visitors came to meet jointly with the school's academic staff for a daily two-week period of oral testing. It was known as "the Inquisition" or "the Agony" to cadets who shuddered to obey the call: "Turn out, first section, First Class!" Six cadets at a time were summoned into the examiner's presence. Three large blackboards were set up on easels, two cadets being assigned to a board. They were given problems to work, and after an allotted time were called upon individually to explain the problems orally or by demonstration. Each cadet had five hours of questions on all subjects covered that year.

After it was over, Robert's sense of relief must have been akin to Jack Mackay's, and if he wrote home he would have said something similar to what Jack told his mother:

"I am at this moment from the examination hall. I have passed satisfactorily to myself on every subject, & the game is now over . . . clear through. Our class will be relieved from duty at the Military Academy this evening or tomorrow at the farthest. I wish I could transport myself this moment among you."

The end of "the Inquisition" that year was marked with a display of fireworks that lighted up the vale as far as Newburgh.

When the grades were reckoned, Robert's rating placed him first in artillery and tactics, but in class standing he had to bow once more to Charles Mason and take second place. In conduct he tied with Mason, who had also received no demerits during the four years.

These young men who stood at the head of their class had the privilege of selecting the branch of service in which they wanted to serve. Robert chose the Engineer Corps, which had all along been his goal.

Graduations were simple at this time, and were attended by only a few parents and friends who stood in the hot sun to watch the awarding of diplomas and listen to the address, usually made by the Secretary of War.

It is certain that none of Robert's family came, for his mother was on her deathbed.

4

ANN Carter Lee had improved so much during the warm spring days of 1829 that her family was encouraged. But before summer arrived, she suffered a relapse and Mrs. Fitz-hugh insisted that she come to Ravensworth, where she would receive every attention.

When Robert stood beside his mother's bed that June day, right after his graduation from West Point, he saw that there was no longer any hope for her recovery. It was an effort for her to talk, but it was evident to all how happy she was to have him with her again. Cousin Sally Lee, who called often to see her, remembered how she watched his every move and seemed content only when he was in the room. Once again he mixed her medicines and saw to her comfort night and day.

The ordeal was not a long one. The indomitable will that had seen them all successfully through the trying years relaxed its grip. With the exception of Mildred, all the children were settled. There was no longer any need for Ann to struggle with poverty and sickness.

On the morning of July 26, 1829, her end came; and Robert, as he stood at her bedside, experienced a sorrow he never forgot. Forty years later he recalled it as keenly as if it had happened, as he said then, "but yesterday."

"Her death is such as might have been expected from her life —exhibiting the resignation and composure of a practical Christian, conscious of having faithfully discharged her duties both to God and her fellow creatures," *The National Intelligencer* wrote of her passing.

Details of the disease that caused her lifelong illness and her death at fifty-six are wanting. In her letters, the only specific sickness mentioned is dropsy. In view of her tendency to chest congestions, and her doctor's recommendation of a warm, dry climate, it is reasonable to conclude that she had tuberculosis, particularly since anemia is present in this disease, and is also one of the causes of dropsy. Tuberculosis was a very common and unrecognized disease of that day, and can possibly also account for the untimely deaths of her sister and two brothers.

Shortly before her death, she made a will, leaving to her daughters ten thousand dollars of the principal of her trust fund. To each of them also went half the linen and wearing apparel. Ann Kinloch received the china tea service, a wardrobe, and title to the three servants she had taken with her at the time of her marriage. Mildred was given Nat, the old house servant and coachman, and because of her musical talent, the piano.

Robert inherited a third interest in an undivided tract of land in Floyd, Virginia, his share worth twenty-five hundred dollars; one hundred acres in Fairfax County; a share in his father's property at Harpers Ferry; and his mother's maid, Nancy, and her children. Mrs. Lee requested that the rest of her property be sold, and the proceeds divided among her three sons. When this was done, each received about three thousand dollars.

On August 6, Robert and Mildred went to stay with their sister Ann Marshall and her husband, leaving Carter to take care of the sale of the house and furnishings.

"I am left by myself to reflect on how melancholy it is that there will soon be no longer a roof under which we can be gathered as our home," Carter wrote his half brother Henry, who was leaving for his post as United States Consul at Algiers. "This happening at the very time of your departure seems to complete the overthrow of that domestic happiness, which after all the heart appears most to rely on. . . . Friends after friends walked out of the house yesterday in tears, & I could hardly retain mine."

On August 11, General Charles Gratiot, Chief Engineer in the Washington headquarters of the Corps, wrote out Order No. 8:

"Brevet 2nd Lieut. Robert E. Lee, of the Corps of Engineers will by the middle of November next, report to Major Saml Babcock for duty at Cockspur Island, in the Savannah River, Georgia."

When the order came, November seemed a long way off, so Robert accepted his Aunt Elizabeth Randolph's invitation to visit at Eastern View. He settled Mildred permanently with the Marshalls, and reached the Randolphs' at the beginning of September. The house was full of young people, the mood was gay, and according to his Boswell, Cousin Marietta Turner,

Robert was soon "as full of life, fun, and particularly of teasing, as any of us."

At the end of October, Robert, with what he called his "Mammoth trunk," boarded the stagecoach for New York, to take passage there on a coastal packet bound for Savannah. With him went Nat, the old servant, who had tuberculosis. The family believed that Georgia's warm climate might cure him.

When he reached Savannah, Robert found Nat a comfortable room, called in the best doctors, and nursed him tenderly himself. But the old man's case was far advanced, and he lived only a short time.

Cockspur Island, twelve miles below Savannah, was a marsh and mud island, so Robert found, located at the mouth of the river, and subject to inundation with the flow of tides. Preliminary surveys for a fort had been made the previous December, but because heat, mosquitoes, and fever limited the working season to the winter months, little else had been done. Major Babcock was still on leave, so Robert returned to Savannah and went to see Jack Mackay, who was stationed with the artillery at Oglethorpe Barracks.

Jack took Robert home to meet his family. His widowed mother, Mrs. Elizabeth Mackay, welcomed Robert warmly and made him feel like a member of her large family by assigning him a permanent room in her spacious house.

Besides Jack there were two other sons, William and Robert. But most pleasing to a man in Lee's situation, there were four lovely daughters at home. Margaret was just twenty, and possessed what was described as "a distinctive personality" which shortly won Robert into the ranks of her many admirers. Next to Margaret was the beautiful Elizabeth Anne, or Eliza, small, dark-eyed, with a talent for drawing and painting; then Catherine, sixteen, vivacious, pretty, and also gifted in art; and Sarah, fourteen, of unrecorded potentialities.

As if these were not enough young ladies to ensnare Robert's susceptible heart, the Mackays introduced him to their relatives and friends. He found Mary Anderson "sweet and bright"; he admired Mary Savage, one of Savannah's belles;

and enjoyed the company of the attractive Sarah and Philippa Minis, whose home was just up the block from the Mackays. He gave Sarah a pen-and-ink drawing of a terrapin and an alligator made during his leisure at Cockspur, which was carefully preserved by Sarah and her descendants.

This was a pleasant interlude before banishment to the forsaken Cockspur, where Robert passed his days in mud and water up to his armpits and his nights at the drawing board or in consultation with Major Babcock. Though he met one congenial person, Lieutenant James A. Chambers, a Marylander and West Point man, the only diversions were cards and chess. Encouraged by the example of Eliza and Catherine Mackay, who passed much of their leisure in art work, he took up pen-and-ink sketching and gave his best works, a death mask of Napoleon and identical drawings of the alligator and terrapin, to these young ladies.

Major Babcock was an older man, in poor health, and for this reason perhaps, was inefficient and lax in his supervision. He was glad to have so "active and intelligent" an assistant, he wrote, capable of taking over direction of the construction of dikes to keep out the tides, a canal to drain the site, and quarters for the officers and men. On February 1, Babcock informed General Gratiot that he had appointed "Bt. Lieut. R. E. Lee, of Engrs., acting commissary of Subsistence of the Post under my command." Four months later he wrote his chief that he was leaving his post "with Lt. Lee forwith, agreeably to your instructions," since, upon the advice of two of Savannah's "most eminent Physicians," he had been ordered "to remove as soon as possible" from Cockspur's "unhealthful situation."

In March, Robert was subjected to keen humiliation by the disinterring of a scandal involving his half brother, Henry. In 1817, Henry had married Anne Robinson McCarty, who with her younger sister, Elizabeth, was considered the richest heiress in Westmoreland County. Anne is described as "handsome" though having a fiery temper and "stormy, undisciplined emotions." With their marriage, Stratford Hall revived the luxurious days of the past. They bought new and hand-

69

some furnishings and entertained in an "elegant and expensive" style. Life at Stratford proved so gay and tempting, Elizabeth McCarty decided to come there to live. She arranged to share the expenses, placed her fortune in Henry's care, and asked the court to appoint him her guardian instead of her stepfather, Dr. Richard Stuart of Cedar Grove. At the time, Elizabeth was just seventeen, and "gentle and even-tempered."

With her coming, Stratford Hall witnessed one final tragic act before it passed out of the Lee family forever. Henry and Elizabeth were "thrown together into a state of the most unguarded intimacy," as Henry wrote later to justify his conduct, and with her he committed adultery, and "blackened with his disgrace everyone that bore his name," a connection of Ann Carter Lee wrote in righteous indignation to his sister. There was a child which tradition states died at birth. Elizabeth returned to Cedar Grove, and investigation of her finances by the court disclosed a large deficit which Henry Lee was ordered to pay.

He was then ostracized by kin and friend, and to him was attached the ironic designation "Black-Horse Harry" Lee. Nothing remained but to sell Stratford and move away. His wife stayed just long enough to sign the deed of sale (the property was bought by Major William Clarke Sommerville), then went her own way.

For a time, Lee made a precarious living by his pen. Then, in 1825, he was appointed assistant postmaster general. But shortly, his enemies were accusing him of duplicity in his politics, claiming that he was scheming against both President Adams and Adams' enemy, Andrew Jackson. Lee had actually long admired Jackson, and in desperation he appealed to him, candidly stating his position and assuming an "unaccustomed humility."

"For his father's sake, and believing also in the sincerity of his contrition, and giving due weight to certain extenuating circumstances," Jackson invited Lee to live with him at The Hermitage, in Tennessee. Lee then became Jackson's "able scribe," composing "some of the finest campaign papers ever penned in this country," it was said, and began sorting the

70

General's military papers with the intention of writing a biography.

When Jackson became President, Lee accompanied him to Washington, and for his loyalty received appointment as "Consul of the Barbary Powers" at Algiers. By this time, Henry and his wife were reconciled and they sailed together to his post. Just before his departure, his sister, the unhappy Lucy Grymes Carter, wrote to him from Bristol:

"You are going a great distance, & we may never meet again. If so tho' we can't help it, the reflexion that we are both unfortunate impresses on me & makes me feel more at bidding you farewell than I thought I would."

After Henry had given a year of excellent service in Algiers and won the admiration of the whole foreign colony, word reached him that the Senate had unanimously voted against confirmation of his appointment, on moral grounds. Though Lee probably never learned it, it was his "connections" who pressed the subject of his unfortunate domestic troubles "upon the Senate in such a manner as to compel Lee's own friends to vote against him," one of Jackson's aides wrote. The President had submitted his name on February 2, 1830, and by March, the scandal had been revived.

After leaving Algiers, he and his wife settled in Paris. Here Lee met Mme. Letizia Bonaparte, who told him "much about the birth and infancy of her great son," inspiring Henry to write a biography of Napoleon, assuming the role of champion as he replied to the "errors and detractions" of Sir Walter Scott's unsympathetic work.

Carter Lee was perhaps the only member of the immediate family (aside from Lucy Grymes), who was not humiliated by the Senate's action. He felt that Henry had "long ago atoned for his sins" and that his rejection was a "gross injustice" dictated by malice.

In an attempt to escape from the law, Carter had bought a farm, and now that Henry and his wife were homeless, he invited them to join him, though he warned that it was a meager existence:

"I have frequently last summer and this Fall eaten potatoes

71

for want of bread, & milk for want of meat. I am gathering a little stock around me, & shall in a year or two be in a condition to write a pastoral, not from the fancies of poets, but the experience of a grazier."

But after Henry had started the biography, Carter felt that it was important for him to stay in Paris "in order that you finish the great work you have undertaken."

The first volume was published in 1837, but the biography was never finished, for this same year Henry died during an influenza epidemic in Paris.

It was not Robert's nature to brood. His spirits were always resilient, and the unsavory affair was soon forgotten in the additional responsibilities of his post and the diverse activities centering around the Mackay house at No. 75 Broughton Street. As a member of the family, he fitted into its plans, was included in invitations, and now that Margaret had accepted the hand of one of her many admirers, Dr. Ralph Emms Elliott, a physician and planter, he became chief escort and companion for Eliza. He did not turn to her to seek consolation for the loss of Margaret, whom he admitted to "love dearly," but because she was an extremely fascinating young woman in her own right.

It was said of George Washington, to account for his many loves, that no Virginian could live among its fair women "in that hale and sociable colony without being touched again and again by the quick passion; and this man had the blood of the lover beyond his fellows." The Virginia of Robert's day was no less "hale and sociable," nor had its number of fair women diminished. In Robert's veins also flowed "the blood of the lover beyond his fellows." At no age and under no circumstance was he able to resist the fascination of a pretty and intelligent girl—in Virginia or elsewhere. In love, as in war, he was his father's son, and he found his heart as easily won by the pretty face, "sparkling, black eyes," and small, fashionable figure of the vivacious Eliza, as it had been by Margaret's "distinctive personality" and "that alacrity in the turn up lip," which he admired.

It would have been hard for any girl to resist Lee's physical attractions. An upperclassman at West Point wrote that he had "the highest type of manly beauty," and yet was "seemingly unconscious of it." Another cadet recalled "the admirable symmetry of his person and the manly beauty of his countenance."

But in addition to these attributes, a fellow officer wrote:

his nature was genial and sociable, and he would join freely in all sports and amusements proper to his age. He was exempt from every form and degree of snobbery. . . . He was a favorite with the ladies. . . . I will not deny that . . . the multiform graces that clustered around him, oftentimes oppressed me, though I never envied him, and I doubt if he ever excited envy in any man. All his accomplishments and alluring virtues appeared natural in him.

A gift for small talk, developed to an art during the years spent almost exclusively in a woman's world, made him even more of "a favorite with the ladies," while from his father he inherited talents as a raconteur, making him equally popular with the men. His friend Hugh Mercer wrote of his sparkling conversation and lively stories, and told how he made his audience "laugh very heartily" while Robert himself laughed "until the tears ran down his face."

With the coming of June, the thoughts of the Mackay family were absorbed with preparations for Margaret's wedding; and Robert, as one of the groomsmen, shared in the excitement which served to further fire his blood and quicken his pulse, and turn his thoughts to a serious consideration of matrimony for himself.

On the twenty-ninth of June, the wedding was held in the parlor of the Mackay home, and by the time the festivities were over, construction at Cockspur had ended for the season, not to be resumed until late November.

This gave Robert ample time to return to Virginia and seek fulfillment of the major decision he had now reached: to ask his cousin, Mary Anne Randolph Custis to be his wife.

5

THE "multiform graces" embodied in the person of Robert E. Lee might have won for him the hand of any young woman he chose. But he was sorely handicapped from a material stand-point by having neither lands nor fortune, while his future prospects were shadowed by the notoriously slow promotion in peacetime, and the army's meager pay. He could therefore offer a prospective wife little more than a wandering existence from project to project, or a life of loneliness if she preferred to remain permanently established.

"Never marry unless you can do so into a family which will enable your children to feel proud of both sides of the house" was an edict Robert had learned in childhood, and one that he was determined to fulfill now in spite of handicaps.

But in this day of strictly advantageous marriages for fami-lies in his social stratum, even the most sanguine of parents could not view an alliance with Robert Lee as expedient. With the revival of Henry Lee's misfortunes, even Robert's good name had been sullied. Mary Custis was therefore probably the only young woman he felt free to approach. It was obvious that she was in love with him, and he was certain that since she was related to the Lees and shared the recent stigma, an offer of marriage would not be considered an affront to family pride. He also knew that since she was sole heiress to a large fortune, his own want in this respect could be more easily overlooked. It was a highly practical choice.

For this frail dark-haired girl with "red-brown eyes" and plain face Robert felt the warm affection Virginians hold for their kin, and he retained a sentimental attachment for her as the playmate of his childhood. It was to prove an unwavering attachment, strengthened by Mary's role as mother of the chil-dren who brought his chief pleasure and comfort in life, and by the compassion he felt for her sufferings and eventual total invalidism brought on by rheumatoid arthritis.

Aside from this affectionate regard, she was highly attrac-tive to him because of her spiritual affinity to George Washing-ton, and marriage to her, as a kinsman wrote, "in the eyes of the world, made Robert Lee the representative of the founder of American liberty." In certain facets of her character, she resembled Ann Carter Lee, and a man who has been bound to his mother by strong ties of affection will often be subcon-

sciously drawn to a woman of similar temperament and attributes.

Like Robert's mother, Mary Custis was devoted to her
parents, and so attached to her childhood home that she was
unable to find complete happiness elsewhere. She was also
sympathetic, loyal, and pious. She was simple and unassum-
ing, without ambition for herself. "Her heart was as unworldly
and artless as a child's," it was said of her. Though at this time
it was unforeseen, she was to prove as heroic as Lee's mother
when afflicted with illness and constant pain.

But here the similarity ended, for Mary was outspoken to
the extent of offending, had a quick temper, a sharp tongue,
and did not take kindly to the stern reverses of fortune.

She shared with Robert a deep appreciation of nature,
"loving the beautiful with an artist's passion—delighting in
the trees, the fields, the hills." She liked to ride her mare,
"Kate," through meadows and glades in search of wild flowers.
She enjoyed working in her mother's famed garden, and could
often be seen there with her white sunbonnet hanging down
her back, "digging and weeding."

Mary and Robert had a common liking for animals, she
favoring cats, a fondness she had inherited from her father.

A contemporary described her as "a young lady of sound
and vigorous intellect. . . . Her education had been in all
respects such as was best calculated to make her happy herself,
and the source of abundant utility and happiness to others." A
school copybook dated 1823, when she was fifteen, has been
preserved, and on its faded pages are seen essays she wrote on
such erudite subjects as "Style, Perspicuity and Precision,"
"Sublimity in Writing," and "Beauty and Other Pleasures of
Taste."

Reading was her favorite pastime, and she was noted for a
discriminating taste in literature; repeatedly she lamented the
demands upon her time which kept her from it. She had considerable skill in painting, and it was felt by those who knew her
best that had she followed art, she would have achieved recognition. "She had the real artist temperament," and everything
practical was foreign to her. She was therefore negligent and

unmethodical, and particularly forgetful, with a special pen-chant for "losing everything that could be lost." Her dislike of routine made her habitually tardy. She professed a total uncon-cern for the dictate of the world of fashion, carrying her indifference for dress to the point of untidiness. Though her tardiness and lack of interest in her appearance were most often irksome to Robert, he seems to have been content to remind her of her foibles merely by teasing her about them, though often provoking her to a sharp retort.

When Robert reached New York, he called on his brother, Carter, living at 15 Pine Street in that city where he had gone in pursuit of a young woman whose beauty had made his head "swim," and whose door he had to pass "twice before I could summon the courage to pull the bell." Carter also hoped to improve his financial prospects by this move, finding "the field for professional men . . . certainly rich and ample." With the prospect of marriage, his whole future seemed bright. Just a few months later, his marriage offer had been refused, and he was longing to go back to Westmoreland, "my favorite spot on earth."

After his visit with Carter, Robert went to Ravensworth to give sympathy and aid to Mrs. Fitzhugh, his Cousin Anna, whose husband, William Henry, had just died of "apoplexy, probably brought on by a blow from his horse." His death deprived the Lees "of a friend we dearly loved and a happy home," Carter mourned.

From Ravensworth, Robert went next to Arlington, only to be told by Mr. Custis that Mary and her mother had gone to Chatham, Mrs. Custis' family home, on business connected with the death of her brother, William Fitzhugh.

When Robert reached the handsome brick house on Stafford Heights, near Fredericksburg, he was somewhat taken aback to find that her uncle's death had "afflicted the sweet girl with a little of that over-righteousness which the blue-lights brought into Virginia," making his mission difficult.

But Chatham's romantic setting among great oaks and blooming terraces that sloped down to the Rappahannock River was ideally suited to courtship, and in spite of her "over-righteousness," Mary found herself listening to the dictates of her heart. It was at Chatham, so tradition holds, that George Washington first met Martha Custis; after she had become a young widow, he successfully courted her there.

It was fitting that Robert, steeped as he was in the Washington tradition and mystically drawn to everything connected with him, should woo Martha Washington's great-granddaughter at Chatham. One day as they sat under the oaks, he asked her to be his wife, and she accepted, simply and frankly, as was characteristic.

Though her mother shared Mary's joy when she heard the news, she was afraid her husband would not approve. He had never admired Light-Horse Harry Lee. Although he did not object to Robert personally, he did not consider him a fit match for his daughter, knowing that he could not support her as she had been accustomed to live.

Mary Lee Fitzhugh Custis was a simple woman, entirely without ostentation and singularly pious in the true meaning of the word. She was generous and kindly, had a keen mind, and a fine taste in literature. As small boys, both Robert and Smith had responded to her warmth, and came to look on her as a second mother. Since Mrs. Lee's death, Smith had made Arlington his home when ashore. But the Major had always been too much engrossed with the arts and absorbed with perpetuating the Washington traditions to take more than a casual interest in the Lee boys. He knew only that he considered neither a suitable husband for his only child.

George Washington Parke Custis was a man of considerable talent, though he failed to fulfill the hope of his foster father "that he might shine in the councils of the Nation." His education was ended abruptly when Washington found it "impractical to keep him longer in college with any prospect of advantage, so great was his aversion to study." He was accordingly put in the army, but upon reaching his majority, he settled down to a life of study and artistic production. Whenever he was not engaged in composing an epic poem to extoll George Washington's achievements, or at work on one of the orations for which he became famed, he was absorbed in painting gigantic pictures of Revolutionary battle scenes with Washington as the central figure; but because of his peculiar technique of starting with his subject's feet and working upward, he often obtained startling results. When he was not painting, he might be found writing a historical drama, several of which were produced successfully in New York. In 1825, he had published his delightful *Conversations with La Fayette*, and was presently writing *Recollections and Private Memoirs of Washington*.

After his visit at Chatham, Robert joined Ann Marshall, "the most interesting of my mother's children," as Carter characterized her, who with her young son and her sister, Mildred, was passing the summer at Newport for her health. Mildred had by this time bloomed into a beautiful young woman who would soon enjoy the reputation of a belle in Baltimore, where the family had settled since "Brother Marshall has given up *parsoning* and betaken himself to law." In addition to her beauty and her "fine taste in musick," Mildred was, according to Carter, "smarter than any of us, and has a passion for books."

Robert may have visited elsewhere during his furlough, but one thing is certain, that he stopped again with Carter before taking the packet to Savannah, for he gave him the news of his engagement. On December 1, 1830, Carter relayed this to Henry, then in Paris: "Some good luck has got among us of late for a wonder. . . . Robert, our dear Robert is engaged to Mary Custis. He has to sigh however till Spring at the distance of Cock-spur Island, when they will be married."

When Robert reached his post on November 20, he found that due to a recent gale a large portion of the main embankment built during the spring had been swept away; the wharf was badly damaged; and the canal that drained the site, choked with mud and debris. He was the only engineer on duty and, with a small crew, repaired the wharf and strengthened the dikes, finishing just in time to withstand a hurricane which swept the Georgia coast early in December. At the end of that month, he received word that Major Babcock had resigned because of his health and was being replaced by First Lieutenant Joseph K. F. Mansfield, an experienced engineer, well equipped to handle the problems of the site. He was a much younger man than Babcock, and more congenial, making life on Cockspur less austere.

On taking over his assignment, Mansfield found that there were missing records and construction plans, unbalanced expense sheets, and verbal contracts. Since Robert was of little use in untangling the confusion, he was set to making a survey of the island, and a plan of the dikes and wharves.

He obtained leave whenever possible, and made the Mackay house his headquarters. Jack had been assigned to duty in Alabama; but Eliza, Catherine, and Sarah were still there, and Margaret, "the Sweet little Madam," as Robert now styled her, came often to visit. Engagement to Mary Custis made no difference in his relations and attentions to these young ladies. One lonely Saturday night at Cockspur he wrote Margaret of his pleasure at seeing her again after an indisposition had confined her to her room:

I am truly happy —— —— Mrs. E. to find that you are again down stairs. And should it always require a similar event to procure me the great pleasure I this morning received I fear my selfishness might lead me to place among my daily wishes, that the preceeding *cause* might never be wanting.

See what a great temptation to sin you will give me. Do spare me the blame of its commission, and add to the pleasure you must constantly receive from making happy those near you, that of sometimes enlivening the dull hours at Cockspur. . . .

I . . . give you my warmest thanks for so speedily gratifying my "fancy with a sight of your handwriting," and for your kindness in sending me the life of Byron. This last I will bring up with me & the cause for so doing I will then explain. It is needless to say what great pleasure I shall then receive from again seeing Mrs. E. . . .

When they were separated, Robert corresponded with the Mackay girls. When together, they kept up a busy social schedule and took part in amateur theatricals and musical dramas. In a letter to Margaret, Robert discussed a potential role:

"I think I could enact the 'Hidaldo' *á merveille.* For by the 9th what a moustache I could have, and the Whiskers could be so increased, & my Spanish would be so pure & flowing. And I am so well acquainted with the costume, air, &c."

But this blissful period was destined for a sudden end when Lieutenant Mansfield decided that the soil composition at Cockspur would not provide a suitable foundation for the type of fortification originally planned. He informed General Gratiot, and asked permission to draw a new plan. Permission was granted, and Captain Richard Delafield was sent to confer with Mansfield.

Until the new plans could be completed and approved, there was nothing to occupy Robert. Because the need for engineers on both private and government projects was pressing, engineering cadets from West Point were often loaned for duty as topographical draughtsmen and surveyors, returning to classes when their jobs were completed. General Gratiot had no intention of allowing Lee to remain idle. On March 26, he sent orders for him to report "as soon as practicable" to Old Point Comfort, Virginia, to assist the chief engineer, Captain Andrew Talcott, who was engaged in completing Fort Monroe.

Robert had expected to be reassigned, but not until the first of July. When his orders came, the Mackay girls and their mother were visiting the J. J. Smith family at Old Fort, near Beaufort, South Carolina. Robert had been included in the invitation, and was intending to join them. But now there was not even time for a hasty trip to say good-by. Much against his will, he had to write his farewells. His letter to Eliza has survived in part:

Cockspur. Wednesday 13th
There has been but one redeeming circumstance in the occurrences of the day Miss Eliza & that has been the arrival of your letter. Indeed I have been dreadfully harassed by these two men, who call themselves Engineers. For you must know that Capt Delafield has arrived & is in high consultation about Foundations, Grillage, Piles & What not. And I have made them more little troublesome plans & worse calculations about weight, cost &c. of

masonry, lime, sand & such stuff than I intend to do tomorrow, "and that's the certain of it." Will you believe that they are still at it, & have just touched upon cranes, with "Lee give us a sketch of that"? But I happened to have my watch in my hand & seeing that it was ten minutes to 11 P.M. says, "Yes Capt tomorrow." And then I takes up this table & placed it by the fire, with pen ink & paper. And I will leave them to themselves & they shall leave us to ourselves. But I can only stay with you while they are present. . . . I have not had the heart to go to Savannah since you left it. Though I was within an ace of doing so last Sunday, when I recollected there was *nobody* there, so I turned on my heel & told Joe to be off & bring me down all letters. And he did bring me down all letters but none from you Miss E. It did grieve me so to see the Boats coming down one after another, without any of those *little comforts* which are now so *necessary* to me. Oh me! I do not know what I shall do for them at Old Point. But you will send some sometimes, Will you not Sweet ———? How I will beseige the P. Office. . . . But Miss Eliza, this parting with all in Broughton St. is dreadful & they so far away too. But I *will* not *yet* think of going without seeing them, though I do not know how I shall compass it. Perhaps, owing to Capt D's arrival I shall be obliged to stay longer. Perhaps I can get to Beaufort. Perhaps your two weeks will be *out* next Tuesday. Perhaps I shall be taken sick. (And you know no one can nurse me so well as Miss C. [Catherine]). . . .

But Captain Delafield did not need his services; neither did Robert fall ill, get to Beaufort, nor did Eliza return early. His departure was made up of conflicting emotions. There was a sense of relief at being freed from an unpleasant assignment, and he looked forward to returning to Virginia. But parting with Mrs. Mackay, who had mothered him so delightfully, with the talented Catherine and "the Sweet little Madam" was hard. The sharpest pang of all, however, was separation from "Miss Eliza (My Sweetheart)," the lovely girl "to whom I am not satisfied in offering my *best*," as he once told her; the girl who had for over a year been the chief companion of his days off, and solace for his lonely hours at Cockspur.

As he stood on the afterdeck of the packet, watching the church spires of Savannah fade into the misty distance, his mood of depression was allayed by hopes of returning soon, perhaps for winter duty, since work at Fort Monroe was suspended during that season. Although he had written Eliza that if ordered to Cockspur for duty, he would *not* come, this was said purely for the pleasure of reading her entreaties to change his mind.

L'homme propose, et Dieu dispose. It was fifteen years before Robert went back to the gracious old house on Broughton Street. But loyalty was an attribute of Robert and the Mackays, and their devotion to one another remained constant for a lifetime, and was carried over into the next generation by close friendships between their children.

Eliza's "little *comforts*" found their way to Fort Monroe, as did letters from Jack, Margaret, and Catherine. Because of his delightful associations, Savannah would always remain for Robert:

"That spot of spots! That place of places!! That city of cities!!!"

6

BEFORE reporting to Fort Monroe, Robert stopped at Arlington, for Mary had written that her father had finally consented to the marriage and she wanted to consult about members of the bridal party, the guest list, and most important, the date.

Smith Lee was there, his fine looks enhanced by "a pair of whiskers," which in the opinion of their sister, Mildred, "brought him out in the new and interesting character of an Adonis." Since Smith was on extended leave, Robert asked him to be his best man.

The evening of June 30 was decided on—provided Robert could get a furlough. When the consultations were over, Robert had to hurry off to his post, leaving his brother with a list of instructions to be carried out in his absence.

Robert found his superior officer, Captain Andrew Talcott, a slender, gracious young man with large luminous eyes, a high forehead, a sensitive mouth, sparse chin whiskers, and a good sense of humor. He was ten years older than Robert, and though scion of a distinguished Connecticut family, had all the warmth of a Southerner. He and Robert were immediately drawn to one another, becoming close friends in a matter of weeks (for Talcott was invited to Robert's wedding), and remained on intimate terms throughout life.

Aside from his attractive personality, Talcott was a man of ability. He had graduated from West Point, No. 2 man in his class, and had since acquired considerable experience.

Just now he was especially sympathetic to romance, since he was courting a beautiful Virginian from Norfolk, Harriet Randolph Hackley (as it happened, a kinswoman of Mary Custis), and he readily recommended the desired furlough. But until that time arrived, he set Robert to ordering supplies, computing costs, and supervising the excavation and grading of the moat around the fort.

When Robert's letter telling that his leave had been approved reached Arlington, it aroused the plantation from its customary torpor. Over the years, the servants had grown lazy under a master who was easygoing and inclined to indolence himself, and most did little more than tend their own garden plots and fish for themselves. It took all Mrs. Custis' vigilance to keep them at dusting, polishing, curtain washing, and cake baking, preparatory to the wedding.

With her key basket over her arm, she took inventory of storage rooms and closets, counting the extra cots, mattresses, quilts, and sheets; checking the table linen, the silver, and dishes. As a result of her tallying, Mary sent an urgent message to Aunt Maria Fitzhugh for the loan of more cots, quilts, mattresses, tablecloths, silver, and candlesticks—and if possible, dining-room servants.

They were welcome to anything she had that would be useful, including four servants, Mrs. Fitzhugh replied, and offered her silver cake baskets as an added touch of elegance for the table.

It was also necessary for Mrs. Custis to be present at the consultations with Miss Brown, Washington's most fashionable dressmaker, for Mary lacked ideas as to what style and material would be most becoming for the wedding gown and the important "second day's dress." Since not even the indefatigable Marietta Turner, who was a bridesmaid, thought to record anything about Mary's appearance other than to say that she was "never lovelier," and the gown was not preserved as was the second day's dress, there are no details as to what the bride wore.

It is possible that, in keeping with tradition, she wore a white satin gown, with "pearl necklace, ear-rings, and bracelet; and pearl ornaments in her hair," as her great-grandmother Martha Custis had when she married George Washington.

Many guests, with their small army of servants, dogs, and horses, came as early as a week in advance of the wedding. Mr. Custis delighted in the role of host, and was at the door to welcome them with all the gracious hospitality of his foster father. He seated them in the hall, ordered refreshment, and told them stories of his Mount Vernon childhood.

Mrs. Custis took the guests to look at the roses that were her pride, the garden that hundreds of strangers came each year to see. Here they admired the delicate buds of the Safronia roses, the single red one that grew under the apricot tree, the teas, the Persian yellow, the damask, and the hundred-leaf and moss roses. They sat in the shade of the large arbor covered with honeysuckle and yellow jasmine that carpeted the ground with fallen blossoms, which the little girls in the party strung into necklaces and garlands.

While members of the bridal party and other guests were gathering at Arlington, Robert, whom Mary had "charged" not to "appear before the *important* day," was fretting at his post, worrying lest the old steamer *Potomac*, so subject to breakdowns and balks, might not get him there on time.

The morning of June 30 dawned clear and shining, but in the late afternoon the thunderheads began to gather. Shortly after the Reverend Ruel Keith, rector of Alexandria's Christ Church, set out on horseback for Arlington, he felt the first big raindrops splash in his face, and before he had gone half a mile, the downpour came. By the time he reached Arlington, he was drenched. Since he was unable to officiate in this state,

84

Mr. Custis took him to his room and gave him dry clothing. This was an ordinary enough occurrence, and would have passed unrecorded, had it not been that Mr. Custis was a short stocky gentleman while the Reverend Doctor was very tall and thin. Dr. Keith's appearance was so highly ludicrous that it caused much long-remembered amusement among the guests.

In spite of the minister's appearance, the ceremony was solemn and formal. Mr. Custis escorted Mary down the stairs, and at a signal from the butler, Nelly Custis Lewis, seated at the piano, began to play softly. Robert and Smith entered the parlor by a side door, and the six bridesmaids and groomsmen formed an aisle down which Mary passed on her father's arm. The vows were taken under a large floral bell hung from the central archway between the family dining room and parlor.

Mary's maid of honor was her childhood friend and neighbor, Catherine Mason, who had Smith as her escort. Then came the cousins: Marietta Turner on the arm of Lieutenant James A. Chambers, who had been stationed at Cockspur; Mary Goldsborough with Lieutenant John P. Kennedy, a West Point classmate presently stationed at Fort Monroe; Angela Lewis (Nelly Custis' daughter), with the irrepressible Lieutenant Richard Tilghman, now with the artillery at Monroe; Julia Calvert with Lieutenant James H. Prentiss, another West Pointer at Fort Monroe; and finally, Britannia Peter—the "beloved Brit"—who, to the horror of staid parents, was in the habit of signaling Mary from her Georgetown home by waving a colored petticoat out the upper window. Her cavalier was Naval Lieutenant Thomas Turner, Marietta's brother.

No guest list has survived, but contemporary recollections and letters indicate that Robert was well represented by the numerous Lees from Alexandria, by the Carters, and all of his immediate family except Mildred, who had, in May, married Edward Vernon Childe of Boston, a lawyer of independent means who intended to "relinquish the law" and "betake himself to literature." They were at this time traveling to Canada, with Paris as their eventual destination.

After the wedding supper there was dancing, and liquid refreshment supplied from George Washington's capacious punch bowl, a present from his close friend, Colonel William Fitzhugh of Chatham, Mrs. Custis' father. The interior of this bowl was decorated with the painting of a ship with its hull resting on the bottom and its masts projecting to the rim. The rule (always strictly observed), was to drink to the hull.

During the festivities following the ceremony, Robert toasted the bride and her attendants, danced, joked, and laughed with them, "his bright eyes and high color" making him "the picture of a cavalier."

On the evening of the second day, Mary wore a *moiré* silk dress in a bold plaid of blue, cerise, and dark green on a cream ground. It was an off-the-shoulder décolleté, with fitted bodice, full skirt, and wide sleeves, and could be worn on less formal occasions with a lace fichu. The dress measurements and bodice laces indicate that Mary was around 5 feet 5 inches tall, and that her waist was 20 inches.

Wedding journeys immediately after the ceremony were still not the fashion, and the guests were expected to stay and participate in festivities for a week or more. The frolic at Arlington lasted until July 5, when the entire company rode over to the house of General John Mason for further entertainment. A week later, the more enduring members of the party and those young officers whose furloughs were not yet up went with Robert, Mary, Smith, Carter, Ann Marshall and her son, and Mrs. Custis to Ravensworth, where Aunt Maria held more receptions and parties in their honor. It was here that Robert took the time amidst the bustle to write to Captain Talcott, disclosing considerably more than just the lack of formality that existed between them:

Ravensworth
13th July 1831

So, Captain, you would not come up to Arlington on that memorable Thursday. But I gave you the severest scolding you have had this many a day, from which I hope you will derive great benefit. However you would have seen nothing strange, for there was neither fainting nor fighting, nor anything uncommon which could be twisted into an adventure. The Parson had few words to say, though he dwellt upon them as if he had been reading my

Death warrant. . . . I am told I looked "pale & interesting" which might have been the fact. But I felt "bold as a sheep" & was surprised at my want of Romance in so great a degree as not to feel more excited than at the Black Board at West Point. . . . We are this far on our way to the Upper Country where I will spend the remainder of my leave. . . . And I hope Mother & Daughter will recover from an attack of Fever & Ague, they have lately undergone. Their health has been re-established though not their looks. . . . I write in great haste with the servant waiting. . . . Remember me kindly to Mrs. Hale. . . . I long to hear Miss Rebecca's "Lee, Lee" & to see whether Miss Katie is still as "Bwack as Wu". . . .

It is a rare young man who, on his honeymoon, longs to hear the baby talk of his friends' children back home. Robert's genuine delight in the company of children, little girls especially, increased with age. At no time in his life was he ever too distracted or too weary to welcome a child to his lap. Then he would gently stroke the hair and kiss the cheek as he listened with evident enjoyment to the artless chatter. Children instinctively sensed his capacity to meet them on their own level, so that wherever he was, in peacetime and war, they sought him out. Already he had found two small admirers at Old Point.

Around the first of August, Robert, Mary, and her maid, Cassy boarded the *Potomac* for the trip to Fort Monroe, where they set up housekeeping in a modest way in a wing of Captain Talcott's house which Robert had asked him to arrange with furnishings bought in Alexandria.

May I trouble you to have the Bedstead placed in the larger room (of the two in the Wing) since *Madam* prefers that, and such other articles as you see fit, the rest can be placed in the small room, [he had instructed.] All Feather beds have been forbid the apartment under pain &c. and as I could not procure a Palliasse, the Mattress must answer for the present. . . .

In November, work on the project was over for the winter, and Robert and Mary went overland to Arlington, stopping first for a visit with Hill Carter at Shirley, then with Ann Marshall and her family in Baltimore, where they stayed a week "& saw it snow every day for our benefit," Robert wrote. They reached Arlington in time for the ceremony of kindling the yule log with the remains saved from the previous year.

Right after the New Year, Robert and Mary received an invitation to attend Eliza Mackay's wedding. She was marrying the handsome and wealthy Savannah attorney, William Henry Stiles, who at twenty-three had become solicitor general of the Eastern District of Georgia. The wedding was to be held on January 4, but the invitation had been delayed and did not reach Arlington until the evening of the third. Deprived of the pleasure of attending, Robert started a letter to Eliza on her wedding day, making a brave show at light-heartedness. At the end of his lament, disguised by a gossamer of forced jocularity, Mary added her congratulations to "one of Mr. Lee's most valued friends," as she called her.

> January 4th 1832
> Arlington

How I would like to say "Mr & Mrs Lee have the honour to accept Mrs. Mackay's kind invitation for Wednesday night." But this cannot be Miss Eliza (My Sweetheart) because it only arrived here last night, by this token that I have been in tears ever since at the thought of *losing* you. Oh Me! Gilderoy you are a lucky fellow to get so bright a New Year's gift this January 1832. Why Man, it is better for you than the gift of life, an Mrs. M. would give *me* such a one every year I would live forever "And that's the certain of it." But Miss E. how do you feel about this time? Say 12 o'clock of the day, as you see the shadows commence to fall towards the East & know that at *last* the sun will set. Though you may not be frightened I 'spect you are marvellously alarmed. And then you know the little Madam's tongue is running so fast & Miss Kate is looking so cunning (Never mind Miss it is your turn next so you need not laugh at your Sister). Well I do wish I could be there. It would do me so much good to be with you all again & see you so happy. I wonder that it has never entered the dull heads of Congress that I ought to be there & that they make special provision for the occasion. But the wretches take no care of "Us youth." And through their negligence you are deprived of my presence & I of your sweet company. If I could but drop in this morning & tell you what a powerful fine thing it is to stand up before the Parson with all eyes bent upon you (except one pair), he mournful & solemn as if he was reading your funeral service. A man feels of so much, & I am sure, he could not add to the stillness of the scene though he were dead. Would this not revive you Miss E.? How your black eyes would sparkle at the description.

Sunday Jany 8th—I was interrupted in my letter Miss Eliza by our receiving information of the death of Mrs. Law Custis & that her remains would [be] . . . deposited in the vault at Mount Vernon. . . . There was a melancholy group of us & my black face looked longer than usual. But perhaps it was because my thoughts were in Broughton St. wondering upon all that was going on there. And how did you disport yourself my child? . . . Do regulate me thereupon in your next. But Mother must feel quite melancholy as she sees her dear daughter leaving home—Tell her I am coming after Miss Kate soon, though stop, our sister of Quincey has arrived & before I determine, I will see her.—If I was a dog I would beat myself—For here has this letter been laying by me a month of Sundays & not yet finished. And I had so many fine things & sweet congratulations to give dear Miss Eliza all of which are now gone out of my head—She however knows how happy I must always wish & believe her to be & will I hope think that this dilatoriness on my part has proceeded from anything else rather than neglect or forgetfulness of her. . . . And now I am excused am I not Sweet ——? Oh Mercy are you really married Mrs. Stiles? The idea is as great a damper to a man's spirits as that of the cholera. . . . There have been some large parties in Washington, but I am a poor old broken down man & attend none of them. . . . Good Bye Miss E.

Yours truly & ever
R E Lee

The contrast in dispositions is so striking, Mary's note warrants quotation:

You see what a small place is left me my dear Miss Eliza to offer my congratulations & wish that your pathway in life may be as bright as our beneficent Creator & father sees best for you. . . . I am now a wanderer on the face of the earth & know not where we are going next & hope it will be East. I suppose you remain in Savannah near your Mother? What happiness! I am with mine now—the past & the future disregarded. I offer my love and congratulations to you & your family on the late joyous occasion. . . .

Your Sincere & Affectionate
M. Lee

Robert's sense of loss prompted him to compare the groom to Gilderoy, the famous Scottish highwayman, whose prize this time was not material, but the gift of life itself—"an Mrs. Mackay would give *me* such a one every year I would live forever" is a comment more significant than jocular. The solemnity of the marriage ceremony always reminded him of the finality of death. In fact, death with its separation from loved ones was much on his mind as he wrote. He strove for a smile when he described his long black face "longer than usual" in the "melancholy group" attending the Mount Vernon funeral, though the truth was revealed when he added:

"But perhaps this was because my thoughts were in Broughton St. wondering upon all that was going on there." He never could bring himself to express the congratulations he knew were due her, pleading lack of time, and then asking tenderly: "And now I am excused am I not Sweet—— ——?"

There was now the question of a gift for Eliza. Mackay family tradition holds that from the cherished set of dishes presented to George Washington by the Society of the Cincinnati, Robert chose a tureen decorated with the Society's emblem and a handsome border of flowers and butterflies in blue on white. However, this is not certain, for among the surviving letters from Mary Lee to Eliza, there is one written from Arlington on November 1, 1847, suggesting that the tureen was presented at this later date, unless she was given two tureens from the set.

In 1847, Eliza was in Vienna (her husband was American chargé d'affaires there), and she wrote to ask if Mary could send her a piece of George Washington's "State" china to show to European friends and present to some admirer of the First President.

I have searched thro' the house & find that our stock of the states china is reduced so low that I cannot send you a whole piece & the broken ones would give a very imperfect idea of the device [Mary replied]. I send you a small tureen of the Cincinnatti which you must value highly as they are getting very rare & it is almost like parting with one of the family to send it so far—Present it where you think it will be most prized & valued.

If this was the only tureen Eliza received, she chose to keep it, and it now can be seen in the collection at Stratford Hall.

The winter furlough lasted until the first of March. As it was drawing to a close, Mary became so reluctant to part from her mother that Robert suggested she stay on until the warm weather came.

All her life, Mary would find it hard to fit herself into any sphere outside of Arlington and her circle of relatives and childhood friends. She did not make new friends easily, like her genial husband, and took little part in the social life at Fort Monroe. She had found more pleasure in her books, her needlework, gardening, and in teaching reading to her classes for Negroes, than she did in card parties and frolics. She enjoyed long walks on the beach "to inhale the sea breeze," but even then she found herself longing "for a little rural scenery."

"What . . . would I give for one stroll on the hills at Arlington this bright day," she wrote nostalgically to her mother.

Joe Johnston had paid a promised visit to Arlington, and when the furlough was up, he and Robert set out together on horseback for Old Point Comfort, since the river was frozen. Robert rode a spirited thoroughbred he had named "Bolivar." Both young men were still in a festive mood when they reached the fort, and proceeded to lead the untrammeled lives of gay bachelors, joined in their expeditions and larks by Dick Tilghman, Ben Huger, Albert Church, Hugh Mercer, and Bob Parrott—"the old set," as Robert termed them—West Pointers, all. With them he played chess, and shared a mutual interest in horseflesh, attending the races whenever possible, or following them through the less exciting medium of the newspapers. They went to the amateur theatricals given on the post, and the "grand parties" that sometimes had such unforeseen conclusions as the one Robert described confidentially to Andrew Talcott: "*Sally* is as blythe as a larke & admitted me (an innocent man) into her bed Chamber a few days after the frolick."

Some evenings Robert made the rounds of the bachelor

quarters, "plaguing" his unmarried friends about their "Dulcineas." He wrote in amusement about two friends whose course in love was not proceeding smoothly, and who might "at any time be found in a corner of one of the . . . rooms, reenacting the Sorrows of Werther." On one occasion he and Joe found a friend who had sought comfort in a bottle "in the middle of the floor trying to get off his uniform. We had to assist his lendings, or his Borrowings rather, for there was nothing his own but his Pants. . . ."

Contrary to a popular concept of Lee, he was neither shocked nor offended by occasional overindulgence, but habitual drunkenness, he admitted, "is *impossible* for me to comprehend." He was aware of the boredom brought on by peacetime garrison life, and knew that certain temperaments resorted to drink in order to stimulate minds grown sluggish with inactivity. He was entirely sympathetic with both kinds of drinkers, though only the occasional imbiber amused him. Of such a friend he punned once: "He looked badly but was in good *spirits*. His constant companion was a phial of Texas whiskey, hermetically sealed to celebrate his meeting with Dick T.[Tilghman] whenever that should take place."

In April, Robert wrote exultantly to Mary:

Let me tell you Mrs. Lee, no later than today did I escort Miss G. to see Miss Slate! Think of that Mrs. Lee! And hasten down if you do not wish to see me turned out a Beau again. How I did strut along with one hand on my whiskers & the other elevating my coat tail! And my whole face thrown into the biggest grin I could muster—Surely that was a sight for Old Pointers to see.

That same month, Captain Talcott returned with his bride, Harriet Randolph Hackley. Hers was the kind of beauty that would have quickened the pulses of a less susceptible man than Robert, so that her presence in the same house was like a rare and heady wine to a connoisseur. He immediately became her devoted cavalier, with an admiration that was open and avowed. He never addressed her as Harriet, but always as "Talcott, my Beauty," "my Beautiful Talcott," and "my Hardy." This was an attention she must have appreciated fully, coming as it did from this officer now designated as "the handsomest man in the Army."

But neither Robert's attentions to the ladies nor his threat of becoming a "Beau" again hastened Mary's departure from Arlington. The river opened, the warm weather came, and with it the bathing season which Robert enjoyed as much for the attractive young women who gathered at the shore as he did for the swimming. But still Mary lingered with her mother. When she did come, he knew they would be crowding the Talcotts and so secured other quarters. Mary made many advance preparations, and wrote often for advice as to what furniture and which servants to bring, finally exhausting Robert's patience.

At last Mary set a date for him to come up and escort her and her mother—for she was unable to bear separation from Mrs. Custis—to Old Point. The *Potomac* had broken down again that week, and Robert asked her with mock solemnity: "What shall I do if she is not forthcoming next Saturday? The manner in which I shall row up the Bay will be curious. The old wretch I am almost afraid to trust her; yet you say everything is for the best, though I must acknowledge it sometimes escapes my poor comprehension to understand it."

Robert took advantage of Mrs. Custis' presence, and made a trip at his father-in-law's request to inspect Smith's Island, one of Mr. Custis' properties. A gale had swept that area in the spring, but Robert found the damage slight. He was received hospitably by the tenants and the lighthouse-keeper, and dined with them on wild birds' eggs (he found the sedge hen's most to his taste), roe, and other local delicacies. On his way back, he visited the original Arlington, an old Custis holding on Maryland's Eastern Shore, and was impressed favorably with the house and its setting.

During the summer, he and Mary took a trip to the Dismal Swamp, and one to Shirley. The rest of the time Mary divided between Old Point and Arlington. Her health was still "only tolerable," for she had been unwell ever since the attack of fever and ague at the time of her marriage.

When she was at the Fort, instead of reading after supper

as had been her habit, she now embroidered petticoats, sacks, and wrappers for the coming baby, while Robert read aloud to her from Maria Edgeworth's *Belinda*. Unlike her husband, she was content to stay home at nights, although "almost every evening there is an invitation somewhere," she told her mother. "Except that we generally get some nice cake & fruit, they would be rather stupid. I suppose it is my fault, but there are not many persons here very interesting."

On September 16, Mary gave birth to a boy whom they named for her father, thereby completely winning Mr. Custis' heart and causing him to hurry down to see his namesake. In his excitement, the delighted grandfather sat "talking & eating oysters at such a rate" that Robert, attempting to compose a letter, complained good-naturedly to his correspondent: "I hardly know what I have written."

The arrival of his first grandchild removed the final barrier between Mr. Custis and Robert, and from that time on he "was ever as a Father to me."

7

THE three years that Robert passed at Fort Monroe afforded him varied experience. Since Captain Talcott was away a great part of the time for consultation on other projects, Robert took over duties which enabled him to design buildings and wharves; award contracts and inspect materials; supervise the preparation of monthly and annual reports; and handle large labor crews.

Socially, he would never be happier, though he often expressed the desire for Jack Mackay's company to complete his contentment. In a letter addressed to "My Beautiful Jack," he revealed the secret of his satisfaction: "Ft. Monroe is a Post by no means to be despised. Its advantages cannot be unknown to a mind like yours, & to comprise many things in one sentence, it is in *Virginia!*"

Despite the distinct advantage of location, the congenial company, and above all the presence of such a rare commanding officer as Andrew Talcott, there were drawbacks which after several years caused Robert to wish for another assignment. Much jealousy existed between the regular-army garrison and the engineers. There were constant conflicts over authority and the letting of contracts, and the engineers' use of quarters in the Fort. The most serious argument was whether the engineers or the regulars should direct the completion of the project.

But at this period, Robert's social instincts were at their peak and his spirits irrepressible. During the winter furlough of 1833, he gaily called upon Mackay, then on engineer duty in Savannah, to picture him

surrounded by my *wife* & *child* after an absence of a month, with so many accounts to settle with the one & to learn of the other. Then if you will place on the perspective a host of sweet young ladies. But stop, what am I speaking of & to whom? Aye, to whom? I fear I should awaken certain recollections, or perhaps recall cherished anticipations; Savannah, a city for which I have great affection might feel through the nerves of its Engineer. Therefore Mack we will change the subject & congratulate you on your happy location. . . . Do you hail from Cockspur or Broughton St.? (I would that I had the choice.) . . .

He complained to his friend that the Washington social season was

duller this Winter than usual. There are a few Parties but no one is decidedly the rage, nor considered a big Lion. Miss Fanny Kemble was the great attraction last week & drew to herself crowded Houses & all hearts. She is a lady of great talent & surpasses any performer I ever saw. . . . On the stage she is beautiful. In the ball room . . . she is next door to homely. Her eye is bright & teeth good but off the stage I could not recognize her as the same being I had so admired the previous night.

Dull or not, Robert was obviously enjoying the season, recounting further how he and James Prentiss (whom he described as "very fat & wrapped in his blue cloth cloak lined with *velvet*, has all the size & importance of a member of Congress") had "foraged the City together some three or four days." Congress, he reported to his Savannah friend, was

95

"hammering on the Tariff" but made "no mention of promoting modest merit in the persons of you or I."

When Jack, who was normally remiss in "regulating" Robert on news of Broughton Street, announced the arrival of Eliza's first child, Robert responded:

You told me that Miss Eliza was the mother of a little Girl, which sounds very *funny* to me, and it was my intention to have told her so myself, as well as to have assured her anew of what she still must be certain of. Do . . . say to the little one [he continued], that I have a young man entirely at her service. The *modesty* which he has inherited from his *Father* forbids him from entering in person, upon so delicate a subject, but he says, without her beauty & brightness his young days will be dark & dreary, & that the Bower of roses which he has planted would be changed to a Hut of willows. . . .

This theme captured his fancy, and when the Talcotts' first child, also a girl, was born this same year, Robert asked the Captain to "inform the little lady of the most fortunate fate that awaits her. The all-accomplished & elegant Master Custis begs to place in her hands, his happiness & his life, being assured that for her he will live! His only misery can be in her frown, his only delight her smile." This letter was the first in a series of annual congratulations to the Talcotts. On the arrival of their second child, he wrote: "*We* have been waiting for this event to decide the sex of our next & now determine it shall be a girl in order to retain the connexion in the family."

But when the number of Talcott offspring had reached six, Robert's theme was well worn, and with a final jest at their expense, he dropped the subject: "You are aware you must look out for *connexions* for *three* of them in some other families. For I had given up some years ago the hope of supplying them, & now doubt if there is any *one* family in Virginia that can keep pace with their number."

During the summer of 1833, President Jackson visited Fort Monroe while inspecting nearby Fort Calhoun, known also as "the Rip Raps." The bustle and excitement occasioned by his visit disturbed Mary, and she complained to her mother: "I shall be truly glad when they all go, & we shall have a little quiet, & Robert will have a little time to be at home. What all the consultations at the Rip Raps have resulted in, except that they are to be finished next summer, I do not know, for Robert is not very communicative on the subject." To Andrew Talcott, who was away, Robert's only comment was: "The President has played the Devil with the plan of Fort Calhoun."

Of the charming informality of Jackson's call upon her and the baby (at present known as "Bouse"), Mary had this to tell Mrs. Custis:

I carried Bouse in to see the President, who took him in his arms & held him for some time. Bouse looked at him with a fixed gaze, put his hand over his nose, but did not pull it hard, & put his finger in his eyes. The old man gave him Rachel's picture to play with, which delighted him much, & then presented him with a half dollar . . . said he was a fine & good boy & that I must take off his shoes & let him run barefoot.

That November, Robert found himself in a situation which far from displeased him. A good number of the garrison officers had been sent off the Seminole War, leaving their wives behind: "I am left to console them, & am in the right position to sympathize with them as Mrs. Lee & her little *Limb* are at Arlington."

Mary's presence was a definite hindrance to Robert's participation in the social events on the post. Since she was bored by them—"we have been quite satiated with tea-drinking lately," she complained—and was unable to understand his enjoyment of them, he felt obliged to refuse most invitations, and spend his evenings reading aloud. In some triumph Mary reported to her mother that he passed most nights in this occupation "instead of attending the card parties which attract so many, but this is *entre nous*." Her absences afforded Lee a freedom he admittedly relished: "Mrs. Custis & Mary have gone to Shirley, which is as much as to say that I am as happy as a clam at high water," he told a friend; but the coming of their first child made these holidays from his family mixed pleasures. He was strongly philoprogenitive, and at the same time that he was consoling the wives of absent officers, he sent

97

this tender lament to Mary: "My Sweet little Boy what I would give to see him! The house is a perfect desert without him. . . . I am waking all night to hear his sweet little voice, & if in the morning I could only feel his sweet little arms around my neck & his dear little heart fluttering against my breast, I should be too happy."

Of this little boy, who became his favorite son, he once wrote proudly to Mary's mother: "He is dabbling in sounds & dipping in locomotion . . . his caps have been taken off & his hair is growing finely. What more shall I tell you of him Mother, but that he is *too Sweet*."

All his children would take this same firm hold, and become "so entwined about my heart, that I feel them with every pulsation," he told Jack Mackay. In later years, they constituted his chief interest and at times, his sole pleasure in life.

That winter was again spent at Arlington, with participation in the festive doings in Washington. "As a stimulus to your blood," he teased Mackay, "I will tell you who were in the District this Winter. The Misses Mason! Miss Teaco prettier & sweeter than ever, Miss Nanie, rather thin & pining for her *Lover* [Smith Lee]. But I laughed at her so much that I believe I did her infinite service, at least she said so." Washington, he reported further, was "filled to overflowing: Bank, Bank, Deposits, Deposits, speeches, Memorials, wrangling & quarreling & *doubling of fists*—very gay. Two or three parties every night. The Ladies by their mild & winning ways at night, endeavouring to calm the storms that rage by day."

In February he returned to Fort Monroe, reporting telegraphically to Mackay: "Navigation closed, came by land, up to my eyes in mud & *alone*." By the end of March, Mary and "the Boo," as little Custis was now known, had joined him, and Robert was writing his superior officer not about sand and rock lime (the burden of their recent correspondence), but about the purchase of a new hairbrush for Mary: "Enclosed is one of Mrs. Lee's old Brushes, with a request to Mrs. Talcott (Mercy what gets into women's heads?) to get her one of the same *kind* & *size*, with a good Point." A little more than a week later he was writing to Talcott again, describing the "grand party at

Capt. Thurston's last night," a frolic he had attended alone since "Mrs. Lee is tolerably well only."

Because Captain Talcott was away from Old Point more than he was there, he had given up his regular quarters; whenever he came back he stayed with the Lees. Now he was returning, with his wife and mother-in-law, and Robert wrote apologetically:

I am glad to hear that Mrs. T. is to pay us a visit—I hope you will be willing to trust yourselves to us while you remain. Your room can easily be cleared out & made ready. Tell the Ladies that they are aware Mrs. L. is somewhat addicted to *laziness* & *forgetfulness* in her Housekeeping. But they may be certain she does her best. Or, in her mother's words, "The Spirit is willing but the flesh is weak."

That spring, although Robert was in an economical frame of mind, he was, as he told Talcott, then in New York,

making another attempt to procure a *full dress uniform* & have to request your assistance in rigging my head. My present *Chapeau* can be altered to the required shape in Norfolk. But I do not know whether I can obtain the necessary trimmings, consisting of a broad lace strap, *Silver Eagle, Gilt lapels* & *ostrich feather.* Mr. King got the chapeau *complete* at St. Johns for $38.00!! (Chapeau $30.00, Plumes $8.00). But as I cannot comprehend *why* they cost so much, unless they are worth it, I have no idea of giving it. If therefore you find that he does ask so much, please get me the *trimmings* as above mentioned & I will have my *old* fellow manufactured into a *new.* But if you find that the hat *proper* is no great additional charge, I would rather have one with everything complete. . . . I also wish you to get me an *undress leather cap*, full across the ears & with a *broad large vizor*, partaking more of an Ellipse than a circle in its formation. . . .
P.S. The circumference of my head is 22⅓ Inches . . .

Andrew Talcott bought the leather cap and the new dress hat, shipping the "precious article" as Robert termed the latter, aboard the *Norfolk.* When he received the bill of lading, he justified the total expense by admitting to the comfort derived from the thought that "we shall be a grand set of Fellows with our gold & silver."

In this letter to Talcott, Robert mentioned for the first time his dissatisfaction with aspects of life at Fort Monroe:

As much as I like the *location* of Old Point & as fond as I am of the Company of some of the Offrs. & of some persons in the neighbour-hood & notwithstanding the great partiality I have for my *Comdg* Offr. (I mean no flattery) & my belief I shall not meet with such another—yet there are so many of the *disagreements* connected with the duty that I should like to get another Post.

During Talcott's absence, Inspector General Wool made a tour of the fortifications. The friction existing between the engineer and general officers is revealed by Robert's bantering manner of describing the visit:

I requested him to commence at once, in order that the three inspections might complete our measure of *Glory* for this week— He accordingly went over to the Rip Raps this morg—But the dose of *heated* Granite, seemed to satisfy his *Punctilio*, & he postponed his annihilation of this side till tomorrow before breakfast—He propounded several wise queries & among them whether there were not quarters for us *outside*, which I take for a premonitory symptom.

But nothing could dampen Robert's exuberance and en-thusiasm for life. That June he was writing spiritedly of his friend Prentiss, "so puffing up with fat, dignity & diplomacy, that his oldest creditors would not know him, which is as much as to say Col. Johnston & myself have made some bad invest-ments." In a tone of eager anticipation he expatiated on the joys of the coming summer season: "As for the Daughters of Eve, in this country they are formed in the very poetry of nature, & would make your lips *water* & fingers *tingle*. They are beginning to assemble to put their beautiful limbs in this salt water, & among the rest we expect some friends of ours."

Complaints now began to be registered in almost every letter to Jack for his failure to include news of his sisters: "Mackay, did I depend upon you my Friend for tidings of your kind family, I should perish, but thank God I have other resources. When you write . . . tell them I am *famishing* for a sight of them. The idea alone thrills through my blood like the neigh of my blooded stallion now does through my ears." In another letter he lamented: "Not one word about them all on Broughton Street, the place I most wished to hear from. Not a syllable concerning Miss Eliza . . . Mackay . . . in your next open your heart a little. Don't be so confounded selfish & keep all knowledge of them in your own person, I pray you."

The year 1834 brought changes to Fort Monroe. In July, all engineers with the exception of one officer were transferred to the Rip Raps, and the completion of the work at Monroe was assigned to the commandant. Andrew Talcott was transferred to a project on the Hudson River, and Robert was put in charge of the work at Fort Calhoun, an uninspiring assignment for a talented and ambitious man. Each year, the riprap foundation sank at least three inches, so all Robert was called upon to do was superintend the piling of more stone upon stone. But as he told his Savannah friend: "You must rejoice, Mackay, instead of being sorry, that I am clear of Old Point, though if there were any probability of being there together, I shall regret it too. . . . I was heartily sick of it, & am rejoiced that it is at an end . . . the jealousy that existed concerning the contract exercised by the Engineers was a continual thorn in my side." Shortly after taking up his "residence" in the shabby quarters at Calhoun, he was addressing Mackay as "Delectable Jack" and recounting uninhibitedly the activities on the post. Among other doings, "we have been *celebrating* the death of the good La Fayette, *all day*."

For a long time, Robert had been disillusioned about promotion, and in writing of Jack's chances he had advised: "Do not wait for me, for there is no prospect." But in October, he had news for his friend: "You may expect my next advices from General Headquarters," he wrote, explaining that General Gratiot had submitted his name for appointment to the West Point professorship of natural and experimental philosophy, to be vacated by Edward H. Courteney. Of his reply to the General, he said to Mackay:

I told him what I tell you now, that a residence in W. P. would be peculiarly agreeable to me, yet I confessed I had no partiality for the duties of the office. But as he had done me the honour, it was

101

not for me to decline, that I would be ready to be relieved whenever he thought proper.

It is evident that Gratiot expected Robert to receive the appointment, and had told him so. For some reason, perhaps political pressures which the General could not foresee, William H. C. Bartlett, his assistant, was appointed instead, and Robert was offered Bartlett's post.

He accepted with reluctance, not only because the pay was less, but because he was well aware that his disposition did not allow him to undertake routine and sedentary duties without chafing restively.

8

WHEN Robert, Mary, and the Boo left the Rip Raps that November, they headed directly for Arlington, though Robert wrote to Andrew Talcott that he intended to rent a house in Washington. This was just what Mary feared, and she was therefore less elated than she otherwise might have been over an assignment so close to home. But until he could find a house, Robert was content to make the trip on horseback to and from his office each day the weather permitted. On nights that were stormy, he stayed at Mrs. Ulrich's Washington boarding-house where Jim Prentiss, Joe Johnston, Jack Macomb, and his cousin Tom Lee made their headquarters. Mrs. Ulrich prided herself on her "select mess," refusing application from anyone she considered "unedifying" to the young officers in whom she took a motherly interest. At this time, the Secretary of War, Joel R. Poinsett (for whom the scarlet Christmas flower is named); Senator William Rives of Virginia; Mahlon Dickerson, Secretary of the Navy; and the eminent South Carolina lawyer, Hugh Swinton Legare, then Congressman, were staying there. Since both Dickerson and Legare were classical scholars, many an evening was passed in discussion of the Greek poets.

One day while riding to his office, Robert passed a blacksmith shop on 20th and G Streets and stopped to watch the smithy, a Mr. Schneider, shoe a horse. From what he observed and learned from questions, Robert decided the man was competent. With his usual explicit instructions, he left his horse to be shod. When he returned that evening, he carefully examined each hoof, then turning to Mr. Schneider said approvingly:

"You are the first man I have ever come across who could shoe a horse by my directions."

Thereafter, for over thirty years, Mr. Schneider took care of Robert's horses and those at Arlington, and made latches, coulters, and other farm implements to Robert's design.

"My heart always warmed at the sight of him," the blacksmith remembered. He found it "pleasant to serve him," for Lee was always ready to listen to any suggestions Mr. Schneider felt free to make.

Robert's house-hunting proved fruitless, for there were as yet few places to live in the capital. The scarcity of dwellings impressed Charles Dickens, who wrote of Washington City at this time: "One might fancy the season over and most of the houses gone out of town with their masters." To the delight of Mary and her parents, Robert agreed to settle at Arlington, which—in spite of assignments in New York, Baltimore, and St. Louis—would always be *home* to the Lees until 1861.

Originally the Arlington estate had been part of a six-thousand-acre tract (including what is now Alexandria) granted to a sea captain in payment for a shipload of colonists brought to Virginia. A month later, the Alexander family exchanged six thousand pounds of tobacco for the acreage, and built a four-room cottage beside the Potomac River. In 1778, John Parke Custis, a son of Martha Washington by her first husband, bought eleven hundred acres from the Alexanders but did nothing with the land except to plant a row of willows along the river. When Mrs. Washington died, the property was inherited by her grandson, George Washington Parke Custis, who moved into the cottage, named his estate "Mount Washington," and began planning the mansion he would build to befit the name and house his inheritances from Mount Vernon. He engaged George Hadfield, the English architect who was in

Washington supervising construction of the Capitol, to draw plans.

Custis started the house in 1802, but since he did not have enough money to complete it, only the wings were built. They remained two separate units until 1816, when the central portion was constructed. Aside from a few trees needed for foundation timbers and overhead beams, none was cut, so that early visitors speak of the house set in the midst of a forest "left to the wildness of Nature."

In 1804, Custis brought his sixteen-year-old bride, Mary Lee Fitzhugh of Chatham, to what he now called "Arlington House," after the older Custis estate on Maryland's Eastern Shore. They lived in the north wing, partitioned into three rooms to meet their immediate needs. The original plan had called for a banquet hall here, but the wing was never changed to conform to these plans. It later became the family parlor and dining room and was always the favorite part of the house.

When the main section was built to connect the two wings, lack of money prevented the interior from being entirely finished until forty years later. Still, the mansion was considered one of the finest residences near Washington—though Robert characterized it as "a House that any one might see with half an eye," and some dubbed it "Custis' Folly." To this house filled with the spiritual and tangible mementoes of his mentor, Robert Lee now came to make his home, inbibing inspiration at the fountainhead.

As he had feared, the new assignment proved onerous; his time was passed in work on reports, accounts, correspondence, and odd jobs about the office. He expressed his opinion of these duties in a letter to "Glorious Jack."

"I should have to lacerate thy *tender heart* with an account of the harassing labours to which thy doughty Bob is subjected. Know my Friend that it is a situation full of pains, & one from which I shall modestly retire on the first fitting opportunity."

And to another friend he wrote: "Your choice effusions are always before me—Do not think that any delay in my responses proceeds from forgetfulness—I *abhor* the sight of pen and paper and to put one to t'other requires as great a moral effort as for a cat to walk on *live coals*."

But the composing of routine letters and reports in no way dulled the sprightly imagery of his personal correspondence, nor did the sense of frustration he spoke of to his closest friends curb the animal spirits. He gave dinner parties at his bachelor quarters, and took his usual active part in the social affairs in Virginia and the capital.

Nor was he above pranks. One day as he set out on horseback for home, he came on his messmate, Jack Macomb. Pulling up, he hailed his friend, and called out: "Climb aboard!" Macomb swung up behind the saddle, and they rode on down Pennsylvania Avenue, attracting a good deal of amused attention as they waved to comrades, and lifted their caps to the ladies. Directly in front of the White House, they met the Honorable Levi Woodbury, Secretary of the Treasury, who stared in astonishment at the two young men on a horse, both bowing to him with great dignity.

On February 5, 1835, Smith Lee married Anna Maria Mason or Nanie, whose charms Robert frequently extolled in letters to Mackay. Of the festivities, he reported to this friend: "We had a grand frolick & have been keeping it up ever since at various places. Next week we are to have it at Arlington, which will be the finale. . . . It is useless for me to tell you of the doings on such occasions, come to Va. & get married & then you will know it."

Of the "doings on such occasions," particularly when released from the vigilant eye of one's spouse, Robert confided to Andrew Talcott:

Your humble servant has returned to a state of rejuvenescency. . . . My brother Smith was married on the 5th & the Bride I think looked more beautiful than usual. We kept agoing till Sunday & last night I attended a Bridal party in Alexandria. . . . My spirits were so buoyant when relieved from the eyes of my Dame, that my Sister Nanie was trying to pass me off as her spouse but I was not going to have my sport spoiled in that way & undeceived the young ladies & told them I was her younger brother. Sweet innocent young things, they concluded I was single, & I have not had such soft looks & tender pressures of the hand for many years.

Between Lee and the cultured and able General Gratiot there developed a warm personal relationship. Aware that his young assistant was unhappy in his post, unworthy of a talented engineer, the General gave him a welcome break in the spring of 1835 when he assigned him to the duties of assistant astronomer in a survey party headed by Captain Talcott; they were to determine the boundary line between Ohio and Michigan, which had been disputed since 1832. Talcott had made a survey in 1834, and for a while it seemed that all contentions were silenced. But now trouble flared up again and an armed clash seemed imminent.

Lee was delighted to escape from the office, and in company with his close friend, see a part of the country that was new to him. In high spirits, he wrote to Mrs. Talcott in Philadelphia:

My Beautiful Talcott,

Instructions have this day been mailed to our Captain to resume at once the survey of the boundary line of Ohio, which is as much as to say that he will start immediately for Lake Erie.

He does not appear to think that he will be absent much longer than a month. His old time & able assistant, Lt. R. E. Lee of the Corps of Engrs. will join him forthwith for same duty, & will be at your home . . . on Wednesday eve.

I give you this notice that you may have all commands for A—— ready which he will be very happy to take charge of, especially if they are in the form of your sweet person. Can't you go & tell him Good bye & find an escort back? . . .

The assignment took much longer than the estimated month, so that it was October before the Captain's "old time & able assistant" returned to Washington. During his absence, his second child was born, a daughter, in keeping with the pattern of alternate sexes he had jestingly promised the Talcotts.

The birth was normal, and Mary recovered quickly, feeling so well, according to Robert's account after his return, "that she could not be restrained, but walked out, rode out, slept with the windows open all night, &c. A cold was the consequence, of which after some time she got better & then took a severe one, which was accompanied by Bilious Symptoms. This being removed, a pain & soreness in the lower part of her body & leggs remained."

When Mary first became sick, she wrote to Robert, asking him to come home at once. Her letter greatly disturbed him, for he thought it dictated by a whim.

But why do you urge my *immediate* return, & tempt one in that strongest manner, to endeavour to get excused from the performance of a duty, imposed on me by my Profession, for the pure gratification of my private feelings? . . . Do you not think . . . that I rather require to be strengthened & encouraged to the *full* performance of what I am called upon to execute, rather than excited to a dereliction? . . . I cannot in conscience do what you ask. . . . I must not consent to do aught that would lower me in your eyes, my own & that of others. . . . I hope therefore that you & your Mother will bundle up your little treasures & commence your tour up the country. . . . You see therefore Molly that every consideration induces you to cheer up & pack up; to lay aside unavailing regrets; to meet with a smiling face & cheerful heart the vicissitudes of life. . . .

This letter should silence for all time the contention that Mary "ran" her husband.

But "Molly" was in no condition to "cheer up & pack up" or to meet her trials with a "smiling face." When Robert reached Ravensworth, which was as far as she was able to get on her "tour up the country," he found her "very low & more emaciated than I could have imagined." The morning after his arrival he had her moved on a bed to Arlington, "in order that she might be nearer Physicians & called in Dr. Lovell in conjunction with the family Physician."

The doctors diagnosed her illness as "rheumatic diathesis," the treatment for which was "fomentation, leeching, cupping, &c." Two painful abscesses formed on her left side. On November 9, Robert wrote in genuine concern to Andrew: "Mary is dreadfully reduced & so weak that she cannot stand." Several days later, he was pleased to report that both abscesses

107

had opened, and that when she moved now, "a soreness is substituted for acute pain."

When Mary was first able to sit up in bed, she found that her long heavy hair had become hopelessly snarled, and to Robert's horror she reached for the scissors and cut it all off. But she was completely indifferent to her appearance, and as soon as her hair began to grow out, and Robert could bear to look at her again, she announced one morning as he was about to leave for the office that she intended to have her head shaved. "I expect on my return to find her bald," he wrote in distress to Talcott.

It was spring before Mary was able to walk, for the abscesses supposedly caused what the doctors described as a "contraction" of the sinews under the left knee. By June, Robert felt that she was improving, though she was then "labouring under an attack of the mumps."

Meanwhile, the children and their various illnesses were an additional trial. Robert told Andrew about staying up all night in order to relieve the baby, little Mary Custis, during an attack of croup; the Boo, recovering from the whooping cough, was "thin & fretful." Both presented teething problems, so that at times the harassed father was subjected to their "whooping, coughing, teething, &c. & sometimes all three together." His confession that baby Mary "had as yet, some little ways about her that do not altogether suit a man of my nervous temperament" is understandable. That the children's querulousness was particularly vexatious to their ailing mother is evident from the closing words in a letter to Eliza Stiles: "My brats are squalling around me so I cannot write more. You know how such musick puts all one's ideas to flight."

When Robert was certain that Mary was on the road to recovery, he reported her improvement with his old gusto: "Her appetite is famous & the partridges, Buck Wheat Cakes, Muffins, &c. disappear at breakfast as fast as the pheasants, chickens, &c. at dinner." During the summer, he took her to the hot springs where she found some relief, though she was lame for many months. This sickness marked the beginning of the rheumatoid arthritis which eventually caused her total invalidism.

During the summer of 1836, Andrew Talcott resigned and entered the field of private engineering. " 'The long agony is over,' and you have at last torn yourself from the Corps," Robert wrote him. "The reflection has made me quite sad, & should it ever be my lot to take a similar step, it will now be done with less regret than formerly." Since Talcott had made his final visit to the engineer office when Lee was absent, he continued: "You may judge at my chagrin at having missed such an opportunity to take by the hand a man for whom I have so high a regard & esteem as the one in question. I was therefore left in ignorance, too, of your future plans, or rather the minutiæ of them, as well as the opinion & feelings of my beautiful Talcott upon the unnatural separation."

Though long overdue promotion to first lieutenant came to Robert that September, Talcott's resignation made him more than usually restive. He had been contemplating a similar step, he told his friend, and if Mary had been well enough that previous spring, he would have made the effort either to find a more congenial post or to have resigned. With her improvement, he professed to be now "waiting, looking, & hoping for some good opportunity to bid an affectionate farewell to my dear Uncle Sam," a sentiment that he would often repeat over the years.

A partial explanation for the fact that he never brought himself to follow Talcott's example is revealed by his admission of a failing he was never able to master: "My talent for procrastination is so good, that I can easily pass a winter or two in commencing a letter," he once wrote. Recognizing this disposition to delay and postpone, he told Talcott now: "I seem to think that said opportunity is to drop in my lap like a ripe pear, for d——l a stir have I made in the matter & there again I am helped out by the talent I before mentioned, I possessed in so eminent a degree."

When Andrew Talcott went to New Orleans in April, 1837, to superintend the improvement of the Mississippi delta, the Beautiful Talcott stayed at home. Robert wrote her to urge: "My Hardy had better come on & consort with my Dame at Arlington. We will be very glad of her entertaining presence, & our children will be in a way of fulfilling their destiny."

On the 31st of the following month, the Lee's third child, a boy—in keeping once again with the established pattern—was born. This son was named William Henry Fitzhugh for the family's loyal kinsman, but his father, possessing a talent for bestowing nicknames, called him "Rooney."

Mary had no complications during or after the birth, Robert told the Talcotts. The beauties she saw in the newborn babe, he readily admitted, were not visible to him: "Her little limb is as ugly as ever, though she thinks his nose is to subside, his mouth to contract, eyes to open, hair to curl, &c., &c., & is in fact to become a perfect beauty."

General Gratiot, the son of an aristocratic French couple, had been born in St. Louis and for this reason was particularly interested in the city's fate. He kept an engineer officer, Captain Henry M. Shreve, stationed there the year round to superintend the removal of snags in the Mississippi, a constant menace to shipping. For some time the river had been cutting a new channel on the Illinois shore and had built up two large sand bars opposite the city, threatening to cut it off from river commerce. What threatened St. Louis threatened the whole Mississippi Valley and the expansion of the West.

In 1836 Congress appropriated fifteen thousand dollars to build a pier that would give direction to the current, and General Gratiot asked Shreve to draw the plans. But snag control was a full-time operation, and another engineer was needed to direct the building of the pier and the cutting of a channel in the Upper Rapids, to allow steamboats to make the passage at low water.

Robert saw in such an assignment the opportunity "to get rid of the office in W.," as he told Mackay, "& the Genl. at last agreed to my going. I was cognizant of so much iniquity in more ways than one, that I feared for my morality, at no time strong."

He also saw the possibility of advancing in his profession, an interest he held mainly for his children's sake. "Of all things in this world, the most bitter reflection to me in after life should I be spared to see them grow up, would be that I had given them reason to think I had preferred my own ease and comfort to their welfare and interest and had not improved such opportunities I might possess for their advantage," he wrote Mary's mother. "Should I fail in my attempts, which is equally probable, I shall have nothing to reproach myself with, or they to regret."

9

TOWARD the end of June, 1837, Robert started out in high spirits for his new assignment, leaving his family, as he reported gaily, "in care of my eldest son who will take them over the mountains somewhere this summer, & his grandmother along with them." In his valise were letters of introduction from General Gratiot to his brothers and sister, and to other prominent families in St. Louis. His assistant, Lieutenant Montgomery C. Meigs of Augusta, Georgia, joined him and they set out for Pittsburgh by way of the Pennsylvania Canal. At Louisville, the captain accommodatingly kept the boat waiting while Robert inspected the progress of the two "stone boats" (used for lifting rock) and the little steamer to tow them, which Captain Shreve had ordered built for the channel work at the Upper Rapids. The journey also took on a new interest when Robert assumed what he called "a responsible charge." He was asked to escort two young ladies traveling alone to St. Louis. One was "a handsome young widow— scarcely over twenty," and the other, her cousin, whom Robert found "young & spritely, quite pleasing in manners & appearance, & sings sweetly & unaffectedly. . . . They are decidedly the most beautiful & interesting *young Ladies* I have seen since leaving Baltimore . . . and served to dispel a part of the tedium of the voyage."

When they reached St. Louis on August 5, he and Meigs

went to what was considered the best hotel, but found it

very crowded, and a dark *dirty* room is the only one we could procure. The dinner was very good indeed, well cooked and well served, but the table is too large and full, and contains too many guests for the viands and servants. This part could be borne with, but the room is intolerable, & so soon as I close this I shall sally out in quest of another. I may be *over* scrupulous in this respect, but I can readily bear the *clean dirt* of the earth, & drink without a strain the mud of the Missouri, & if necessary could live in it & lie in it. Domestic filth is revolting to my taste.

With the distractions of the journey over, Lee found himself suffering acutely from homesickness: "Oh, what pleasure I lose in being separated from my children. Nothing can compensate me for that. I am very anxious to get back, & my desire to be again in the midst of you and Mother and the children and the rest is sometimes uncontrollable. You must give a great deal of love to all of them. Kiss them all for me." His thoughts, he found, kept "returning more forcibly & longingly" to his children. "Tell the Boo," he wrote, "that I have closely inspected all the little boys on my journey, & have looked long & wistfully to see if any were like him. It was all in vain, & my feelings were each time sadder than before." But as he became engrossed in the challenge of his new assignment and in roughing it on the frontier, an experience foreign to a Virginia gentleman, the pangs were lessened, though thoughts of the little ones at Arlington were always there. When he went to the Des Moines Rapids several weeks later, he asked Mary to be *certain* to "tell Mr. Boo that I see plenty of Indians paddling their canoes along the river, dressed in all their finery & blankets & some not dressed at all." Of his daughter, whom he now called "the Little Woman," he inquired tenderly: "How is the little darling with the bright eyes?"

When Mary and the children returned to Arlington after a summer passed with relatives, she wrote Robert about her problems with their five-year-old son, who had inherited two Lee traits—willfulness and temper. Though he was sympathetic and acutely aware of the boy's right to both characteristics, he replied in concern:

Our dear little boy seems to have among his friends a reputation of being hard to manage—a distinction not at all desirable. . . . I have endeavoured in my intercourse with him to require nothing but what was in my opinion necessary or proper, & to explain to him temperately its propriety, at a time when he could listen to my arguments, & not at the moment of his being vexed & his little faculties warped by passion. I have also tried to show him I was firm in my demands, & constant in their enforcement, & that he must comply with them, & I let him see that I look to their execution in order to relieve him, as much as possible, from the temptation to break them. Since my efforts have been so unsuccessful, I fear I have altogether failed in accomplishing my purpose, but I hope to be able to profit from my experience. You must assist me in my attempts, & we must endeavour to combine the mildness & forbearance of the mother with the sternness and, perhaps, unreasonableness of the father. This is a subject on which I think much, though M [mother] may blame me for not reading more. I am ready to acknowledge the good advice of the text books, & believe I see the merit of their reasoning generally; but what I want to learn is to apply what I already know.

Robert's first reactions to St. Louis were unfavorable. He considered it the "dearest & dirtiest place I was ever in. Our daily expense about equals our daily pay." But two months later, he was willing to make this gallant exception, "and that is in favour of the pretty girls, if there are any here, & I know there are, for I have met them in no place, in no garb, in no situation that I did not feel my heart open to them like a flower to the sun." By the middle of August, though, when the stone-boats and steamer, supposed to have been sent on in less than a week after his stop in Louisville, had still not come, he was ready with more complaints about the westerner: "They are the greatest people for promising & not fulfilling, that I ever saw. Never hesitate to undertake anything, but completing is another matter. So you will see instead of being nearly done with our examinations here, we have not commenced them."

While waiting for the equipment, he revived a subject he had discussed earlier with Andrew Talcott: his desire to have a seal ring made with the family arms and motto. He asked the Captain to "choose a handsome & proper stone, Carnelian,

113

Rock Crystal, or what you prefer, & have it richly but plainly set in a gold ring about 2¾ inches in circumference in the interior." (Small fingers for a man his size.) "Do not let the seal be too large, though what the proper size is, I could not tell without seeing one."

The stoneboats and steamer did not arrive until the end of August, a time when the river had fallen so low that Robert was fearful the season would be entirely fruitless. Nevertheless, he took his survey party up the river. At the mouth of the Des Moines, their little boat, the *Pearl*, ran aground, so Robert decided to survey this area first. Stores and equipment were removed from the steamer to a vacant one-room log cabin which they rented for "half a dollar a week" from a man named Allen, whom Robert styled "the nabob." But "the men & eatables so completely filled its single apartment that Meigs & myself took up our blankets & walked a short mile to the City of Des Moines composed of the worst kind of a small log cabin which contained the Proprietor & the entire population." This was Allen, "a hard featured man of about *fifty*," so Robert described him, "a large talker, and has the title of *Doctor*, whether of Law, Medicine or Science, I have never learned but I infer all three." He offered the two engineers "the privilege" of spreading their blankets on the floor at night. Robert claimed the good fortune of having found the "softest puncheon" for his bed.

When the surveys in this area were finished, they went on to the Upper Rapids, working "downward with more comfort, as we found a better class of people & better accommodations, besides having the whole range of an old steamboat or two sunk on the rocks, whose upper decks were out of the water. I assure you we were not modest," Robert admitted, "but fell without difficulty into the manners of the country, & helped ourselves to everything that came our way." Meigs recalled that after a day's work, the larder was frequently replenished by someone fishing off the stern of the wreck for "blue catfish, pike, and pickerel."

This survey was completed by the end of September, and the party, hailing a passing steamboat, returned to the Des

Moines River, where, due to a sudden rise in the water, they found the *Pearl* afloat, and returned in her to St. Louis.

Robert now began his work in the harbor. Mayor John F. Darby saw him almost daily, and wrote that

his time was occupied in making surveys, preparing drawings, and planning the manner of doing the work in the driving of piles and filling in with brush and stone, and in making revetments. . . . He went in person with the hands every morning about sunrise, and worked day by day in the hot, broiling sun—the heat being greatly increased by the reflection from the river. He shared in the hard task and common fare and rations furnished to the common laborers—eating at the same table in the cabin of the steamboat used in the prosecution of the work, but never on any occasion becoming too familiar with the men. . . . He also slept in the cabin of the steamboat, moored to the bank near their works. In this same place, Lieutenant Lee with his assistant, Henry Kayser, worked at his drawings, plans and estimates every night till eleven o'clock.

Henry Kayser, the United States Surveyor General of Public Lands, had been appointed as Lee's assistant in charge of surveying; Lieutenant Meigs supervised the draughting.

After the findings were mapped, Robert decided to use the river to destroy its own works. He planned the construction of two piers or dikes. One would extend from the head of Bloody Island (so called from the number of duels that took place there), perpendicular to the Illinois shore, and divert the river back to St. Louis, thereby concentrating the current where the channel required deepening. He estimated the cost at $63,574. The second dike would be built at an angle from the foot of Bloody Island in order to direct the full force of the diverted current against Duncan's Island, thus removing this two-hundred-acre sand bar that the river had been steadily building since 1818. Estimated cost: $80,680. To protect Bloody Island against the current, enabling it to become a permanent landmark (it was also a sand bar), Lee estimated that an additional $14,300 would be needed. No allowance had been made for the cost of the channel in the Upper Rapids, so the total appropriation of $65,000 was, as Robert told Mackay, "barely sufficient" to commence the works. "One half is already spent in S. Boat, Stone Boats, Pile Drivers, &c."

By the time Robert had completed his surveys, he was more reconciled to the West, finding the country near the Upper Mississippi especially beautiful, with soil "so fertile, trees so grand & verdure so rich." The people were "rough, but they will polish as soon . . . as they . . . begin to thrive. There are some quite pretty & flourishing villages . . . & when you consider that it has been only three years since the greater part of them were founded, you will allow the inhabitants deserve some credit."

When the end of the season came, navigation was closed, so Robert and Meigs made the journey home by stagecoach over the Cumberland Road from Springfield, Ohio, via Wheeling, Virginia, to Cumberland, Maryland. It was a rugged trip in winter. The passengers huddled together for warmth, their legs buried up to the knees in straw, to keep from freezing. Meals at the coaching inns were often poor and always expensive. Often passengers were tricked into going back to the coaches before they had been served, for meals were paid for in advance.

At Frederick, Maryland, Lee and Meigs took their first train ride, boarding the cars of the Baltimore & Ohio, which had been operating just a short time; part of the way the train was horse drawn. The two engineers parted company in Washington, and Robert reached Arlington just in time for Christmas, a season made more joyous by the presence of his three children for whom he had bought gifts along the way.

Lee spent this winter partly on leave and partly on duty at the Washington office. It was a busy time for Robert, preparing for the coming season's work on the Mississippi. He and his German assistant, Henry Kayser, corresponded weekly about the adjustment of vouchers, the letting of contracts for piles and timbers, the caulking of the *Pearl*, the quarrying and transportation of stone, and the construction of a scow and "Pile Engine." At New Albany, Lee let contracts for the building of a steamboat and four large scows, and in Washington he engaged John Lowry to superintend the pile driving.

There were also extensive domestic preparations since Rob-

116

ert had persuaded Mary to accompany him, bringing both boys, but leaving the "little Woman" with her grandparents. "Are there any houses for rent now, and what are the prospects for getting lodgings?" He asked Kayser. Just before they left, he wrote again: "If you find the present Landlady . . . will keep a boarding House in the Building of Genl. Clarke the ensuing year, *engage* the rooms of Mr. L. Clarke for me. . . . I take it for granted that the rooms . . . are *un-furnished*. Please write to me at Louisville as I may find I can get cheaper and better furniture there than in St. Louis."

About the twentieth of March, the Lees with the servant, Kitty, to keep the boys in hand, and a variety of trunks, valises, and hampers, and Mary's precious box of books, left for Baltimore to visit the Marshalls. At the suggestion of her parents, Mary and Robert had their portraits painted by the distinguished American artist, William E. West. He was pleased to have as his subject the nephew of Bernard Moore Carter, who had recently celebrated West's portraits of Mrs. Patterson and Lord Byron in a long and laudatory poem published in Paris.

Robert had his sittings first, for Mary thought she would prefer to have Sully. But when she saw Robert's portrait, she wrote home: "His picture is a very fine likeness & a fine painting," and she then consented to sit for West. Robert wrote Mrs. Custis that Mary was having her first sitting on March 24, "with the hope that he may be successful, and that you may have something to look at while she is away."

It is evident that West found inspiration in working with Robert. Effortlessly he captured the sparkle in the brown eyes, the fleeting smile, and the bright spirit in a face so handsome it needed no flattery. But Mary's picture seems labored and spiritless. The lower part of the face appears to have been worked over often in attempts to soften the straight mouth and sharp chin, and gives the impression that it was left unfinished.

In Baltimore, Robert met Lieutenant Horace Bliss of the Engineers, "laying on his oars," and hoping to find work with a railroad survey. Lee persuaded him to join his party and take charge of the operations at the Rapids, for Meigs had found work closer to home.

But just as they were ready to leave for St. Louis, both the

Lee boys took sick, delaying departure ten days. On April 2, Robert wrote to Henry Kayser that he believed they would be able to start in two or three days.

When they reached Pittsburgh, Robert was buying keel boats, which he was having fitted up with quarters for the men, and utensils and equipment, but he found time to write to the Beautiful Talcott to let her know that Pittsburgh was "the darkest, blackest place" he had "ever put foot in. Even the snow, milk & everything intended by nature to be white, not excepting the rosy cheeks of the pretty girls, partake of its dingy nature, & I am afraid my complexion is ruined!"

At Cincinnati, the Lees remained long enough to buy furnishings for their rooms, shipping it aboard the steamboat *Moselle*, on which they fortunately did not take passage, since it blew up a short distance from the city. Several days were spent in Louisville, inspecting the steamboat and four scows Lee had previously ordered, and "to partake of a wedding and the good things attending it." A number of Virginians had settled in this city, and the bride, it happened, was a friend from the Old Dominion.

Robert and his family reached St. Louis the first day of May. The trip had been a pleasant one on the whole, Robert wrote "My Hardy." "The boys stood it manfully & indeed, improved on it, & my Dame, taking advantage of the frequent opportunities to nap, and refreshed by the good viands of the West (it would make your mouth water if I was to dilate upon the little roast pigs & sausages) defied the crowding, squeezing & scrambling." They found that the rooms Henry Kayser had engaged for them in the Clarke mansion on First and Vine Streets had not been saved, "which was perhaps just as well," he told Harriet, "as the furniture intended for them . . . had taken a different course from the one projected."

They found other rooms in the same building, bought more furniture, and at the invitation of Dr. William Beaumont, the army surgeon who also lived in the house, took their meals with him and his family. The doctor was, as Robert described him, "at the head of his profession here, so that he can administer food & physic in just proportions."

To the delight of the little Lees, there were three young Beaumonts with whom they joined forces in the pleasures of steamboating in the parlor. "As drumming was the mania at Old Point, riding & driving at Arlington, so steamboating is all the rage here," Robert told a friend. "They convert themselves even into steamboats, ring their bells, raise their steam (High pressure) and put off. They fire up so frequently, & keep on so heavy a pressure of steam, that I am constantly fearing they will burst their boilers."

This year the water level in the river fell so slowly that it was July before they could consider blasting at the Rapids. Robert accompanied the crew, but as soon as they arrived, the river made a sudden rise, so he left Lieutenant Bliss in charge and went back to St. Louis. After another month, the water was still high, so Lee laid the men off and prepared to give up for the season. Then in September, the river suddenly fell. Taking Mary and the boys with him this time, he hurried to the Rapids and set the men to blasting.

On his arrival, he noticed many indications of an early winter: leaves had fallen, the prairies were enveloped in smoke and flame, and large flocks of geese and brant were flying south. Before another month was out, ice appeared on the river —"in the language of the natives, strong enough to *bear a dog*" —so he discharged the main body, keeping a gang of forty, after six of his watermen had promised to stay. "But alas on Monday our chief man," he wrote, "backed out after ½ hours trial. Tuesday a second took his leave, Wednesday the remaining four shook their heads & shivered." Then a snowstorm came, and they "began pulling up our stakes in earnest." He regretted the short season, but was consoled by the fact that the little work done proved the practicality of deepening the channel.

The Lees and Horace Bliss found quarters in the city of Montebello, which consisted of a single house, a stable, and a hen coop. The way of life of the young Yankee couple who comprised Montebello's entire population was a revelation to someone reared in the South, and Robert confessed that it made him "nervous" to see a well-educated and refined young

119

woman who kept volumes of Sterne, La Rochefoucauld, and Bryon on her shelves, work so hard. Not only did she sew, wash, and mind her child just starting to walk, but she cooked for three boarders besides themselves, and for occasional passengers from steamboats that stopped there. Her task was made doubly hard, Robert commented drily, because Bliss ate up the pumpkin pies as fast as she could make them.

The abundance of game in this region astonished him, coming as he did from a countryside that had known the reckless hand of the white hunter for nearly two centuries. One could hardly keep from stumbling over the partridges, he wrote Mackay, who was an enthusiastic hunter. Hare and squirrel were without number, there was an abundance of woodcock and pheasant in season, turkeys and deer were just beyond the back door, and now the river was beginning to be covered with ducks. As for fishing—one could engage in this sport from "years end to years end."

Despite the small appropriation, Lee managed to make a start in the harbor. He began with the dike from the foot of Bloody Island, and before the end of June, two rows of piles had been driven in the river bed, the space between them filled with small stones, sand, and fascines, "and the slopes and crest above this plane revetted with stones placed on their edge, and well bound together, so as to form a revetment of from a foot and a half to two feet thick," Lee reported to General Gratiot. The exterior was made of a matting of brush, with butts and branches so interwoven with the piles that it formed a solid facing.

Before the season ended, almost the full length of this dike had been built, and on September 13, the *Missouri Republican* reported: "Already the beneficial effects of the work are very evident, there being at least 13½ feet of water on the bar opposite the city at low water; whereas during the last season there was but 6 feet, and boats now approach directly to all parts of the city above the market-house, instead of making a circuitous navigation as formerly." On the second dike, Lee was able to drive only two rows of piers before ice began to drift downstream and end the work.

120

The previous October, the city of St. Louis had supplemented the small federal appropriation with fifteen thousand dollars, and when Congress adjourned in July, 1838, without further allotment, the city authorized Lee to use this sum, an act which provoked an immediate controversy, fought mainly in the local press. It shortly assumed major proportions with political overtones, since an election was approaching, and accusations of slowness due to incompetence were hurled in Lee's direction. Then the city rescinded the offer of the funds. When Lee was asked for a comment on this action, he replied:

"They have a right to do as they will with their own; I do not own the city. The Government has sent me here as an officer of the Army to do a certain work. I shall do it." This was his only recorded statement during the entire altercation.

The capers of the candidates on election day amused him, even if their pre-election antics had not. He observed that all hacks, steamboats, and grog shops had been hired by the different candidates and parties, who decorated them with signs, banners, and bunting. Speechmakers exhorted the populace, and companies of fife and drum marched through the streets. The Whigs and Democrats each marshaled their forces to the polls with bands of music and flying colors. The city was in a ferment, and one might have thought it besieged.

As to the results of the election, Robert expressed the contempt he always held for politics and politicians:

The "Van-ites" have carried the day in the State, although the Whigs in this district carried their entire ticket, & you will have the pleasure of hearing the *great expunger* [Thomas Hart Benton] thunder from his place in the Senate against banks, bribery & corruption. While on the river I cannot help being on the lookout for that stream of gold that was to ascend the Mississippi, tied up in silk-net purses! It might be a pretty sight, but the tide has not yet made it up here.

After the election, when tempers had cooled and feeling between the Locofocos and Whigs had returned to normal, the city once again granted Lee the use of its money, and the editor of the *Republican* commended "the Superintendent" for having "deported himself throughout our election, as every government officer should, but as very few at this day do, taking no part in the contest."

Jack Mackay had suffered what Robert felt was a "gross injustice" at the hands of the "Sovereigns" in Washington, and in his friend's behalf he wrote to General Gratiot to learn the amount of the appropriation that had been granted for the improvement of the Savannah River, what the department's plans were, and whether they could use "a good man and true . . . to take charge of the business." It was perhaps through Robert's instance that Mackay was made superintending topographical engineer on "constructions of Harbors in Georgia."

But at the moment, Mackay was considering resignation, and though Robert believed there was justification, he urged Jack not to let the politicians bother him, reminding him of Don Quixote's injunctions to Sancho Panza when, upon being questioned as to the cause of certain odors, he had slid from his mule in fright: " 'Let it alone Sancho, I tell you, the more you stir it, the more it will stink.' " Robert added: "The manner in which the Army is considered and treated by the Country and those whose business it is to nourish & take care of it, is enough to disgust every one with the service, & has the effect of driving every good soldier from it, and rendering those who remain discontented, careless, and negligent."

It has often been said that Lee restricted his reading solely to works of history and an occasional military biography for variety, while some biographers have gone so far as to claim that he was solely a man of action and read nothing at all. His letters to Jack Mackay prove beyond all doubt the fallacy of these statements and show that Lee was familiar with the work of Shakespeare, Goethe, Voltaire, Cervantes, Dickens, and other literary masters.

On the first of August Robert received his commission as captain of engineers, "a tardy promotion" which he looked upon with mixed feelings. At the suggestion of Mary's mother, he had been considering settling on one of the Custis estates. Procrastination had kept him from taking this step; the promotion now would make it all the harder for him to leave, if he really did intend to do so. In words that echoed Light-Horse Harry's desire for an obscure retreat, Robert replied to a congratulatory message from the Beautiful Talcott's mother:

I do not know whether I ought to rejoice or not at the cause of your congratulations, as in all my schemes of happiness I look forward to returning to some quiet corner among the hills of Virginia where I can indulge my natural propensities without interruption, & I suppose the more comfortable I am fixed in the Army, the less likely I shall be to leave it.

Despite preoccupation with his work on the river, he was still devoting thought to the Lee ancestry. Andrew Talcott had doubted the accuracy of the sketch of the Lee arms and motto and had hesitated to have the seal ring made. In August, Robert applied to his Cousin Cassius for help:

I believe I once spoke to you on the subject of getting me the Crest, Coat of Arms, &c., of the Lee family, and which, sure enough, you never did. My object in making this request is for the purpose of having a seal cut with the impression of said Coat, which I think is due a man of my large family to his posterity, and which I have thought . . . might as well be right as wrong. . . . I once saw in the hands of Cousin Edmund, for the only time in my life, our family tree, and as I begin in my old age [he was thirty-one] to feel a little curiosity relative to my forefathers, their origin, whereabouts, &c., any information you can give me will increase the obligation.

So sit down one of these hot nights & write it off for me, or at any rate the substance, and tell my cousin Philippa not to let you forget it. I wish you would at the same time undeceive her on a certain point, for, as I understand, she is labouring under a grievous error. Tell her that it is farthest from my wish to detract from any of the little Lees, but as to her little boy being equal to Mr. Rooney, it is a thing not even to be supposed, much less believed, although we live in a credulous country, where people stick at nothing from a coon story to a sea serpent.

Cassius replied at once, assuring Robert that his silence was not due to forgetfulness but because the information had been mislaid or carried off by some other member of the family. He had found an engraving of the arms and a sketch of the genealogy compiled by William Lee in 1771, both of which he enclosed. He concluded his letter with a message from Cousin Philippa, "who was amused at your vanity, for she says she must really look upon it as such, if you really pretend to [compare] your little boy with hers."

When Robert wrote next to Talcott for advice about some problems with the river, he sent copies of the genealogy and crest, and asked him to check them. He also asked Andrew to select him a watch: "I should like a thin, plain gold hunting watch, & a good time keeper; by thin, read not thick; by plain, no ginger bread or Filimigree. A hunting watch with a good second hand, I should prefer, & the price would be something, though for a good one, I would give a pretty high one."

In spite of the oppressive heat that summer—it was "hissing hot," Robert told Jack, and Cockspur was a "shady grove" by comparison—Mary was well, and as happy as she could ever be away from Arlington. She passed much time with her books, writing to her mother that she had been "reading some beautiful poetry by Coleridge, Shelley, Wordsworth, some French books lent me by Mr. Cabanné & other little things, among them Goldsmith's *Life* & poems." She was greatly interested in the unusual garden flowers that grew there, often securing the promise of a root or cutting to take back to Arlington. When she went with Robert to the Rapids, she walked over the prairie with Mrs. Bliss (who had joined her husband), hunting wild flowers and gathering the ripe seeds to plant in the garden at home.

Her mornings were spent in attempts to teach the Boo to read, write, and spell, but she found it "hard to induce him to sit to his lessons" with a mischievous younger brother around. In one letter to her mother, she apologized for her thoughts being so "disjointed" and "stupid," but at the moment this little boy was "playing around me pulling my pens, paper & ink & is now trying to throw his Papa's hat out of the window. . . . I wish I had some of the little ones [Negroes] here to amuse Rooney all the time Kitty is washing; I find it rather tiresome to nurse all day such an unsettled brat." But this was not his father's opinion, she admitted: Robert was convinced "there is not such another child in all Missouri & that he would not exchange him for the whole State."

124

The Beaumonts soon became their closest friends, Robert's heart opening readily to the handsome and congenial Mrs. Beaumont and her lovely daughter, Sarah. Most evenings were spent with this family, whose chief diversion was music. Sarah played the piano, another frequent guest, Major Ethan Allen Hitchcock, the scholarly grandson of the leader of the Green Mountain Boys, was an accomplished flautist, Mrs. Beaumont sang, and Robert turned the pages of the selections from "Oberon" and other of their favorite operas.

Hitchcock's visits attest to the superiority of the company, for he preferred to read in the large library of philosophical works that he took with him everywhere, than to pass his time "idly" with "unrewarding companions," as he wrote. It was his habit to remove "dullards" from his quarters by reading to them from Hegel or Spinoza; and at gatherings, to escape the tedium of "unenlightened minds," he would steal off to the woods, a favorite volume hidden under his coat.

Although Robert's financial statements and reports were mailed to Washington in October, settlement of the "Island accounts" delayed him until after January 1, 1839. It was then too late and hazardous to take the cold overland trip, for Mary was expecting a child in June.

Late in December, Robert learned of General Gratiot's dismissal. "I believe the news of his death would have been less painful to me," he admitted. On December 6, Gratiot had been discharged for "having failed to pay into the Treasury the balance of the moneys placed in his hands, in 1835, for public purposes, after suspending therefrom the amount which he claims to be due him on settlement of accounts. . . . "

On December 23, Robert wrote to him:

> I recd a letter this morg from my brother giving me information of your separation from the Army and the command of our Corps. The rumour which had reached me of this distressing event, I could not before credit, nor can I now realize its truth. I am yet unacquainted with all the details of the transaction, but when I call to mind your zeal and integrity in the discharge of your duties, your service rendered, and labours performed . . . I can neither comprehend or account for a result that has deprived the Country of so able an officer, or the service of so bright an orna-

ment. . . . I hope I need not assure you of my deep sympathy in what concerns you or the warm interest I take in the feelings of Mrs. G—— and your daughters, in all of which I am joined by Mrs. Lee. Do present us to them in the most affectionate manner. . . .

There was no doubt where Lee stood. He at once suspected that Gratiot's dismissal was the result of political intrigue; that someone else wanted Gratiot's post, and the accusation was a pretext to remove him.

Robert talked with the General's brothers to see what action could be taken, and when Gratiot came to St. Louis, had conferences with him. These talks convinced Robert "that nothing was farther from his intention than the idea of defrauding the Govt. of a single cent."

Lee's sense of justice was outraged, and he came to the General's defense by writing letters in his behalf, so that his "hitherto unsullied name, should be justified to the world."

This outspoken advocacy of Gratiot's cause did not tend to endear Lee to the "Sovereigns" in Washington, nor further his chances of recognition and promotion. When he took Mary and the boys home that spring, he stopped in Washington to gather all records and papers that the General would need for his defense.

The case did not come to trial until 1841, and though Lee wrote then, "all expect a favorable issue. God grant it may be so," his expectations were too sanguine. Gratiot's name was eventually cleared, but he was never restored to the army roster. He worked as a clerk in the General Land Office in Washington until his death in 1855. Lee believed that the reason he had not won his case was that he had "failed in the beginning of his controversy to penetrate the designs of his enemies & study to refute them."

This served to make Robert more than ever discontent with the army. But he did not ever forget his father's fatal mistake in leaving the service. Too, he was haunted by a fear of poverty, also born of his father's errors. His prudence and caution kept him from taking what he called "the desired step."

126

Another important reason for staying in the army was the satisfaction he found in the camaraderie: "You have often heard me say," he wrote Mary, "the cordiality & friendship in the army was the great attraction of the service. It is that, I believe, that has kept me in it so long, & it is that which now makes me fear to leave it. I do not know where I should meet with so much friendship out of it." Friendship was precious to Lee, as it had been to his mother.

That winter the eminent French astronomer and explorer, Joseph Nicholas Nicholett, came to St. Louis. He was making a geological and geographical survey of the territory beyond the Mississippi, and Robert gave Henry Kayser permission to work with him on his maps and calculations. Astronomy had been Lee's favorite subject, and he was therefore greatly interested in the man and his work.

With the first signs of spring, Mary talked of little else than the return to Arlington and reunion with her parents. Robert dreaded the thought of parting with his children again, and wrote Mrs. Custis to persuade her and "the Major to break up and campaign with us. You know, Mother, a man ought not to be separated from his children."

Unfortunately, such a happy solution did not materialize, because Mr. Custis refused to go so far from home and his affairs. Robert had to apply for a leave.

On May 1, they left St. Louis. It took just eleven days to reach Arlington, but it had been a "tiresome trip" for Mary, and a confining one for the boys, who were, according to their father, "noisy and quarrelsome."

Robert was able to stay at home just long enough to renew his acquaintance with his daughter, visit Smith, and have a brief reunion with his sister, Mildred, who was visiting America.

The last week in May he parted sadly with his children, and leaving Mary with many parting injunctions for their care and training, started off for the "Western Metropolis." He was, as he said,

"Turned out upon the world again as a *lone man*."

127

10

BY the time he had reached Louisville, Lee was already home-sick.

> To be alone in a crowd is very solitary [he wrote Mary]. In the woods I feel sympathy with the trees and birds, in whose company I take delight, but experience no pleasure in a strange crowd. I . . . must again urge you to be very prudent and careful of those dear children. If I could only get a squeeze at the little fellow turning up his sweet mouth to "keese Baba!"

Reflecting on Mary's preoccupation with other matters, and the indulgence of grandparents, he admonished her:

> You must not let him run wild in my absence, & will have to exercise firm authority over all of them. This will not require severity, or even strictness, but constant attention and an unwaver-ing course. Mildness & forbearance, tempered by firmness & judg-ment, will strengthen their affection for you, while it will maintain your control over them.

This advice did not arise from Lee's inclination to preach, as some biographers have contended. He did not have to look far to see the results of willfulness and impetuosity among his imme-diate family. There was every reason for him to worry about headstrong little boys.

The eighteenth of June brought him another daughter—"a little long-nosed fellow waiting for my first benediction," he described her unflatteringly to Jack Mackay. She was named Ann Carter, though her father referred to her now as "Little Raspberry" in a jocular attempt to hide his anxiety over a small birthmark Mrs. Custis had mentioned in her letter announcing the baby's coming.

"With what a bountiful hand are these *responsibilities* dis-tributed!" he told his Savannah friend, yet he wrote to Mary's mother: "I am very anxious to see this one as none of the descrip-tions . . . I have yet had have satisfied my fraternal longings. Does the mark you mention fade at all, or retain its original hue? It has been some *Whim Wham* of that *Mama* that has caused it I am certain. But I'll take her as she is. . . ."

A month later Mary was well enough to go with her mother across the Blue Ridge to visit Kinloch. "Nothing less than an entire stage or omnibus would contain them," Robert insisted. This statement was less facetious than suspected, for Edward Carter Turner, the master of Kinloch, entered tersely in his journal for July 27: "At night Mrs. Custis & Mrs. Lee (her daughter) with a squad of children, negroes, horses and dogs arrived."

Not until August was the water in the harbor low enough to permit work on the dike at the head of Bloody Island. But a land speculator named Morris claimed that the improvements would create a shoal on the Illinois side, thereby injuring property values for his projected city of Brooklyn, still on the plat, and stopped the work by an injunction. The press urged Lee to continue in defiance of the court order, but Morris and his friends, to show that they were in no mood to be crossed, rolled a cannon out to the working site. Lee reported the enjoinder to the United States district attorney, asking that it be vacated, and advised the new chief engineer, Colonel Joseph G. Totten, of the action. The injunction did not prevent the city from continuing the work, so on October 7 it was resumed under Henry Kayser's supervision, using equipment "loaned by Capt. R. E. Lee. Corps of Engrs. as Agent of the U. States, to the City of St. Louis, according to the instructions of the Chief Engineer of September 18, 1839." The work continued until the cold weather came, when Kayser reported completion of 2850 feet of the dike—the exact amount Lee had counted on finishing that season.

After completing his arrangements with the city for the use of government equipment, Lee joined Horace Bliss at the Rapids. He stayed in the town of Galena, where he met Dick Tilghman and General Brooke. Of his meeting with the General he wrote to Joe Johnston, who had also known him at Fort Monroe:

. . . We had much sport in fighting the battles of Old Point again. But it was done temperately & in a temperance manner, for

129

the Genl. has forsworn strong potations, and our refreshment consisted only of soda-water & ice-cream, delicacies that had been untasted by the Genl. for the last *nine* years, & four times a day did we pay our respects to the fountain & freezer.

Lee found Tilghman considerably changed since he had last seen him.

Dick had been up to Dubuque to let out one of his roads, and, finding some spare days on his hands, "accoutred as he was," he plunged into a pleasure-party for the Falls of St. Anthony that came along in fine spirits with music playing & colours flying. Would you like to hear of his apparel [he asked Johnston]? A little short-sleeved, short-waisted, short-skirted brown linen coat, well acquainted with the washboard, and intended for a smaller man than our friend; a faded blue calico shirt; domestic cloth pants, a pair of commodious brogans, a hat torn, broken & discolored. Now hear him laugh as he presents himself for a dance, arms akimbo, and you have him before you.

When Dick's leave was up, Robert, having nothing better to do, accompanied him back to his headquarters at Burlington. Here he met "Dick's *Red She*," a squaw with whom Tilghman had been living. Lee accepted the facts with none of the prudishness history has ascribed to him, which has given rise to the tale that even as a boy he was prone to advise his elders on their moral conduct. He gave Joe an impartial account of Dick's derelictions, including a suggestion of secret amusement: "He . . . looks thin & dispirited, and is acquainted with the cry of every child in Iowa. He is well practiced in . . . promiscuous sleeping, and is a friend to Quakers, or rather their pretty daughters."

During the summer Lee was offered a teaching post at West Point, but since he had not changed his opinion of "the *disagreements* attending the duties of an Instructor," he refused it. When a brother officer wrote him of Colonel Totten's disappointment, Robert told him: ". . . My inclinations led me to prefer some work of construction. . . . It would have been uncandid to have induced him to believe that I possessed the taste & peculiar zeal which the situation requires, nor can I see what qualifications I possess that renders me more fit for this duty than others."

By the time the winter weather suspended work at the Rapids, two thousand tons of rock had been removed—"a tolerable season's work," Lee thought. On his return from the Rapids, he was ordered to inspect improvements on the Ohio River—"studying mud and water," he termed it. From the Ohio he was to continue on down the Missouri to "hunt snags" which he insisted were "no game, but spoil sport and boats too." He went aboard the *Malta* which had "93 cabin passengers, a fair lot of Lady freight, and 20 children." On the Missouri River, the steamboat ran aground on a sand bar, in full view, as it happened, of an apple orchard laden with ripe fruit, which proved a sore temptation to old and young alike, who passed the time projecting methods and means of getting ashore to pick it.

To while away an evening, Robert started a letter to Mackay, rebuking him kindly for having been so remiss in his correspondence:

Why Man you have not written to me any time, I had almost said, these five years. And were it not for accident, so to speak, and the *A. & N. Chronicle* I should know no more of you than the man in the moon, who if all is true that is said of him must be the biggest blockhead in the Universe, and yet is as well informed on the present subject as your friend on the Missouri.

But his verbal ramblings were cut short for, as he explained: "The *gentlemen* have put out the fire with the *extract* of *tobacco*, and the ladies are putting their little pledges to bed which produces an uncomfortable commotion." Musingly, he added: "It is a little remarkable that as often as I travel *up* these rivers with the fair part of humanity I never travel *down*. I wonder if it is explained upon the same principle that Sam Weller accounts for never seeing dogs around a sausage factory. *That they are used up.*"

On his return to St. Louis he made up the annual reports and passes, and when these had been mailed, he was ready to start, on November 18, to inspect the Lower Mississippi, the Arkansas, and the Red River.

Aside from the companionship of the refined and well-educated Henry Kayser and the Beaumonts, there are few particulars of Lee's social life in St. Louis. Since neither Mackay nor Talcott had acquaintance among the officers and civilians there, there was no intimate to whom he could describe the frolics, weddings, and "grand parties" he must have attended. But from his letters to Kayser, written from home, it is evident that his circle of friends was large, for besides the favorite Beaumonts to whom he always sent love, there were similar messages to be delivered to the Kingsburys, MacGinnises, Chocteaus, Skinkers, Gratiots, Cabannés, to Alexander Kayser, Henry's brother, to Mrs. Sarah Irwin, and to a young woman identified only as "one of my sweethearts, Miss Louise D."

Robert did give a glimpse of himself when he went to call at the house of his cousin, Major John Lee, who was on court-martial duty there. He complained that too often he was placed in the uncomfortable role of a third party, as a certain Captain Clarke was "laying as close seige as the customs of civilized society will admit of" to a young lady house guest of the Major's wife: "I never go there, day or night, raining or shining, that he is not close by her rocking chair and she in it. I have had to petition that they be punished with separate rooms for it is against my principles to flush a pair in such a covey, or to be Bally ragged from the House."

After finishing his inspections of the rivers, Robert was free to start for Arlington, gleeful at what he termed his "escape from the West."

"I felt so elated when I found myself within the confines of the Ancient Dominion," he told a cousin, "that I nodded to all the old trees as I passed, chatted with the drivers and stable-boys, shook hands with the landlords, & in the fulness of my heart—don't tell Cousin Mary—wanted to kiss all the pretty girls I met." It was a hard journey, he told Kayser, but he managed to arrive in time for Christmas, though the joy was shattered this year by the tragic death of Ann Marshall's little boy.

Robert had been home only one day when he received an urgent summons to Baltimore. His nephew, about the same age as Boo, while playing outside the front door had been run over by a dray, his "head entirely *crushed* by the wheel," and his body hardly recognizable except for his clothes. The shock temporarily deprived Mrs. Marshall of her reason. By the time Robert was ready to leave Baltimore, taking with him the boy's remains to place them beside Ann Carter Lee in the ivy-covered graveyard at Ravensworth, his sister had improved, but her health was shattered by this tragedy, and like her mother she would be an invalid for the rest of her life.

It was a season beset with distress, some of which revived unpleasant memories: Bernard Moore Carter died, and his will named Robert and his brother, Carter, sole executors of his estate. Robert disqualified himself, but this did not spare him the trials of hearing the complaints of dissatisfied heirs, or of trying to satisfy them. There also arose the irksome problem of support for his half brother Henry's widow, who was still living in Paris. Whatever income she had up to this time was now cut off, and she was entirely dependent on Carter, who had been sending her money "from time to time as she wanted it, hoping his business might furnish enough to supply her wants." She would be needing regularly from nine to twelve hundred dollars a year, a sum Carter could not afford, so he turned to Robert and Smith for advice. It was found that none of them could spare any fixed amount consistently, although Robert wrote that he was willing to "cheerfully appropriate all that is not necessary for the support of my own family." Since this was so uncertain a means of support, the brothers decided it would be best for "our poor sister in Paris," as Robert called her, to return to her family, the Richard Stuarts of Cedar Grove. Although Carter prided himself on his ability to compose letters, it was Robert who had to write to both Mrs. Lee and Dr. Stuart.

It was during this winter at Arlington that Robert took his eldest son for a walk one snowy day. For a time father and son were able to stay side by side, but as they entered the grove where the snow lay deeper, the boy fell behind. When Lee turned to look back, he saw Custis imitating his every move, taking long strides to fit into his father's tracks. Lee was amused, and related the incident to friends, smiling as he said:

133

"When I saw this, I said to myself, 'it behooves me to walk very straight when this fellow is already following in my tracks!'"

This little story was taken by Lee's first biographer and embroidered with such sententious overtones as to rob his remark of its warmth and humor, and the pun.

He was assigned to Washington for temporary duty in the engineer office that winter. Most of his time was passed in correspondence with Kayser to settle the quarterly accounts, and to try to reduce expenses. He asked his friend to sell the mules and "*any thing* else that you can get a fair price for," carrying his economy so far as to give up his post-office box and cancel his newspaper subscription. These letters also contained instructions for personal business, among them the collection of a loan to a Mr. St. John, on whose note Lee had accepted four thousand dollars in St. Louis city bonds.

It was evident that Robert did not intend to forego the pleasures of the social season. In January, he sent an order to the New York haberdasher, Samuel Frost, asking him to have made: "1 dark fancy coloured dress coat; 1 pr. black dress pants; 1 black silk dress vest; also, 1 dark blue Mil: frock coat, Engr. buttons, Capt: shoulder straps, made accds to regns; 1 pr. dark blue uniform pants, blk. velvet stripes 1½ inch wide down outside seams; to button up in front. 1 black cassimere vest." To the order he appended the note: "Please let the cloth and making be of the best quality & put the cost at the lowest cash price."

The middle of June found him still in Washington, awaiting further appropriations from Congress. He was certain, he told Kayser, that no more money would be voted for internal improvements. He therefore asked his friend to tell Mrs. Beaumont that if she found their furniture in her way, she was to "just despatch it to the Auctioneer & let him dispose of it."

As Lee predicted, Congress did not approve further funds. He wrote Mackay on July 23 that since "the few works under this Dept. are for the present *dished*," he was going to have to go west and "sell off all the Pub. property belonging to the works & wind up the concern." He was not looking forward to the trip, he told his friend, for "the rivers are all low, weather hot & country sickly, & I am afraid I should have to go all the way over land." In addition, he was not feeling in his usual "best of health." During the winter, he had what was diagnosed as rheumatism, and as it was still with him, he decided on his way west to stop at the White Sulphur Springs and see if he could not find relief in the waters.

He received his orders on July 24. Before leaving he put his "Dame and the little Lees in the carriage" and started them on their way over the Blue Ridge, once again "in charge of my *eldest* Son."

Robert took the stagecoach to Staunton and through Buffalo Gap—a part of the route he would recall twenty-one years later when on his way to command the Confederate operations in western Virginia.

He reached the White Sulphur on August 3, and was pleased to find there "the beautiful Miss Bettie & Mattie" Mason, of whose "health & happiness" he wrote enthusiastically to their mother. But to Mary he said:

"I am not very well & I hope a little delay here may prevent greater detention hereafter & that thereby I may avoid more serious indisposition. I have regretted the whole way that your mother did not accompany me."

Also among the guests were some Baltimore acquaintances for whom he admitted he had "always felt a repugnance." But now that his window looked down on their cottage, and he was "compelled to witness their ridiculous pride, superciliousness & shallowness, it amounts to an annoyance."

Robert stayed at the springs for eight days before continuing his journey. He reached St. Louis in the midst of the worst of the heat and mosquitoes and rather than fix up his old quarters in the Meriwether Clarke mansion, he took a room at the New Hotel.

Each day at dinner, he was amused by the antics of a newly married couple.

He was a loafer about Natchez [Robert wrote]. She is very pretty . . . but she has not yet laid aside the manners she acquired in her belleship. Sits during dinner expanding her large eyes & pouting

135

her pretty lips & has all the appearance of one that has not found matrimony what it is cracked up to be. . . . Today while busily engaged with his grouse & champagne he was much startled by the announcement of her intention of going to Europe, but recovered himself sufficiently after one swallow to beg permission to accompany her.

This was the only bit of interest he could find to include in a letter to Bettie and Mattie Mason. He apologized for having "to inflict upon them a letter before they will give me one of their bright epistles," but

like the Indian gathering cocoanuts I shall be forced to throw sticks in the trees until the natives in self defense hurl down the fruit in return. I warned them that I would have no adventures to relate & that they must expect nothing interesting to occur to so plain a man as myself. . . . A sleepless night or two, the attacks of the Mosquitoes & their Allies, the loss of a dinner or a draught of muddy water, are the only topics I could use to excite their attention or sympathy.

His first task in St. Louis was an inspection of the dikes in order to make an official report on harbor conditions. He found that the pier from the foot of Bloody Island still confined the water to the Missouri shore and had directed the current against the head of Duncan's island with such force as to wash away

a large portion of the head and eastern face. . . . The deep water now extends close to it, and admits the largest boats to the lower part of the city. The depth of the water on the Illinois side is diminishing proportionally, and the shoal formed under the influence of the pier from the foot of Bloody Island is extending itself down the river, and assisting the operation of the pier itself. Both piers, however, require to be finished. The upper ought to be strengthened and extended down the river, and the lower completed. . . .

To Mayor John Darby, Lee expressed "his chagrin and mortification at being compelled to discontinue the work. It seemed as if it were a great personal misfortune to stop, when the work was about half finished." In this project where he had been the supervising engineer, it was disappointing for him to be unable to see it through. He had met the challenge with enthusiasm and interest. He had studied Holland's system of dikes, and obtained from Andrew Talcott some ideas in use on the Hudson. He had, in fact, expended so much mental and physical energy on the project that he was able to speak of himself during the previous season as "fast wasting away, & there is but little left now but nose & teeth." But the result of Lee's careful planning and calculation was a system which is the basis for the harbor control at St. Louis today.

After finishing his report, he had a few idle days before boarding the *Rosalie* to go upriver and dispose of the equipment at the Des Moines base, so one evening,

feeling lonesome, as the saying is, and out of sorts, I got on a horse and took a ride. On returning through the lower part of town, I saw a number of little girls all dressed up in white frocks and pantalets, their hair plaited and tied up with ribbons, running and chasing each other in all directions. I counted twenty-three nearly the same size [he described the scene to Mary]. As I drew up my horse to admire the spectacle, a man appeared at the door with the twenty-fourth in his arms. "My friend," I said, "are all these your children?" "Yes," he said, "and there are nine more in the house, and this is the youngest." Upon further inquiry, however, I found they were only *temporarily* his, and that they were invited to a party at his house. He said, however, he had been admiring them before I came up and just wished that they were all his in reality. It was the prettiest sight I have seen in the West, and perhaps in my life.

After disposing of the Rapids apparatus, Robert returned to St. Louis to find buyers for the harbor equipment; most of it was bought by the city, which planned to complete the project.

Around the end of October he was free to leave for home, reconciled in a measure by his final interview with the Mayor who assured him in "appropriate terms" of "the great obligation the authorities and citizens generally were under to him, for his skill and labor in preserving the harbor."

Within thirteen days after leaving St. Louis, he arrived at Arlington. He was given a short rest before being sent to inspect Forts Macon and Caswell in North Carolina, and Fort Moultrie in South Carolina. He left home on November 22, expecting to be gone two months. He hoped to make a short stay in Savannah, for which he went prepared. But the Engineer Department was so anxious to get his report in order to present it to Congress as the basis for their request for appropriations that he "could not in conscience take even the few days that it would have required to look in upon you," he explained to Jack Mackay, now stationed in Savannah.

By the eighth of January, he was back in Washington. When Congress voted the funds for his recommended improvements at the North Carolina forts, he commented: "God grant that they may be *applied* by some one else. I have seen enough of that Sovereign & independent Commonwealth!" But he was kept in suspense for some time, not knowing whether his next assignment would be North Carolina or Fort Hamilton, New York, for Colonel Totten was more inclined to reticence than the genial General Gratiot had been.

And while he waited, there came

another little Lee, whose approach, however long foreseen, I could have dispensed with for a year or two more. However, as she was in such haste to greet her Pa'a, I am now very glad to see her, & although she has not conformed to the order established by her predecessors, for you must know we have been very precise in arranging them in pairs of boy & girl, & came out of her turn, yet I must play the forgiving father & excuse her first offense. To add to the confusion created in the wigwam by this unprecedented breach of discipline, the aforesaid couples prepared themselves with most obdurate colds, & opened upon this newcomer with such an incessant barking, that all my care & attention were required to keep them from her captivating presence. By dint of sugar and hoarhound candy with an occasional sprinkling of Pease's, the cause of their embargo has been removed & they now by authority hunt her in full, tho' with not so annoying a cry.

The young lady in such haste to greet her Pa'a was another black-eyed brunette. She was named Eleanor Agnes but was always called Agnes, though in her early years she was known best as "Widdy" and "Wig." In her father's eyes, she promised "to be the prettiest of the flock"; his instinct proved unerring.

But the *pater familias*, who found himself converted into "a horse, dog, ladder, & target for a cannon by the little Lees" while attempting to concentrate on his correspondence, was not sufficiently deterred by the arrival of the fifth little Lee to forego his "necessary attentions," as he called them, to the pretty girls. In his estimation, these were fully as "imperative" as his attentions to his Uncle Sam.

Robert was never at a loss to discover fascinating young women, no matter where he was. As he admitted to Henry Kayser, "you are right in my interest in pretty women, & it is strange that I do not lose it with age. But I perceive no diminution." Feeling that he should temper this admission, he cautioned his friend: "Young men, however, ought not to lead them into indiscretions, & fighting duels or shooting each other can't remedy it." Even Mary was to write of him: "No one enjoyed the society of the ladies more than himself. It seemed the greatest recreation in his toilsome life."

Among those who came most often to visit at Arlington was Martha Custis Williams, or "Markie," a great-great-granddaughter of Martha Washington. She was a beautiful and talented girl, still in her teens when her role in Robert's life became an important one. She symbolized for him the eternal woman, the ideal that he had found embodied first in Margaret and Eliza Mackay, and the Beautiful Talcott. Throughout his life up to the very end, there were always such symbols, as necessary to his well-being as other nourishment.

This role of gallant and perennial lover is endowed with rich inspiration, and is never dulled by satiety or marred by disillusion. Burdened as he so often was by the tedious routine of uninspiring assignments that asked of him no imagination and little ingenuity, and gave none of the rewards of creative work; fated as he was to have a continually ailing wife and children whose symptoms he had to hear and worry over, year after year; and oppressed by a sense of having failed to make his mark in life, the beauty, youth, and bright spirits of these girls were needed stimulants.

When Markie was not at Arlington, she and Robert kept

up a regular correspondence, the importance of which has sometimes been underrated. Though none of Robert's letters to her compare to the colorful, lusty letters to Jack Mackay, Andrew Talcott, or Joe Johnston, they do point up facets of Lee's many-sided character.

Since correspondence with these three close friends was at this period irregular, a letter to Markie provided Robert the opportunity to indulge his delight in fanciful imagery: "The rest of our heroes are poised high on the wings of love, gazing on the Divinities of their worship, for though they strike like the falcon, they woo like the turtle." And to keep his perspective young: "Mr. Daniels is wrapped up in his blushes & philosophy," and "Mr. Gibson's lady love has found one more to her liking . . . & he has consoled himself with a *horse!*" Letters to Markie gratified his pleasure in small talk and harmless gossip: "The Dr. has come out in a new wig & is more captivating than ever;" and they gave him an opportunity to discuss the social activities in which he took so much interest: "Balls, fireworks & tableaux have been frequent. The Polka has been the favorite dance & Miss Matilda Church a great belle." He was also able to express the words of gallantry and love which flowed so easily. In his imagination, he told Markie: "I have followed you in your pleasures, & your duties, in the house & in the street, & accompanied you in your walks to Arlington, & in your search after flowers. Did you not feel your cheeks *pale* when I was so near you?"

Markie's letters, written in a bold and unfeminine hand, always brought him "infinite pleasure." Admittedly he thumbed through his stacks of daily mail in the hope of finding one of her "bright epistles" to break the tedium of routine and divert his thoughts. Of one such letter he told her: "I have thought upon it, slept upon it, dwelt upon it (pretty long you will say) & have not done with it yet."

Preoccupation with his "necessary attentions" to his newest favorites did not mean that the old ones were forgotten. It is apparent from his letters to Jack Mackay and his continued attempts to pry news from him concerning Eliza, that she was very much in his mind. Proving that Robert was remembered,

140

too, she sent him a watch guard of her making. "It is one of the many mementoes that reach me like Angel's visits, to say I am not forgotten," he wrote, and preferred to keep the guard wrapped in the note that accompanied it than to risk wearing it out.

Frequently when Markie came to Arlington, she brought several of her younger brothers and sisters along to romp with their Lee cousins. Orton Williams soon developed a special liking for Agnes Lee, and she became his favorite girl playmate. When weather prevented the children from being out-of-doors, they played games in what was known as the "Big Room," the unfinished drawing room in the main part of the house, where they stored discarded furniture from Mount Vernon—"three venerable presses . . . filled with old & mouldy books, a half broken table, an ancient harpsichord, & several wooden chairs," and Mr. Custis' unfinished paintings. "Many & many a time in our childish days of course," Agnes wrote when she was fourteen, "have we ridden round & round on stick horses, making stables in the niches in the arches, & behind the old pictures & making houses of vast extent with the old furniture." When they had tired of active games, they would cluster around "the nursery fender to tell fairy tales."

While the Lee children were contending with "obdurate colds" during the winter of 1840–41, the adults in the family had "the *Grippe*," very prevalent at the time. "It has attacked my head & now I am under the operation of the mustard plasters & blisters," Robert told Henry Kayser. "Tomorrow I am to have 20 leeches & the next day God knows what. Some periods of the day the pain is almost unendurable. . . . The old President is very ill with it & in great danger." Six days later, on the night of April 4, President William Henry Harrison, kin to Robert through the Carters, died, and Lee wrote that Washington was "filled with anxiety, grief & gloom."

He was relieved to learn that his next assignment would be the superintending of repairs and renovations at Forts Hamilton and Lafayette, situated on the Long Island shore of "the Narrows" in New York Harbor. He received his orders late in March, but the effects of the grippe were lingering, and he was unable to leave home until the second week in April, reaching New York in the midst of a great storm on the night of the tenth. A week later, he was ordered to include in his supervision the repairs on two batteries, Morton and Hudson, on the opposite shore of the Narrows.

There was an epidemic of measles at Fort Hamilton, so Mary delayed her departure from Arlington. Then it was found that the house they were to occupy needed repairs and cleaning. Since it was unfurnished, in mid-June just prior to her departure Mary shipped a load of furniture, mainly pieces from Arlington, though some had been specially made by Green, the well-known Alexandria cabinet-maker.

Lee's duties were multifarious. Since there was only a single clerk for the entire project, and but one foreman at each fort, Robert took over a large part of the official correspondence, the bookkeeping, and all the draughting. It was also necessary for him to visit each of the construction jobs daily, which he did by means of a small boat called the *Flash*.

It was on one of these trips that he spied a little terrier swimming about in the Narrows; she had presumedly fallen off some passing ship. The Lee children were delighted with the dog and named her "Dart." She soon established a reputation as an excellent ratcatcher to rival the cat. During their stay at Fort Hamilton, Dart had puppies, one of which the children kept and called "Spec." Lee refused to have its ears and tail cropped —as Dart's had been—considering this an unnecessary cruelty. This ingratiating little dog became an important member of the family and earned the privilege of accompanying them to church.

One Sunday it was noticed that the little Lees were far more interested in Spec than the sermon. The following Sunday, Spec was shut in the upstairs front room where from an open window he watched sadly as the family went off without him. At length, he jumped out the second-story window, and landing unhurt, raced down the road, reaching the church just as the Lees were going in. To the children's delight, the dog was permitted to sit with them, and they were careful not to give him undue attention. Ever afterward, wherever they lived, Spec was allowed to attend Sunday service.

Besides doing his own work, Lee was keeping up an exacting correspondence with Henry Kayser over the details of the settlement of the Mississippi project. When the city decided to finish the dikes under Kayser's supervision, Lee furnished advice at his friend's request, carrying on the work by proxy. That winter, a limited amount of construction was continued at the Narrows, so the Lees were unable to go to Arlington for the holidays.

Christmas morning, the children were awake at four o'clock, "discussing the contents of their stockings & could not be induced to sleep again," Mary wrote her mother. The long and exciting day was pleasantly climaxed by turkey dinner at the house of their "agreeable neighbour," Colonel Stanton and family.

Mary was unwell during most of her stay at Fort Hamilton, taking almost no part at all in the social life of the garrison. Her disinclination to join the festivities and "frolics" no longer kept Robert from participating with his usual zest; he also included the New York theater and Italian opera (where he heard "Pico & Borghese"). One thing Mary did enjoy was the opportunity to make frequent shopping expeditions to the city, causing her thrifty husband to fear that he would be "ruined" by her "bargains in remnants & worsteds."

Robert enjoyed the companionship of two younger officers at the Fort—Lieutenant John Sedgwick of Connecticut (to fall in battle at Spotsylvania while opposing Lee); and Lieutenant Henry J. Hunt of Michigan—both West Pointers. Hunt thought Lee "as fine-looking a man as one could wish to see, of perfect figure and strikingly handsome. Quiet and dignified in manner, of cheerful disposition, always pleasant and considerate, he seemed to me the perfect type of *gentleman*."

Hunt shared Robert's amusement over the controversy dividing the congregation at St. John's Episcopal Church, of which Lee was vestryman. The Tractarian movement had reached America, and Puseyism was the bone of contention. On the post, the Low Church members (of which Lee was one), strongly suspected the rector of High Church leanings.

Robert was never willing to involve himself in public controversy, and now, Hunt recalled, he always contrived in some pleasant way to avoid any expression of opinion that would commit him to either faction. One evening he came into the quarters of one of us youngsters where a number of officers and one or two neighbors had assembled. Soon the inevitable subject came up and was discussed with considerable warmth, and on the parts of two or three, with some feeling. Captain Lee was quiet, but to those who understood him, evidently amused at the efforts to draw him out.

When someone finally asked him his stand outright, instead of giving a direct reply he turned to Hunt and said in his most "grave and impressive" manner:

I am glad to see that you keep aloof from the dispute that is disturbing our little parish. That is right, and we must not get mixed up in it; we must support each other in that. But I must give you some advice about it, in order that we may understand each other: Beware of *Pussyism! Pussyism* is always bad, and may lead to unchristian feeling; therefore beware of *Pussyism!*

The apparent innocence of the statement made it all the more pointed, and the emphasis, Hunt recalled, as well as the "ludicrous turn given by the pronounciation, and its aptness to the feeling that one or two had displayed, ended the matter in general bursts of laughter, for the manner more than the words conveyed his meaning."

This now became a joke at Hunt's expense: whenever they met, Lee would look at his friend "in a grave way, shake his head, and say,

" 'Keep clear of this *Pussyism!* "

Mary and the children returned to Arlington in the spring of 1842, to enroll young Custis in Fairfax Institute, a boys' boarding school in Virginia. Robert was reluctant to part with his favorite son, but knew that the boy needed regular discipline; he regretted only that there was not a good school closer to New York. Up to this time Mary had taught the boys, a most creditable undertaking that must have often tried her patience, for by now Rooney, according to his father, had grown into "a large hearty fellow that requires a tight rein."

When Mary set out for Virginia, Mrs. Fitzhugh, who had been spending several months with them, went with her. It was

Mary's intention when she came back to Fort Hamilton to bring her mother with her. This arrangement, Robert declared, made her "the happiest of women" for, always "particularly fond" of killing two birds with one stone, "this will enable her to kill *three* with one stone!"

Shortly after Mary and her mother returned to the Fort, Robert received a letter from his cousin, Hill Carter. To Mary's disgust, Hill had neglected to include any news of his family, an oversight she blamed on Robert, accusing him of having failed in his last letter to *ask* Carter for news. In his reply Lee wrote:

> Why could you not have told us how all were at Shirley & what Cousin Mary & the little Hills were doing? My dame made many an exclamation at these omissions which I echoed back in the profoundest manner, notwithstanding which the sin of omission was visited upon poor innocent me, because "that was just my way" & "so unsatisfactory."
>
> I offered to go & make a personal examination if she would only get me a leave of absence, but that would not satisfy her. Do have some regard for my situation the next time [Robert begged].

That year Christmas was spent at Fort Hamilton, too, for the work, an extension of the repairs, kept Lee busy until after the new year. Not until February, 1843, was he free to escort the family to Arlington.

11

IN March, Robert returned alone to Fort Hamilton, describing himself after his arrival as "very forlorn" without his children. When Mary joined him at the end of April, only Rooney and Agnes were with her, for young Mary and Annie had stayed at Arlington with a governess-tutor.

That summer, they had a pleasant visit with Henry Kayser, who came to see them before sailing to Germany for his bride; and the routine of Robert's work was varied by a few weeks spent in temporary duty in Rhode Island, and by a trip to West Point where he had been asked to draw plans for a new cadet barrack. Before the summer was over, Mary took Rooney and Agnes back to Arlington to await the arrival of her sixth child.

On October 27, "a young Robert Lee . . . made his appearance at Arlington, much to the surprise & admiration of his brothers & sisters," Lee wrote a friend. As to the newcomer's beauties, he could only say:

"He has a fine long nose like his father, but no whiskers."

Robert left Fort Hamilton on December 20, taking the completed plans for the barrack with him. He had looked forward to "a little holy-day, but upon my arrival at the Dept. the Col. even before reading the report I handed him put into my hands an order which will furnish me with occupation until I shall be obliged to return to Fort H."

Totten assigned him the job of verifying the titles to lands occupied by federal fortifications and batteries.

He had only one night at home to make the acquaintance of his namesake. The next morning he left for the South and did not return until mid-January. Once home again, he went to work each day in the office until ordered back to New York on April 15. Gone were those delightful winter months passed in kicking up one's heels at two or three gay parties a night, in extended festivities at weddings, and evenings of flirtation under the guise of a single man! The new regime did not subscribe to the philosophy that the souls of its young officers were made more content and their wits sharpened by diversion.

In 1843, the old system of selecting the board of visitors for the United States Military Academy from the ranks of distinguished citizens as well as army personnel was abolished. The members were now only army officers, chosen by the President. When the board assembled to attend the examinations that began on June 10, Captain Robert E. Lee was on the roster, and his fellow Virginian, Winfield Scott, who had recently been promoted to commanding general of the armies, was its President. Other members included Captain Erasmus D. Keyes and Brevet General William J. Worth, who had been the commandant of cadets in Robert's day.

Though Keyes was a lowerclassman when Lee was attending West Point, they had known one another, and now passed much time together discussing, Keyes remembered, "the topics of the day, and all subjects relating to the Union and the dangers that threatened it." Keyes was a Massachusetts man, ardently Northern in his sentiments, which he did not hesitate to express. He was amazed to find with what "candor and fairness altogether unusual with his fellow Southerners" Lee treated his opinions. He was still further surprised when Lee nominated him for the post of Instructor of Artillery and Cavalry, left vacant by a resignation. Keyes would always remember this act: "He did not ostentatiously stoop from his high estate to elevate a suppliant and give him a conspicuous position, nor did he afterward claim to have made me." When Keyes thanked him, Lee made him feel that he owed him nothing. "Such a favor, so graciously bestowed, produced in me a sense of gratitude that nothing could change," Keyes wrote.

During Robert's daily association with General Scott, their acquaintance ripened into a warm friendship. They had often met at parties in Washington where the pompous Scott, who loved fine uniforms, large horses, and flattery, was in great demand among that city's hostesses. Though fond of hearing his own praises, he in turn bestowed praise on those he considered deserving. He had a shrewd eye for men, and Lee's character and abilities now impressed him strongly.

When Robert returned to Fort Hamilton, he found that the Talcotts had come to stay with them until their house in New Brighton was ready, and to his further delight, Markie arrived. During the beautiful autumn days, the season there that Robert liked best, Jack Mackay came, remaining with them until December.

Jack's lung congestion, which Robert had once cautioned him to "look a little to" and take better care of himself, had by this time developed into pulmonary tuberculosis. Lee always held some doubts about the wisdom of doctors and the efficacy of their medications, and told his friend now:

"If you will be sufficiently prudent this winter, you will be completely restored by spring. Avoid all medicine as much as

147

possible, adhere strictly to the diet & course of life that you find agrees with you & give yourself a *fair chance*."

"Esculapius himself could not have given you a more learned prescription or Polonius better advice to his son," he added.

After Mackay had gone, Robert wrote optimistically to Markie: "Dry toast & a rocking chair have made a man of him & he feels strong enough to get married which I suppose will be his next adventure."

The works closed early in December this year, so Christmas was spent at Arlington, though Robert was again assigned duty in the Washington office. In an apology to Jack for having failed to write him sooner, he revealed his attitude toward the irksome duties that occupied his time:

But could you see my list of correspondence upon Whigs, Democrats, Congressmen and Officers, you would [not] wonder at my horror at the sight of pen, ink, and paper, and with what perfect disgust, I pick up my hat between 4 & 5 P.M. with the firm determination of doing nothing till the next morning, except to go home, eat my dinner, play with the little Lees, & rest. At 8 next morng I am again in the saddle to go through the same routine.

He was therefore delighted to return to Fort Hamilton, even though little work was carried on because the imminence of war with Mexico over the boundary of Texas and a threat of one with England over the Oregon boundary were occupying the Department with other matters.

Troops under General Zachary Taylor were already encamped at Corpus Christi, awaiting further orders, and the Pacific and Gulf naval squadrons had been alerted to prepare for a blockade of the east coast of Mexico. At a cabinet meeting on May 9, 1846, President Polk urged the members to pursue a war policy. Only George Bancroft, Secretary of the Navy, declared that he would "feel better satisfied in his course if the Mexican forces had, or should commit any act of hostility." That very night, there was received in Washington a dispatch recounting General Taylor's skirmish (on April 25), with a large force of Mexican cavalry, which resulted in nine American casualties. This was all that was needed for Polk to act with a clear conscience. On May 11, he sent Congress his war message, and two days later that body issued a formal declaration of war.

This summer passed quickly and pleasantly for the Lees. Mary's parents brought young Mary, Annie, and the Boo with them when they came for a visit. Robert found that his oldest son had grown, though as he told a friend, he is "not yet as tall as I am, nor has he as much beard or whiskers." Rooney was the one who had grown fast, and was now "a big double fisted fellow with an appetite that does honour to his big mouth."

In September, they had a brief visit with Jack Mackay, who had stopped off in New York to consult with the army doctors. Robert and Mary called on him at his hotel room, and were shocked to find him "quite feeble poor fellow," as Robert wrote. They urged him to come back with them to Fort Hamilton, but he was not able to do so until he had returned from duty with the topographical engineers at Newport. The result of Jack's medical examination was a two-year sick leave.

Toward the end of September, Robert was appointed to a board of army engineers meeting in New York City to decide on the best means of fortifying Sandy Hook and New Bedford harbor.

Regardless of the constant demands made upon Robert's small income (reduced by seven hundred dollars in the last four years), by his rapidly increasing progeny, which that autumn promised to "equal in number the days of the week"; and his plaints at the shortage of money which kept him, he now maintained, from ever realizing his dream of settling on the land, he found himself that October "in the disagreeable situation of having some three thousand dollars that I do not know what to do with & do not like to keep profitless." He wrote to Kayser for his opinion on investing in either St. Louis city bonds or Missouri state bonds: "You know I am not looking for a speculation, but for a safe investment that will pay regularly without any trouble." Kayser suggested that he loan the sum to individuals, and though Robert admitted that the higher rate of interest would be to his advantage, he had scruples against it:

"There is nothing more unpleasant than to be running after a poor man to squeeze a little money out of him." He decided to invest the sum (it proved to be five thousand dollars), in Ohio state bonds which would yield "about 6½ per cent."

Mary had planned to leave for Arlington around the twenty-first of November, even though Robert would not be able to accompany her. During the afternoon prior to her departure, while she was at a neighbor's saying good-by, Rooney, who had been forbidden to leave the yard without permission, told never to go near the public stables without his father's consent, and warned by Lee's Irish orderly, Jim Connally, never to touch the cutting box when he did go in the stables because it was feared some accident would "befall him owing to his recklessness & thoughtlessness," broke all three rules.

After amusing himself for a while by admiring the horses in the stables, Rooney took a turn at the "patent straw cutter . . . worked with great power by a crank, & in his zeal for work cut off the ends of the fore & middle fingers of his left hand just above the nail," his father described the accident to Henry Kayser. He was taken at once to the post hospital, but the surgeon was absent and Rooney had to sit for an hour and a half, holding up his bleeding fingers; his stoicism amazed officers and orderlies.

That night, when Robert returned from a meeting with the engineer board he found Rooney sitting up waiting for him, "cheerful as usual," and making light of the accident. The extent of the injury was kept from Mary, and Lee learned of it only after she had left the room.

All that night, and every night for weeks afterward, Robert sat by Rooney's bed to see that the bandages were not disturbed while he slept. At first, there was considerable hope of saving the fingers, but after two weeks "vitality became extinct in the middle finger, & 3 weeks in the fore finger. . . . He has been watched night & day for fear of his hand being disturbed, but our care has been unavailing in saving his fingers." He confessed that he was aghast at the thought of his handsome son being "maimed for life." He expressed his sufferings in letters to Kayser and to Boo, then away at school: "I cannot describe the pain it has caused me. God grant that you & yours may be forever preserved from such & all other evils," he said to his St. Louis friend, while to his son he wrote:

"If children could know the misery, the desolating sorrow with which their acts sometimes overwhelm their parents, they could not have the heart to thus cruelly afflict them. May you never know the misery I now suffer."

Several months later, he was relieved to be able to tell Kayser that "though Rooney had lost the use of two of his fingers, he has the perfect use of his hand. They have healed up so well that the disfiguration is less than I anticipated."

This was the second time he had suffered acutely over permanent injury to one of his children. When Annie was about three, she picked up a pair of pointed scissors carelessly left within her reach, and in playing with them, blinded herself in one eye. Because of her misfortune (which seemed to shadow all the Anns in this family), she became all the more dear to her father, who treated her with a tenderness which even precluded the bestowing of a nickname: to him she would always be the diminutive—his gentle Annie.

Rooney's accident delayed Mary's departure until the first of the new year, a period of waiting she found irksome. On December 29, she wrote to her mother, complaining that she could hardly get a moment "to *think* or *read*" because of the "clamour" of the children. The journey home was trying, for little Rob was sick, but it was more agreeable than it might have been because of the "diverting" presence of a major general who escorted them.

Robert delayed answering Mary's letter that announced their safe arrival at Arlington and dwelt upon the superior company of the major general. His excuse was "a grand party at the Colonel's from which I could not absent myself." His spirits were still high when he replied, and he indulged in a bit of humor, which was something rare in his letters to Mary, joking her about the major general, and wondering how she could ever be satisfied with anyone of lesser rank.

Without his children he was again lonely, and wrote them:

151

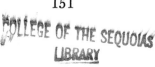

I am very solitary, and my only company is my dog & cats. But "Spec" has become so jealous now that he will hardly let me look at the cats. He seems afraid that I am going off without him, and never lets me stir without him. Lies down in the office from eight to four without moving, & turns himself before the fire as the side from it becomes cold. I catch him sometimes sitting up looking at me so intently that I am for a moment startled.

For his meetings with the board of engineers, Robert rode each day into New York, alternating between two of his horses, Tom and Jerry, that he was breaking to the saddle. New York was very snowy, he told Jack Mackay, and sleighs had replaced hacks and omnibuses for public transportation. These were crowded,

indeed there was no lack of customers at sixpence a ride, and you might be accommodated with a lady in your lap in the bargain. Think of a man of my forbidding countenance having such an offer. But I peeped under her veil before accepting & though I really could not find fault either with her appearance or age, after a little demurring preferred giving her my seat. I thought it would not sound well if repeated in the latitude of Washington, that I had ridden down B.W. [Broadway] with a strange woman in my lap.

Not long after this irrepressible admission, news reached him that the little Lees did now equal in number the days of the week. Back on schedule, it was a girl this time. She was named Mildred Childe in honor of Robert's beautiful and brilliant sister.

"I hope to come on soon to see that little baby you have got to show me. You must give her a kiss for me," he wrote Rooney.

On March 28, 1846, under orders from the United States government, General Taylor marched his troops to the Rio Grande, opposite the Mexican settlement of Matamoros. Seeing a possibility for promotion, Lee was anxious, he told Mackay, to join the army in Texas, and in May he was called to Washington for that purpose. But on the seventeenth of May, General Mariano Arista evacuated Matamoros, Taylor crossed

152

the Rio Grande and took possession, and for a time it seemed that the "war" was over.

Robert was sent back to Fort Hamilton, "to make ready this place and New [York] for the reception of the English. The late treaty however will settle all our difficulties with them & I expect will also [prevent] the appropriations that were designed, so I shall have nothing more than my ordinary business," he wrote in haste and disappointment to Henry Kayser.

He was right about the treaty, but not his prospects of settling down to "ordinary business." In July, he was ordered to turn over his post to Major Delafield, and report to Washington before going to Texas to join General John E. Wool, the vigorous little New Englander who was organizing a second army to reinforce "Old Rough and Ready," Robert's fourth cousin, Zachary Taylor.

153

⇛ III ⇚

The Halls of the Montezumas

1846 ★ 1848

III. The Halls of the Montezumas

O<small>N</small> A<small>UGUST</small> 1, 1846, Lee, about to set off for the battle fronts, made his will, an instrument that he left unchanged to the end of his life. It showed him to be worth more than anyone would have suspected from his consistent frugality and frequent allusions to lack of money. More, perhaps, than he cared to acknowledge. Recently he had written his brother, Carter:

"I was never poorer in my life & for the first time have not been able to pay my debts. . . . My expenses have been increased $300 by Custis' schooling & there seems to be no end to the calls for money."

But his investments in stocks and bonds totaled $38,750, and the value of some small tracts of land he had inherited from his mother was an additional $2,000. He still owned the slave, Nancy, who lived with her children at the White House, a Custis estate on the York River. But slaves could not be counted as assets, since Lee regarded slavery as "a moral and political evil," and stipulated that his should be "liberated so soon as it can be done to their advantage & that of others." Excluding the value of the slaves, his estate constituted at least $40,000, a considerable fortune for that day.

It was not, then, the lack of money that kept him from leaving the army and settling on the land. In addition to the income from his investments, Mary owned stocks, bonds, and land.

But there was in this the hand of destiny. Had he resigned from the army, he could have become either a successful civil engineer or a Virginia planter, unknown to the world generally. It took war and its strange conditions to stir the latent seeds of greatness, causing them to bud and flower. When the time came, he proved, like his father, "to have come out of his mother's womb a soldier"—ingenious, daring, inventive, audacious, personally brave, and gifted with a keen sense of the strategic. All these qualities were awakened by the challenge

157

of a coming battle. His sensitive nature revolted at the sights on a field after combat, and his compassion was aroused by contemplation of the distress war brought to women and children. But he found the abstract concepts of a campaign as absorbing as a well-played game of chess.

These conflicting sensations caused him to write to his wife and son of the horrors of a battlefield, to exult over the success of his batteries in breaching enemy walls, and to utter paradoxically in the midst of one bitterly fought engagement in the Civil War:

"It is well war is so terrible—we should grow too fond of it!"

Robert had little sympathy for this war with Mexico. He was too familiar with the iniquities of politics to be fooled by the bellicose utterances of the press and politicians of both nations. "It is true that we have bullied her. For that I am ashamed," he wrote. He was not alone in this view: Colonel Ethan Allen Hitchcock, as he sailed down the Rio Grande with General Scott, confided to his diary: "My feeling toward this war is no better than at first. I still feel that it was unnecessarily brought on by President Polk . . . I believe expressly aimed to get possession of California and New Mexico. . . . Now, however, as war is going on, it must . . . be carried on by us aggressively, and in this I must be an instrument."

Young Lieutenant Ulysses S. Grant was "bitterly opposed to the policy toward Mexico," regarding the war that resulted "as one of the most unjust ever waged by a stronger against a weaker nation."

Like Grant and Hitchcock, Lee was an instrument, and like them, he chose to do his part handsomely.

He made ready quickly to depart for Texas. He wrote a farewell letter to Eliza, causing her to comment bitterly to her sister Catherine: "This is a terrible business!" He paid his sister Ann a visit, and as he passed through Washington, stopped to say good-by to Mr. Schneider, the blacksmith. Then he packed his camp chest and trunk, including his traveling chess set, and a bottle of fine old whiskey, a parting gift from a lady. To this bottle there hangs a tale.

Lee's first biographer, J. W. Jones, implied, when he told the story, that Robert included the whiskey in his trunk only to keep from offending the friend. The triumphant climax to this tale was Lee's return from the war, with the bottle unopened. Since this story's publication in 1872, it has often been repeated as illustrative of Lee's total abstinence, each biographer overlooking the fact that the liquor was presented for an emergency, and not as solace for loneliness. The bottle returned untasted because the one time that Lee needed a stimulant—when he fainted from exhaustion and a minor wound—General Scott supplied him with brandy from his own flask.

Accompanied by his faithful Irishman, Jim Connally, Lee went first to Charleston, South Carolina, and from there on September 4 took passage to Savannah. He wrote to Mary from the steamer, talking once again of his desire to be fixed "permanently" in "some humble home" rather "than to be living this roaming life in the world we do. But then the desire to educate the dear children & bring them up as they may think they are entitled to, keeps me as I am, as my pay is enough for our support, & my private income can be devoted to them. I hope all is for the best."

In Savannah, he called at No. 75 Broughton Street, finding only Catherine at home, keeping house for Jack and William. He was "much tempted to lay over *one* day" in order to see the other girls, but "resisted" with that firm discipline he wielded over himself, and took the stage to Mobile where he and Jim boarded the steamer *James S. Day*, bound for New Orleans, reaching there on September 9.

Since there was considerable uncertainty about obtaining saddle horses in Texas, he and Jim looked over the New Orleans market. They found a sorrel mare, "part blooded & of fine size" which had "a tremendous walk . . . fine trot & canter" that Lee bought for himself, and called "Grace Darling." For his man Connally they selected a dark bay, "deep-chested, sturdy & strong," which Jim named for himself. On the day they were to sail for Texas, as they were walking to the steamer, Robert saw for sale another mare whose beauty he could not resist. As he told Mary:

"I had not time even to mount her, but made Jim walk her

before me once or twice, paid the man his price, & sent her aboard the boat. She is only 5 years old & seems very docile. . . . Tell the boys she is cream colour with a fair mane and tail & I have christened her *Creole!*"

Once the boat was under way, Robert's thoughts turned to his children, and he began to worry about their training and manners. From the ship's saloon he wrote Mary:

I have seen so much annoyance occasioned by bad children since my departure, that I shall be ashamed for you to take Rob any where until you can get him under better controul & better behaved. Indeed, I think several of them might be improved in that respect. You must therefore set seriously to think upon the dear little creatures & see what you can make of them.

When they landed at Port Lavaca, Texas, he and Jim saddled up and set out, leading Grace Darling, for Robert was anxious to ride Creole. He found her to have "a fine walk, delightful canter, & fast trot & never starts or stumbles," leaping all ditches and gullies without hesitation.

At the settlement of Lavaca, on the road to Gonzales, they spent one night with an amiable French couple named Monod, whose charm and hospitality Robert never forgot. Madame's quantity of privileged cats amused him, and put him in mind of the petted ones at Arlington.

After ten days of hard travel, they reached San Antonio. When Lee reported to General Wool's headquarters he was sent to help Captain William D. Fraser, also an engineer, collect tools and material with which to build bridges and improve the Eagle Pass road on the way to the Rio Grande, for the passage of troops, artillery, and wagon trains.

Before leaving San Antonio, Robert visited the ruins of the Spanish mission, finding it inhabited only "by bats & swallows," and the Alamo, in a similar state of decay, though its chapel he thought exhibited "the remains of some magnificence." He also enjoyed the swimming, for "the river is clear & rapid. . . . As I go in very early or late, am not interrupted by Senoras or Senoritas," who came there to wash clothes and to bathe. Though he admired the dark eyes and beautiful teeth of these women, they were otherwise not to his taste. "I have

160

been told there were some handsome ones but have not seen them," he wrote.

On September 28, General Wool's army, consisting of 2,829 men, 2,000 horses, and 1,112 wagons, filed through the Grand Plaza, colorful with its motley throng of "wild looking Texans," Mexicans in gay serapes, Lipan Indians in paint and feathers, and Spanish señoritas. The long march to the Rio Grande was completed by October 9, the rapidity of the passage being attributed solely to "the indefatigable exertions of those two distinguished officers, Captains Lee and Frazier."

From their encampment on the riverbank, Robert wrote to Mary on October 11: "We have met with no resistance yet. The Mexicans who were guarding the passage retired on our approach." Telling her about the preparations being made for the crossing into enemy territory, he went on: "There has been a great whetting of knives, grinding of swords, & sharpening of bayonets ever since we reached the river," for rumor had it that batteries and a brigade of lancers lay hidden in the thicket of mesquite on the Mexican shore.

The morning after this letter was written, the engineers supervised the laying of wagon-bed pontoons across the Rio Grande, while Captain John A. Washington's battery covered the enemy bank. At a bugle blast, three hundred blue-clad dragoons under Colonel William S. Harney, their carbines held high to prevent wetting, plunged into the river and swam their horses over, landing unchallenged. The troops watching anxiously from the Texas side broke into a "prolonged cheer," and the entire army then started over on the pontoons, going into camp again as soon as it reached the Mexican side.

That afternoon a message announcing the news of General Taylor's capture of Monterrey was brought to General Wool's tent by a Mexican soldier, under a flag of truce; an eight-weeks armistice had been declared, and during that time United States forces were to remain where they were. During the fighting at Monterrey, as Robert would learn later, Markie's father, Captain William George Williams, a topographical engineer, was mortally wounded.

Regardless of his orders, General Wool took up his march

161

the next morning, passing through the little adobe village of Presidio del Rio Grande and on to the settlement of Nava, where Lee and several other officers stopped at the principal houses in search of corn, eggs, chickens, and sweet potatoes. He failed to record whether the quest was fruitful, but did mention that a number of the young women with whom he talked were "quite pretty" and had "fine teeth and eyes, small feet & hands, & in their simple dress of a chemise & petticoat looked quite interesting."

The next camp was made near the Alamos River; then they moved on to San Fernando and Santa Rosa, and finally Monclova. Here, General Wool went into permanent camp to await the termination of the truce, when he planned to advance on Chihuahua.

Robert found "the delay rather irksome to me than refreshing, for I am one of those silly persons that when I have anything to do I can't rest satisfied until it has been accomplished. And it has appeared to me that we have been losing time important to us & granting a season of preparation to the Mexicans"—which was what it proved to be.

The town house of Don Sanchez was placed at General Wool's disposal, and he took his dinner there each day with some dozen of his officers. "He has kindly insisted upon my being a constant member," Robert told Mary. But aside from having his meals there, Monclova held no attraction for Lee, who found his inability to speak the language a serious handicap, though he admitted that those Mexicans he had met seemed "well-informed & gentlemanly . . . [but] their feelings are naturally not mine nor very friendly to us."

Just before the armistice ended, he did accept a dinner invitation from "Don Munchez, the nabob of Monclova. I shall see his pretty daughter, & tell Miss Mattie I will give her a kiss for her." When the truce was over, he was pleased to move on, "as I was heartily tired of our present camp."

Instead of advancing on Chihuahua as planned, General Wool was ordered to move on to Parras de la Fuente and wait there for further instructions. On November 24, the army moved out, leaving four volunteer companies to guard Monclova. After a 9-mile march, camp was made at Castagna, a cattle ranch. During the night, a norther came roaring down the valley, upsetting loaded wagons, blowing tents away, and causing the horses to stampede. It appeared to Lee that the cornfield in which his tent was pitched would be swept out into the desert.

Ten days of marching brought the army to Parras, an oasis of some eight thousand persons, nestled at the base of a high mountain. Since the garrison had already vacated the citadel, the entry was peaceful, and cordial relationships were established between the Americans and the townspeople. Parras ladies of position flocked to the camp to invite the officers to their homes. Two weeks passed uneventfully. Then, on December 17, an express from General Worth asked Wool to reinforce him, as Santa Anna was about to attack the forces at Saltillo.

The long roll sounded on the drums, the buglers blasted "Boots and Saddles," the sick were removed to the safety of the citadel, and the wagons were packed. Within two hours, the army was ready to march. Four days later, they had reached Agua Nueva, 17 miles south of Saltillo: in this time, 144 miles had been covered—a considerable record. Then it was found that the report of Santa Anna's movements was false; the engineers selected a permanent camp near nine springs of pure water, and the army settled down to await orders.

Christmas drew near, and Robert's thoughts turned to his children and home. He spent Christmas Eve writing a long letter to Boo and Rooney:

I hope the good Santa Claus will fill my Rob's stocking tonight, that Mildred's, Agnes's & Annie's may break down with good things. I do not know what he may leave for Mary but if he leaves you one half of what I wish, you will want for nothing. I have frequently thought if I had one on each side of me riding on ponies, such as I could get you, I would be comparatively happy. . . .

I have three horses, Creole is my pet; she is a golden dun, active as a deer . . . and considered the prettiest thing in the army; though young, she has so far stood the campaign as well as any horse of the division. Jim measured one leap she made at

Monclova over a gully & said it was 19 feet. I am afraid of being obliged some day to give her too hard a ride while she is so young & break her down.

Right after breakfast on Christmas morning, the long roll sounded once again in the infantry camps and "Boots and Saddles" among the cavalry, for a scout had come to headquarters with word that he had just missed capture.

Robert lay on the ground, with Creole, saddled, beside him. He kept his telescope trained on the mountain pass from which the road emerged. He could see clouds of dust swirling over the plain as horsemen raced at top speed, for the dragoons had galloped off to meet the enemy.

Out of the dust rode not Mexicans but the Arkansas cavalry, or Rackensackers, as they were known in army slang, claiming to have just routed a large body of mounted soldiers which had charged them while they were on picket. The dragoons could see what was presumably enemy cavalry still lurking in the distance. Through field glasses, however, they saw that the enemy was nothing more than a large band of mustangs.

Back in camp, as Robert told the tale, the horses were unsaddled, "the fires kindled & the cooks went to work," going on with the interrupted preparations for the Christmas feast. Three of the staff messes had united and invited General Wool, Colonel Churchill, and other high-ranking officers to join them.

By the time the egg-nog was prepared and the table ornamented with the evergreen pine [Robert continued], dinner was announced & the guests assembled. I assure you I was surprised myself at the handsome appearance of the feast under the indulgent colouring of candle light, nor did McAlpine's pine leaf ever appear brighter to the eyes present than when it wreathed a large basket of sweet oranges flanked by three bottles of the genuine anchor brand. . . . We drank many patriotic toasts, nor were our wives & sweethearts forgotten, & the evening passed off very pleasantly.

For the occasion, Lee took from his camp chest "the Revolutionary knives & forks" that had been part of General Wash-

164

ington's field equipment. One was placed at the setting of each officer. He asked Mary to be sure to tell her father that the utensils "were passed around the table with much veneration & excited universal admiration."

To this encampment letters from Arlington eventually found their way, keeping Robert in touch with the family's activities and interests. Mary had decided to buy a piano so that young Mary could take lessons.

"Tell her she must learn some handsome tunes by the time I come, & Annie & Agnes too."

He wished that he had all his daughters with him to "wrap up in my blankets each night. What a comfort they would be. . . . But I am afraid Millet would kick too much for me." When he learned that his faithful little terrier was grieving at his absence, he asked:

"Can't you cure poor Spec? Cheer him up—take him to walk with you, and tell the children to cheer him up."

With the volunteers aching for a fight, wishful thinking caused a rash of false alarms. Headquarters was not unwilling to believe these reports of enemy approaches, for it seemed reasonable that the Mexican army must not be far off. Three days after Christmas, there was another alarm that caused General Wool to move his troops to Encantada where he could receive better support, but again no enemy materialized. One evening around the first of January, headquarters received positive assurance that Santa Anna had just crossed the mountains and was then encamped 20 miles away. Lee was with General Wool when the message came and volunteered to investigate. Wool instructed him to take along a native guide, and ordered a company of cavalry to meet Lee at the outer picket line.

From a nearby rancho, Robert secured a Mexican boy to act as his guide, but in the dark he missed the picket post and his escort. Unwilling to lose time by going back to look for them, he rode on. When he and the boy came to within about 5 miles of the place where the Mexican general was supposed to be camped, they noticed wagon and mule tracks in the road. Though Lee could find nothing to indicate the presence of artillery, he felt these signs might be evidence of a reconnaissance or forage party which had by then returned to the main army. But in view of so many recent false alarms, he did not like to take the tracks as proof and decided to ride on until he met their first picket post.

After riding several more miles, he still found no pickets and concluded that he had somehow missed them and must now be well inside the enemy lines. As if in confirmation, he saw campfires flickering on the hillside. The guide became frightened and begged him to turn back, but Robert was still unwilling to accept what he saw as evidence of an enemy encampment. He told the boy to wait for him there, and rode on toward what appeared to be white tents.

Very shortly, he found himself in a small town. He rode down the main street, which led to a stream, and stopped on the bank. He could hear the sounds of talk and laughter incident to a large camp. Peering closely into the darkness, he saw that the white objects were sheep, and then he knew that the sounds did not come from soldiers but from the drovers and teamsters sitting around the fires. He then crossed the stream and found that there was also a herd of cattle and mules being driven to market, which accounted for the tracks in the road.

In his halting Spanish he talked with the men, learning that Santa Anna had not yet crossed the mountains. Satisfied that they had spoken the truth, he thanked them and galloped back to his guide, and then on to headquarters, where a considerable uneasiness had arisen for his safety.

"But," Robert laughed when he told the story afterward, "the most delighted man to see me was the old Mexican, the father of my guide, with whom I had last been seen by any of our people, and whom General Wool had arrested and proposed to hang if I were not forthcoming."

Although it had been a 40-mile ride, after a three-hour rest, Lee volunteered to lead a body of cavalry beyond the point where he had met the drovers, in an attempt to discover some clues to the enemy's position.

Several days later came still another report of Santa Anna's approach, causing General Wool to withdraw to Buena Vista.

But Robert was not destined, at the beck and call of false rumor, to spend his time laying out new campsites every day on the miserable wastes. Around January 11, he was ordered to proceed to Brazos Santiago, an island about 35 miles northeast of the mouth of the Rio Grande, to join the commander of the invading army, General Winfield Scott, who was then preparing to attack Vera Cruz.

Accompanied by Jim Connally and a small escort, Lee rode Creole the entire 250 miles, stopping briefly in Monterrey, where Robert visited the grave of Markie's father. There he found or was given Captain Williams' belt, which he forwarded to Markie later.

Lee was attached to Scott's headquarters as a member of his general staff, which included Colonel Totten, Colonel Hitchcock, and Major John Lind Smith, with whom Robert had recently served on the board of engineers. To his delight, he found Joe Johnston among the topographical engineers. They shared a cabin on the General's ship, the steamer *Massachusetts*, when she sailed on February 15 for Lobos Islands, designated by Scott as the general rendezvous for his troop and supply ships. Lee had left Creole and Grace Darling (he had sold Jim) to come on in the ship expressly fitted up for horses, but afraid that his mares would not receive proper care, he asked Jim Connally to go with them. He always had concern for the welfare of his animals, and this time, to keep Creole and Grace from falling with the roll of the ship, he had special slings made to pass under their bodies. "I took every precaution for their comfort," he assured his boys, after minutely describing the slings, "provided them with bran, oats, &c."

On the way to Lobos, the *Massachusetts* stopped for a day at Tampico, where Scott and his general staff, resplendent in full uniform, "glittering in their gold-seamed pantaloons and embroidered coats," landed amid much fanfare which tickled the General's vanity. The troops that had come here to join Scott were drawn up on the banks of the Rio Panuco, and fired a salute as the party passed; at the landing the artillery waited as an escort. Although a handsome gray charger "richly caparisoned" was there for Scott to ride, he ordered a dragoon to lead it, since he preferred to walk imposingly in the midst of his escort, while the Governor's Island band played "Hail Columbia," "Yankee Doodle," and "Washington's March."

The General went into conference with his commanders when he reached his temporary headquarters, so Robert and John Lind Smith toured the city. "Poor Joe" Johnston was so weak that morning from his bout with seasickness he could not get up from his bunk.

To ride about the city's fortifications, Lee hired a little pony which paced nicely, he wrote his sons, although it would jump and try to run away every time Robert's sword struck its flanks. He and Smith walked along the beautiful river front, stopping often to watch the boys playing about the boats and swimming their ponies, sights which made Robert yearn for his own children.

After the monotony of army and shipboard rations, it was a temptation to sample the native foods. The oranges and sweet potatoes pleased him most, he told Boo and Rooney, but Major Smith found the thick, frothy chocolate so delicious he could "hardly be got away from it."

On Sunday morning, February 21, the sloop-of-war *St. Mary*, which had already reached Lobos Islands, opened her "bull dogs" in honor of the *Massachusetts'* arrival. The sea was so heavy it was impossible to land, and "my poor Joe is so sick all the time I can do nothing with him," Robert told his sons in a letter he could "scarcely write," the ship was rolling so badly.

Close to noon on March 5, the old walled city of Vera Cruz with its distinguishing landmark, the Moorish castle of San Juan de Ulloa, was sighted, and the American ships dropped anchor at Anton Lizardo. That afternoon, General Scott and his staff, Lee among them, with Generals Pillow, Worth, and Patterson, accompanied Commodore Conner on the steamer *Champion*, to reconnoiter the coast for the most practical landing place.

As they turned a point of the long reef on which the castle stands, Colonel Totten, looking through his glass, called out that the castle was "manning their batteries." He handed the glass to Major Smith, who said:

"They are using their sponges; we shall have a shot presently."

A minute later, they saw a small white puff, and a shell came screaming in their direction. It fell short, as did the second shot; but a third burst just above them, scattering pieces uncomfortably close. The fourth shell passed directly over, falling into the water just a hundred yards beyond.

A staff officer wrote in his journal that night: "We were in a ridiculous position. Commodore Conner had stopped the boat and we were in danger . . . without means of defense, and with all our officers of rank aboard. If a chance shot had struck our engine, we should have cut a pretty figure!" Regardless of their "ridiculous position" they selected the little island of Sacrificios, a few miles south of the city, as the most suitable anchorage.

It was a thrilling moment for the Americans when, a little before sunset on March 9, sixty-seven surf boats and several cutters, each carrying from seventy to eighty men with their arms, shoved off from the ships anchored at Sacrificios, and moved in a semicircle toward the shore.

The sea was unruffled and glistening; the sun flashed on the bright muskets and bayonets, and the mist that had all day surrounded the snow-capped peak of Orizaba drifted away, revealing the mountain's rugged outline. The American bands played "The Star Spangled Banner" and "Hail Columbia," and the men left behind on the ships cheered.

The first boat to scrape the shingle was the cutter carrying General Worth, recently distinguished at Monterrey. He leaped over the side into the shallow water—the first man to wade ashore. His First Division of Regulars formed into battle line, charged the sand hills, topped them, and planted the American flag in the dunes. On the other side was an empty landscape—not an enemy in sight.

When the men aboard ship realized that the landing had been unchallenged, there arose "a shout, such as only seamen can give, joined in and prolonged by such portions of the army as had not yet landed."

Now began a busy time for Lee. He was included in what General Scott called his "Little Cabinet." During a "death-bed discussion," as Scott termed it, they decided that it was less costly in lives to lay siege to Vera Cruz than to take it by storming parties. With this point settled, the engineers began to open trenches and place batteries, work that was impeded by the impenetrable thickets of thorny mimosa and small cacti which had to be cleared, by a norther which hit the coast and whipped the sand into stifling clouds, and by the plague of fleas. "If one were to stand ten minutes in the sand, fleas would fall upon him in hundreds," one man recalled.

The edginess that prompted men to interpret every cloud of dust as an approaching enemy horde, and to see lines of Mexican cavalry in distant bands of mustangs, was not limited to the volunteers in General Wool's army—it was present at Vera Cruz, too. On March 19, Lee and Lieutenant P. G. T. Beauregard were going back to camp along a trail through the bushes. As Lee turned a corner, he came suddenly upon an American soldier on guard, who challenged:

"Who goes there?"

"Friends!" cried Lee.

"Officers!" shouted Beauregard at the same time.

But without waiting to hear the response, the picket leveled his pistol at Lee and fired. The ball passed between his left arm and his body, so close that the flame singed the coat.

When the story of the near-tragedy was reported to headquarters, General Scott was furious at such carelessness and refused to listen to Lee's intercession in the man's behalf.

After the batteries were finished, Scott decided that he needed more heavy guns to use against the city walls, and borrowed six cannon from the warships. Lee was ordered to place and construct the battery for these pieces, and to have it ready to open fire on the morning of March 24.

The guns were landed on the twenty-third, and in order to finish the earthworks in time, Robert had to impress the sailors who came ashore to help man them. But here he met stubborn resistance from the seamen, who argued that they had not "enlisted to dig dirt." Their captain protested to Lee that it was an "outrage" to set his boys to this kind of work.

"They don't want dirt to hide behind. They only want to get

170

at the enemy, and after you've finished your banks . . . we will get up on top where we can have a fair fight."

Lee then showed his orders from Colonel Totten, and pushed the work in spite of the grumbling.

The naval battery was ready right on time. Among the officers who came ashore with the guns was Smith Lee, attached to Commodore Perry's flagship, the *Mississippi*. Robert was present to direct the fire, and no matter which way he turned, he said afterward, his eye always reverted to "Rose."

"I stood by his gun whenever I was not wanted elsewhere. Oh! I felt awfully, and am at loss what I should have done had he been cut down before me. I thank God he was saved. He preserved his usual cheerfulness, and I could see his white teeth through all the smoke and din of the fire."

He had placed three 32-pound and three 68-pound guns in this battery, he explained: "Their fire was terrific and the shells thrown . . . were constant & regular discharges, so beautiful in their flight & so destructive in their fall. It was awful! My heart bled for the inhabitants. The soldiers I did not care so much for, but it was terrible to think of the women & children."

Other sensitive men were sharing these feelings. Hitchcock wrote in his diary: "I shall never forget the horrible fire of our mortars . . . going with dreadful certainty and bursting with sepulchral tones often in the center of private dwellings—it was awful."

Among the relief for the naval battery was Raphael Semmes, Commodore Perry's flag lieutenant. As he puffed his after-dinner cigar, he watched Lee and the other engineers repairing the defenses, like so many specters moving about in the starlight. Unable to sleep, he sat and watched the shells give the "doomed city no respite," and shuddered, too, as he heard "the scream of female voices as one of those engines of destruction" exploded in some home. Lee's battery kept up its unremitting fire until the morning of March 26, having by then thrown one thousand paixhan shells, and eight hundred round shot.

The Mexican batteries were silenced, and the white flag

was carried to General Scott's tent in Camp Washington. The sailors, naval officers, and engineers emerged from the shelter of the sandbags, and collecting in groups on top of the parapets, viewed the damage through their telescopes (Robert had to borrow one as his was lost).

At this time, the old navy captain who had objected to the use of earthworks sought Lee out.

"I suppose the dirt did save some of my boys from being killed or wounded," he conceded. He paused a moment, then stepping closer, lowered his voice and said confidentially:

"But the fact is, Captain, I don't like this land fighting anyway. *It ain't clean!*"

Robert was amused, and told the story with relish to friends after his return home.

During the quiet that followed on the morning of the twenty-seventh, Robert wrote a note to his brother whom he had failed to see again before Smith returned to his ship. He wanted to assure "dear Rose" how thankful he was that he had been spared. Further, he had several favors to ask. He was evidently intending to do some entertaining to celebrate the surrender, for he requested Smith to buy "a box or two of claret, one of brandy & four coloured shirts" from a French bark anchored with the fleet. To keep him from being overcharged, Lee stated that the price of the shirts was "seventy-five cents (I have two of them), and the brandy, thirty-seven and a half cents per bottle"—he had obviously bought brandy before, too. Would Smith also buy him a good telescope from the fleet, as he was "woefully at a loss" without his.

Though religious freedom was guaranteed in the terms of the capitulation, the Mexicans were reluctant to reopen their churches. In order to prove that the Americans intended to keep their word, General Scott asked the bishop for the use of two churches in which his chaplains might hold services. Reassured, the Mexicans then opened all the churches and on Sunday, April 4, Scott decided to set the example by attending mass.

There were no pews in the little church he selected, but a long bench was placed against one wall for the use of Scott and his general staff. Before the service began, Lee, sitting beside the General, noticed Lieutenant Henry Hunt in his "dilapidated, old campaign dress" standing near the door. Robert motioned to his friend to come and sit next to him.

When the ceremony was about to begin, an acolyte passed lighted candles to each American officer, and when the clergy filed in, Scott and his staff were asked to take part in the procession.

Lieutenant Hunt recalled that Lee walked with becoming dignity and assurance, "as if the carrying of lighted candles in religious processions was an ordinary thing with him." The elaborate ceremony reminded the younger man of the squabble over "High Church" at Fort Hamilton. Gently he touched Lee's elbow and was rewarded with a "rebuking" look, but when he repeated the touch, Lee inclined his head slightly and whispered,

"What is it?"

"Captain Lee," Hunt faltered.

"Well?"

"I really hope there is no *Pussyism* in all this!" Though Lee did not reply, his eyes twinkled, and the corners of his mouth twitched in his effort to preserve his gravity.

2

ON April 10, Robert went aboard the *Mississippi* to visit Smith. "I had scarcely been able to see him before, & wished ere commencing work to have one night with him. He was very well, but what a place is a ship to enjoy the company of one's brother!"

On April 12, Lee left Vera Cruz with General Scott and his staff. They rode along the National Road that led to Jalapa, the capital of the state of Vera Cruz. The country was rugged and barren. A shortage of wagons had compelled every man to carry his own equipment, and Robert noticed that the roadsides were littered with haversacks, shirts, jackets, cooking utensils, and other surplus articles discarded by the advance troops.

When they neared the Plan del Rio, a few forest trees appeared, and the serrated profiles of the distant mountains announced the approach to the fabled Highlands. Directly ahead lay the high passes strongly fortified by Santa Anna. The right of his line, Robert explained to Mary, rested on terrain "unscalable by man or beast, and their left on impassable ravines" which the Mexican general had left unfortified in the sanguine belief that not even a goat could pass over it. "The main road was defended by field works containing thirty-five cannon," Lee continued. "In the rear was the mountain of Cerro Gordo, surrounded by intrenchments in which were cannon, & crowned by a tower overlooking all—it was around this it was intended to lead our troops. I reconnoitred the ground in the direction of the ravines on their left, and passed around the enemy's rear."

It was while scouting this area with a guide, John Fitzwalter (or Fitzwater), so daring he was known to the Mexicans as "Juan Diablo," that Lee met an uncomfortable adventure. He had noticed a well-beaten trail, and following it, came to a spring where in the moist earth he saw fresh impressions of boots. While they were examining the ground, they suddenly heard approaching voices. Lee stepped back quickly and dropped flat behind a fallen tree beside the spring, while Fitzwalter retreated into a low thicket. Shortly, a group of Mexican soldiers came up to the spring to drink and fill their jugs and canteens. They were in no hurry to leave. They joked and chatted, and several of them sat down on the fallen tree—their backs no more than three feet from Lee. Then more soldiers came, and though some drifted back to camp, still others took their places so that at no time during the afternoon was the spring deserted.

For Lee, hardly daring to breathe, not knowing when some keen eye might suddenly notice his colored shirt, the minutes dragged like hours. Once a shadow fell across him as a Mexican jumped over the log. He missed Robert by inches, but failed to observe him. Even when the shadows began to lengthen, a few soldiers still lingered.

It was almost dark before the last trooper seemed to have gone, although Robert still did not dare move for fear there might be one more. When the absolute quiet reassured him, he eased himself stiffly from his hiding place and made his way back to headquarters, finding that Fitzwalter had been able to escape earlier.

The next day, Lee pushed his reconnaissance further, and that night at a conference held in General Scott's "hut of brush" he reported that although the enemy was strong on the main road, he felt he could be turned with highly favorable results. Immediate preparations for battle were begun, and Robert, as he wrote home, passed the night

in constructing the battery, getting up the guns, ammunition, &c. . . . Soon after sunrise our batteries opened, and I started with a column to turn their left, and to get on the Jalapa road. Notwithstanding their efforts to prevent this, we were perfectly successful, & the working parties following in our footsteps cut out the road for the artillery. In the mean time our storming party had reached Cerro Gordo, and, seeing their whole left turned & the position of our soldiers on the Jalapa road, they broke & fled. Those in the road laid down their arms. . . . All their cannon, arms, ammunition, and most of their men fell into our hands. The papers cannot tell you what a horrible sight a field of battle is.

In this terse account, he was modestly silent about the importance of his part in these movements and his responsibility for their success.

On the afternoon of April 17, he had led General Twiggs' division over the tortuous terrain, during which time Twiggs "consulted him with confidence and adopted his suggestions with assurance." After dark, he had located the battery on the crest of Atalaya and superintended the placement of three heavy guns. Then, with but a few hours' rest, he had set out at sunrise to lead Colonel Bennett Riley and his Second Brigade, in charge of turning the enemy's left. This advance had been through a continual heavy fire, "when the musket balls and grape were whistling over my head in a perfect shower." The imminence of sudden death had brought his children to mind: "I thought of you, my dear Custis," he wrote his son afterward, "and wondered . . . where I could put you, if with me, to be safe. I was truly thankful you were at school."

While Riley's troops were reforming for the charge on the

battery on the Jalapa road, Lee went among the wounded Mexicans and had them carried to a house beside the road where they could be attended by their own surgeons. While on this errand of mercy, his attention was attracted by the grief of a small girl, "her large black eyes streaming with tears, her hands crossed over her breast." He asked her the cause of her distress and learned that her brother, a young drummer or bugler, lay with a badly shattered arm under a mortally wounded soldier. Lee had the dying man removed, and the boy carried into the field hospital. The girl's gratitude touched him deeply: "Her plaintive tone of *'Mille gracias, Signor'* . . . still lingers in my ear," he wrote a week later. After seeing to the care of the enemy's wounded, he broke a way through the chaparral, and mounting Creole, joined the pursuit, finding his mare so "fierce . . . I could hardly hold her."

In General Scott's official report of Cerro Gordo, he wrote:

I am compelled to make special mention of the services of Captain R. E. Lee, Engineer. This officer, greatly distinguished at the siege of Vera Cruz, was again indefatigable, during these operations, in reconnaissances as daring as laborious, and of the utmost value. Nor was he less conspicuous in planting batteries, and in conducting columns to their stations under the heavy fire of the enemy.

Since Colonel Totten was still in Washington, where he had taken Scott's victory report, and Major John Lind Smith was in poor health, Lee became in practice the senior engineer. Scott's good opinion of him was raised even higher by observing him in action; he called upon him constantly for advice, and relied heavily on his suggestions.

General David E. Twiggs, "that grand-looking old man, six feet two inches in stature, with long flowing white hair, and a beard . . . like Aaron's," wrote in his report:

Although whatever I may say may add little to the good reputation of Captain Lee of the Engineer Corps, yet I must indulge in the pleasure of speaking of the invaluable services he rendered me from the time I left the main road until he conducted Riley's brigade to its position in the rear of the enemy's strong works on

Jalapa road. . . . His gallantry and good conduct . . . deserve the highest praise.

And Colonel Riley had this to say: "Although not appropriate within the range of this report, yet, coming under my immediate observation, I cannot refrain from bearing testimony to the intrepid coolness and gallantry exhibited by Captain Lee of the Engineers, when conducting the advance of my brigade under the heavy fire of the enemy."

No other officer was singled out for so much praise in this one action. For his "gallant and meritorious conduct" in the battle of Cerro Gordo, Lee was brevetted a major, to date from April 18, 1847, though he did not learn of it until many months later.

The victorious army now moved on to Jalapa, some 18 miles beyond Cerro Gordo. It was a steady climb through barren countryside until they reached the elevation of 4,000 feet, where as if by magic the slopes were covered with luxuriant green growth. Fields of corn and clumps of banana trees appeared, and neat white houses set in flower gardens. Streams of clear water meandered through the fertile valley, and tropical shrubs and small trees bloomed along the roadside.

When Robert reached the city, he wrote to Mary:

Jalapa is the most beautiful scenery I have seen in Mexico. . . . I wish it was in the United States and that I was located with you & the children around me in one of its rich, bright valleys. I can conceive of nothing more beautiful in the way of landscape or mountain scenery . . . whenever we looked back the rich fertile valley below was glittering in the morning sun and the light morning clouds flitting around us; reaching the top, the valley appeared at intervals between the clouds which were below us, and high over all towered Orizaba, with its silver cap of snow.

At Jalapa Robert found Joe Johnston recovering from wounds received while on reconnaissance with the advance troops at Plan del Rio. Joe, who possessed a predilection for accidents in peacetime and wounds in war, had been shot in the arm and groin. Both bullets had been removed by the time Robert saw him, and he was resting easily. He was being

177

nursed by his nephew, Preston Johnston, a gunner, whom Joe, being childless, cherished as a son.

Soon after his arrival, Robert was ordered to join General Worth at Perote, a fortified castle 10 miles distant, and assist with the inventory of property left by the decamping Mexican troops. Lee was amused to find among the cannon a piece inscribed "The Terror of the Americans." The size of the castle amazed him. It covered 25 acres, and although there were "within its walls nearly three thousand troops, it is not yet full," he wrote. When he had first looked up at the turrets he was surprised to see that the American flag floating there had a green union, explained by the fact that it had been made from a Mexican flag, which contains no blue.

On April 26, the First Brigade under Worth moved out of Perote and took the road to Puebla, "the City of Angels," where Santa Anna had now massed his forces. Lee, with Lieutenants Tower and Mason of the engineers, rode with the advance.

But the entry into Puebla was peaceful, for at the news of the American approach, Santa Anna had retired to Mexico City. The men began a three-month wait—"protracted and irksome," General Scott declared it—for the arrival of additional supplies, mules, wagons, money, and most important, men, for at Jalapa all volunteers whose one-year enlistments were expiring, had been released.

The Polk administration had placed General Scott in command of the invading armies, but reluctantly, because his politics differed from theirs. Throughout the whole war, therefore, the War Department did everything at all times to hamper him, failing to send promised reinforcements and withholding money, ammunition, supplies, and transportation. Now it proposed the greatest indignity of all—to supersede him with Senator Thomas Hart Benton, whom Lee had once characterized as "the great expunger." At this crowning insult, Scott sent in his resignation: "Considering the many cruel disappointments and mortifications that I have been made to feel I beg to be recalled." But wisdom triumphed over party conniv-

178

Robert E. Lee When Superintendent of West Point

This portrait was painted by Ernest L. Ipsen in 1931, after careful study of contemporary descriptions of Lee. It now hangs in the United States Military Academy.

Ann Carter Lee, the Mother of Robert E. Lee

This painting was questioned for years chiefly because the eyes
were blue, and Mrs. Lee had brown eyes. Cleaning revealed
that blue had been painted over the original brown; it also
brought to light the inscription on the miniature, "George
Washington to his dear Ann."

General Henry ("Light-Horse Harry") Lee,
the Father of Robert E. Lee

This painting is attributed to William E. West, after an earlier portrait by Gilbert Stuart. In the collection of Mrs. George Bolling Lee.

Mary Custis Lee, Wife of Robert E. Lee

In March, 1838, after she had seen the William E. West portrait of her husband, she consented to sit for West. Earlier, she had confided to her mother that she would prefer to have Thomas Sully paint her portrait.

COURTESY WASHINGTON AND LEE UNIVERSITY

Robert E. Lee at Thirty-One

By this time Lee was known as "the handsomest man in the
Army." This portrait is by the distinguished American artist,
William E. West. On March 24, 1838, Mrs. R. E. Lee wrote to
her mother: "Robert has taken one sitting which I am going
down to see today." She characterized the finished picture as
"a very fine likeness & a fine painting."

Mary Lee Fitzhugh Custis,
Mother-in-Law of Robert E. Lee

At sixteen, she became the bride of G. W. P. Custis. Robert E.
Lee looked upon her as a second mother. She had a fine intellect and excellent literary taste. This Cephas Thompson portrait is in the collection of Mrs. George Bolling Lee.

George Washington Parke Custis,
Father-in-Law of Robert E. Lee

This grandson of Martha Washington and adopted son of George Washington was a man of letters and a painter. The portrait by C. B. Fevret de St. Memin is in the collection of Mrs. George Bolling Lee.

Stratford Hall, Va., Birthplace of Robert E. Lee

In the southeast chamber where Richard Henry Lee and Francis Lightfoot Lee—both signers of the Declaration of Independence—were born, Robert Edward Lee came into the world on a cold January day in 1807. He lived here only until he was four.

Arlington, the Custis Home

Robert E. Lee visited here often as a child. He was married to his cousin Mary Anne Randolph Custis in the north parlor in 1831. Six of their seven children were born here.

Robert Edward Lee, Jr.
("Rob")

Lee's youngest son, who left the University of Virginia to go into the Army of Northern Virginia as a private in the artillery. He rose by his own merits to the rank of captain. His father strongly opposed nepotism and refused to have his sons on his staff, as other officers did; he wanted them to be promoted on their own ability.

COURTESY
MRS. WILLIAM HUNTER DE BUTTS

Mary Custis Lee
("Daughter")

Lee's second child and eldest daughter.

COURTESY THE CONFEDERATE
MUSEUM, RICHMOND, VA.

Mildred Childe Lee

This vivacious youngest daughter was named for her father's favorite sister. His pet name for her was "Precious Life."

COURTESY THE CONFEDERATE
MUSEUM, RICHMOND, VA.

Robert E. Lee When Superintendent of West Point

His friend, Robert W. Weir, Professor of Drawing at the
Academy, persuaded Lee to sit for a portrait. It was painted
at night, since this was the only time Lee was free. This painting is in the collection of Mrs. William Hunter deButts.

Catharine Mildred Lee

Robert E. Lee's talented younger sister, to whom he was deeply attached. She was an accomplished musician and a student of literature. She lived most of her life in Paris. This nineteenth-century painting of the French School is in the collection of Mrs. George Bolling Lee.

Anna Maria Goldsborough Fitzhugh
(Mrs. William Henry Fitzhugh)

To this beautiful woman, described by a contemporary as "one of the finest looking women I ever saw, fit to grace a throne, with charming manners and conversation," Robert E. Lee turned often for advice and comfort. The Thomas Sully portrait is in Mrs. George Bolling Lee's collection.

William Henry Fitzhugh

This handsome young man gave aid and counsel to Ann Carter
Lee and her children all his life. His sister became Robert E.
Lee's mother-in-law. The Thomas Sully portrait is in the collec-
tion of Mrs. George Bolling Lee.

The United States Military Academy,
West Point, N. Y.

This view was drawn by George Catlin, the famed painter of American Indian life, around 1825, the year Robert E. Lee entered the Academy.

Robert E. Lee Just Before the Mexican War

This picture was taken from a daguerreotype made when he was about thirty-nine. He is wearing the uniform of a Captain of Engineers.

Harriett Randolph Hackley Talcott

Robert E. Lee greatly admired this lovely woman, who was the wife of his superior officer at Fort Monroe. He spoke of her always as "The Beautiful Talcott," and addressed her often as "My Hardy." This Thomas Sully portrait is in the collection of George R. Talcott.

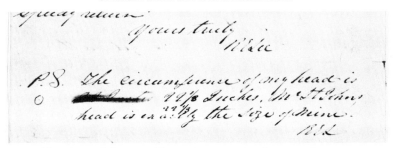

Portion of Letter From Lee to Andrew Talcott, 23 May, 1834

The postscript corrects the error that Lee's head was a "massive" 23½ inches. It reads:

"P.S. The circumference of my head is
22⅛ Inches, Mr St Johns
22⅓
head is exactly   the size of mine.
REL"

Early View of Savannah, Georgia

Much as it must have looked when Robert E. Lee went there
on his first engineering assignment in November, 1829. This
tempera painting by Firmin Cerveau is in the collection of the
Georgia Historical Society, Savannah.

COURTESY GEORGIA HISTORICAL SOCIETY

Death Mask of Napoleon

Drawn by Lee during leisure hours a
Cockspur Island, Ga., where he was sta
tioned, and given to Eliza Mackay.

COURTESY CHARLES F. MILLS

Another Sketch Made While
Stationed at Cockspur Island

Lee gave identical drawings of the terrapin and alligator to Eliza Mackay and
Sarah Anna Minis, whose family were
neighbors of the Mackays.

COURTESY GEORGIA HISTORICAL SOCIETY

ing, and the Benton scheme was dropped. The War Depart-
men, however, did not hurry with Scott's requisitions.

On the first of August, Robert rode out with General Scott,
Colonel Hitchcock, and an escort of dragoons, to the ancient
Aztec city of Cholula. "Our gay cavalcade . . . glittering in
their red, and blue, and gold presented a pleasing and ani-
mated picture." On the summit of a natural mound, the Aztecs
had built a pyramid 200 feet in height, and on the apex they
had constructed a large temple. Scott and his party rode to
the top of the mound, and "hitched our horses beneath the fine
old forest trees" that grew there. They visited the Spanish
church built in 1666 on the temple site, and from the terrace
viewed Cholula's extensive ruins. The evidence of the city's
former size and grandeur prompted General Scott to remark:

"Gentlemen, we are looking at what was long, in point of
civilization and art, the Etruria of this continent!"

In Puebla, across from General Scott's headquarters in the
Palace, was the cathedral. It contained thirty altars, richly
carved and decorated with frescoes, each a complete church in
itself. On the Feast of Corpus Christi, the General and his staff
attended high mass there. "A full choir, consisting of something like a hundred voices, and a variety of musical instru-
ments electrified us by the most splendid of church music," one
of his officers wrote that day in his journal.

But the stay in Puebla soon began to pall for the men and
officers who had counted on holding their Fourth of July cele-
brations in the "Halls of the Montezumas." On August 6,
General Franklin Pierce arrived with twenty-five hundred
men, including a detachment of three hundred marines under
Colonel Watson. This brought Scott's forces up to about thirteen thousand men, and though other troops would probably be
coming shortly, he decided not to wait any longer but to push
his army forward by divisions, with twenty-four-hour intervals
between them, on the way to the capital.

With this order, Puebla was at once in a ferment: couriers
and orderlies dashed about in all directions, and the sounds of
preparation were present in every camp. General Twiggs was

given the honor of the first move, and just before sunrise on August 7 he drew up his veterans in the Grand Plaza. But instead of addressing them as more windy generals would have been tempted to do, he simply removed his hat, waved it above his white locks, and cried:

"Now my lads, give them a Cerro Gordo shout!"

There arose a simultaneous huzza that rattled the Palace windows, "and before its echoes had died away, the division, with its bands playing and banners flying, was in motion."

The next day, General Scott and his staff rode out of Puebla. By the eleventh, they had reached Ayotla, on the shores of Lake Chalco, where Robert noted Indian women, entirely oblivious of the warlike preparations around them, paddling to market in their tiny canoes laden with fruit, and chrysanthemums of many colors.

General Scott now found his advance checked by the enemy's outer line of fortifications. El Peñon, an isolated, steep hill, inaccessible on one side and bristling with cannon and breastworks on the other, commanded the direct road to the capital, while Mexicalcingo, a fort to the left of El Peñon, guarded the San Augustin road. Lee's first reconnaissance indicated that there was no passing between the two causeways because of boggy ground, and that the only course lay in seizing the two forts by a front attack. However, two officers from General Worth's headquarters, out scouting, discovered an abandoned road near Lake Chalco. Though rough, it was practical for the passage of artillery and wagons, and was so little known that Santa Anna had taken no precautions to fortify it. When this report was forwarded to Scott, he abandoned his plans for an attack and started his army along the old road.

When the troops reached San Augustin, scouting on the part of the engineers disclosed that the enemy's right rested on the fortified village of San Antonio and his left extended through marshy ground, partially inundated, while between the two roads lay an extensive field of lava or pedregal, forming an apparently impassable barrier against the approach of artillery or cavalry. His second fortification had been placed in the town of Churubusco, 2¼ miles from San Antonio. To the left of San Augustin was a road that passed through the villages of Contreras and San Angel, on its way to Mexico City, but near Contreras the enemy had established an intrenched camp on an eminence, the Padierna, thus obstructing this passage.

When General Scott arrived in San Augustin, he sent out separate reconnoitering parties under Lee and Mason, each with an escort of dragoons. Lee was ordered to see whether there might be some way of crossing the pedregal to the San Angel causeway, and Mason was to discover whether the Acapulco road via San Antonio was as well fortified as reported. Both parties encountered the enemy. One American was killed in Mason's party, but Captain Philip Kearney, who covered Lee's reconnaissance, lost only a single horse during a "handsome little skirmish" with Mexican troops.

That night at a meeting held in Scott's headquarters to consult upon the *modus operandi*, Lee and Mason each presented a plan. Mason proposed carrying San Antonio with the bayonet by means of a flank movement, but it was Lee's opinion that there would be fewer casualties if they passed through the pedregal and up the San Angel road, for he believed it was possible to make a crossing of the lava field. Raphael Semmes was present at this council, and commented later on the importance of Lee's contributions:

"The services of Captain Lee were invaluable to his chief. Endowed with a mind that has no superior in his corps, and possessing great energy of character, he examined, counseled, and advised with a judgment, tact, and discretion worthy of all praise. His talent for topography was peculiar, and he seemed to receive impressions intuitively, which it cost other men much labor to acquire"—a gift that would serve him well when he came to command an army in the War Between the States.

The next morning, in accordance with Lee's recommendations, General Scott sent General Gideon Pillow, supported by Twiggs, to open the road in the direction of Contreras and San Angel. Lee, in charge of reconnaissance, was ordered to start before the main body of troops, taking with him the engineer company and five hundred men from Pillow's division, to improve a mule track across the pedregal. Shortly after noon, this road had been opened to a point that brought them within the range of the Padierna. When General Twiggs drove back the enemy picket line, Lee selected a position for the two batteries. While he directed the fire from these batteries, he stood beside young Preston Johnston's gun, and as he stood there, a solid shot took off the boy's leg. During the night he died.

After dark, General Persifor F. Smith summoned Lee to a council with Generals Cadwalader and Shields. It was evident to them that the enemy at Padierna expected the attack to come from the front. It was logical, then, to make a feint in front and attack simultaneously from the rear. When Smith expressed his desire to communicate this plan to General Scott, Lee volunteered to carry it to him, supposing him to be at the village of Zacatepec, 3 miles away. It was then about eight o'clock and raining hard.

With a small escort, Robert set off on foot across the treacherous lava field, likened by one imaginative observer "to a sea, which having been lashed into fury by a tempest, had been suddenly transformed, by the wand of an enchanter, into stone." He had to feel his way around blocks of volcanic rock and across gullies which he could find only when the waste was illuminated by flashes of lightning.

When he reached Zacatepec, he found that Scott had returned to San Augustin. There was no choice but to go back the 3 miles over the pedregal. Scott was writing his daily reports when Lee, drenched and exhausted, came into his headquarters. The General was amazed to see him, for, as he wrote:

Of the seven officers despatched since sundown, from my position . . . on this side of the volcanic field . . . not one has succeeded in getting through these difficulties increased by darkness. They have all returned. But the gallant and indefatigable Captain Lee, of the Engineers, who has been constantly with the operation force is (eleven o'clock P.M.) just in from Shields and Smith . . . to report.

Colonel Hitchcock, who was sitting with Scott when Lee

182

arrived, wrote in his diary for August 19: "At night Captain Lee—'the' engineer—came to town to report to General Scott the opinion of General . . . Smith that he could make a movement at 3 A.M. and storm the enemy's batteries. This plan was approved, and, though it was raining hard all night, Lee went back." The Colonel failed to give the reason for Lee's third crossing of the pedregal. Shortly after his arrival at headquarters, General Twiggs had limped in with a report, after having lost his way in the lava, narrowly missed capture, and injured his foot. It was necessary for Twiggs to return to the San Angel road in order to gather his men together for the coming movement, and Lee offered to guide him.

Of Lee's three treks across the pedregal that stormy night, General Scott wrote that it was "the greatest feat of physical and moral courage performed by any individual, in my knowledge, pending the campaign." And Robert's friend, Henry Hunt, noted incredulously: "I would not believe that it had been made, that passage of the pedregal, if he had not said he made it."

As planned, at precisely 3 A.M. Smith's troops were put in motion up the ravine to the enemy's rear, while Colonel Ransom of the Ninth Infantry, with Lee to guide him, occupied their attention in front. Colonel Riley led the rear assault, rushing headlong into the fort and taking it in exactly 17 minutes by the watch.

When Lee entered the captured work, he found Joe Johnston there, as he described him, "his frame shrunk and shivered with agony," for he had just learned of his nephew's death. At the sight of Joe's grief, Robert "burst into tears, and expressed his deep sympathy as tenderly" as a woman would have done.

In the knowledge that this victory could be completed only by a rapid follow-up, Scott now ordered San Antonio to be taken. This was carried more easily than was expected and the Americans swarmed out onto the causeway in time to cut the Mexican retreat in two, continuing unchallenged until they reached the Churubusco bridge, where a large mass of the enemy's infantry offered stubborn resistance.

Scott then sent General Pierce, with Lee to guide him, to attack the enemy's right and rear. Robert gave an account of his movements in a letter:

. . . Apprehending a fire from the batteries to . . . the rear, I drew out towards the City of Mexico until I reached the large hamlet on the Mexican road about three fourths of a mile in the rear of the bridge. . . . Gen. Shields formed his line obliquely to that of the enemy who, not to be outflanked, had drawn out from his entrenchments and extended his line from the bridge to nearly opposite our left. . . . Our troops being now hotly engaged & somewhat pressed, I urged forward the Howitzer party . . . who very promptly brought the pieces to bear upon the head of the columns with good effect. Perceiving that the enemy's cavalry were showing themselves on our left, & that our force was greatly outnumbered, I hastened back to the General-in-Chief, who directed Maj. Sumner to take the Rifle Regt. & a squadron to the support of that wing [which again Lee would guide].

Modestly, he failed to mention that Shields had established his right on the point that Robert had recommended, for that General had, he acknowledged, "the utmost confidence" in Lee's "skill and judgment."

When the Americans noted a waver in the Mexican fire at the *tête de pont* at the head of the bridge, they rushed in at the double quick and carried it with the bayonet, meanwhile turning their artillery upon a nearby fortified church or convent. The effect of the fire was speedy and decisive: the enemy put up signals of surrender on all sides.

When those officers whom Lee had served during the last thirty-six hours came to write their reports, they again made special mention of his services, though he continued to regard them as of small consequence. Typical of this attitude is a letter written to his brother:

My Darling Rose,

. . . Your commendations upon the conduct of the Army in this war have filled me with pleasure; they justly deserve it. . . . As to myself, your brotherly feelings have made you estimate too highly my small service, & though praise from one I love so dearly is sweet, truth compels me to disclaim it.

184

But General Smith wrote in his report:

In adverting to the conduct of the staff, I wish to record particularly my admiration of the conduct of Captain Lee of the Engineers. His reconnaissances, though pushed beyond the bounds of prudence, were conducted with so much skill, that their fruits were of the utmost value—the soundness of his judgment and personal daring being equally conspicuous.

General Twiggs reported: "To Captain Lee of the Engineers, I have again the pleasure of tendering my thanks for the exceedingly valuable services rendered throughout the whole of these operations." And General Shields said: "It affords me pleasure, and I but perform my duty, too, in acknowledging my great obligations to Captain R. E. Lee, Engineer Corps."

General Scott, in Report No. 32, while acknowledging his obligations to the staff, personal and general, singled out Lee to bestow upon him additional praise: "Captain R. E. Lee (as distinguished for felicitous execution as for science and daring). . . ." Later Lee received official notification that as of August 20, 1847, he had been brevetted a lieutenant colonel.

3

THE day after the battle at Churubusco, a commissioner from Santa Anna called upon Nicholas P. Trist, chief clerk in the State Department, whom Polk had appointed a special agent to negotiate for peace, to propose a truce. While awaiting the expiration of this armistice (which the Mexicans observed by strengthening their fortifications), General Scott, Colonel Hitchcock, Lee, and other members of the official family passed their time pleasantly in the palace of the archbishop, set in a garden planted to orange trees, jasmine, and oleander, and built on a knoll overlooking the village of Tucubaya where wealthy families from the capital had their villas. Several English families among them invited the officers to their homes for tea, supper, billiards, a swim in their spring-fed baths, or for evenings of conversation spiced with choice wines and excellent cigars. "What a country to dream in!" Colonel Hitchcock sighed as he described its beauty in his diary. Tucubaya was indeed lovely, provided one could ignore the hilltops bristling with cannon, and the rattle of caissons and the tramp of boots.

One day as General Scott stood on the terrace, he noticed the enemy in considerable force around Chapultepec, half a mile north, a former palace of Montezuma but now the Republic's military academy. Scott was now certain that the peace talks were a farce, proposed solely to allow the Mexican general time to reorganize his forces.

By September 6, it was apparent that the Americans had been duped. That evening, Scott summoned his Cabinet to consider the best means of attacking the capital, and specifically, how with fewer than eight thousand men to outmaneuver Santa Anna's eighteen to twenty thousand troops. Informed by Trist that the truce was formally at an end, Scott ordered Lee to make a reconnaissance over the city's approaches. He found works in preparation everywhere, a report so disconcerting to the general that he rode out with Robert to see the extent of the fortifications himself. He concluded that he must attack at once, before the enemy had time to finish its reorganization. At a council of war, he announced his determination to strike the first blow at Chapultepec even though Lee and John Lind Smith (recently returned to duty), doubted the effectiveness of artillery against the walls; they believed it could do no more than demolish the upper part of the main building, making it necessary then to reduce it with storming parties. Regardless, orders were issued on the spot: General Twiggs was to make a feint before the gate at dawn, while Lee was to put the four heavy batteries into position immediately.

The fire opened early the next morning and continued all day; its only effect was to disable seven pieces of the enemy's light artillery. To make plans for the direct assault, Lee went out that afternoon to reconnoiter. Shortly after his return, Lieutenant Beauregard brought him word that General Scott wanted to see him. With Beauregard and Tower, he rode to the palace, finding Scott in a dudgeon. He demanded to know why Lee had not immediately reported the effects of the artillery on

186

Chapultepec. Lee replied that his reconnaissance had prevented him from doing so. Did Lee believe that the enemy could repair his guns during the night? Lee did. Then the assault must be made tonight. And Scott stalked from the room.

The engineers held a hasty consultation, deciding that there was not time before darkness fell to prepare for the attack. Lee was delegated to advise Scott of this conclusion. The General agreed to defer the assault until morning. His mood was affable when he returned with Lee to sit with the engineers, and after he had listened to their reports he outlined his plan. As they were leaving, Scott asked Lee to come back later for a council.

When Lee returned, General Scott asked him to make a sketch of the plan described earlier. The idea proved so daring that after the meeting broke up, General Worth said confidentially to Colonel Hitchcock:

"We shall be defeated." And after the others had gone, even the lion-hearted Scott admitted to the Colonel:

"I have my misgivings."

Instead of resting, Lee returned to his batteries to prepare them for the work ahead. By dawn, when they went into action, he had been without sleep or rest for forty-eight hours.

General Scott watched the preliminary bombardment from the roof of Count Alcortez's house. Around eight o'clock he sent the order to cease fire, and set the troops in motion. Then Generals Pillow and Quitman, with a battalion of marines, and the storming parties with Lee as their guide, set off up the hill. The Glorieta, a redoubt halfway up, was soon carried, though not without some loss of life and the wounding of General Pillow. Clarke's brigade from Worth's division was then pushed forward, and two young officers, Lieutenants George Pickett and James Longstreet (destined to be closely associated with Lee fifteen years hence), seized scaling ladders, and rushing on with their men, placed the ladders against the walls of Chapultepec and entered the fort. Longstreet was badly wounded as he advanced with the colors in his hand. At practically the same minute, the marines and a New York regiment swarmed over the walls, and all resistance was at an end.

Lee now appeared with General Scott and his personal staff on the terrace of the academy.

"Men," thundered the Commander in Chief, "I could take each one of you to my bosom!"—words that were received with enthusiastic cheers.

But their stay was brief, for the General wanted to see how Worth was progressing in his attempts to carry the city gates on the San Cosimo causeway. When they reached the highroad, Lee rode ahead to reconnoiter near the gate, and received a wound, of which the only mention is in General Scott's Report No. 34. It is not known where he was wounded nor how badly. He apparently thought little of it, for he returned to General Scott, rode with him along the line of Worth's advance, and then suddenly fainted—as Scott reported: ". . . from a wound and the loss of two nights' sleep at the batteries." He was revived by cold water and a drink of brandy from the General's flask, and removed to a dressing station.

A good night's sleep restored him, and he joined Scott and his staff at an early breakfast and rode with them to the capital, which had surrendered the night before. Here, they found the streets filled with a gay throng, and almost every house hung with streamers and flags. It seemed to the Americans more like a grand festival than the entry of the foe.

Except for some small scattered resistance, the battles in Mexico were at an end. While the army rested and waited for reinforcements and supplies, the engineers surveyed and mapped the city and nearby defenses and battlegrounds. One day during a lone excursion outside the city, Lee met an old Mexican who, as he approached, began unwinding his lariat. Robert suspected that he intended to lasso him, so quickly drew his pistol and placed it in front of him. Observing the action, the Mexican dropped the lariat, and greeting Lee most cordially, passed on by.

At the invitation of the city council, General Scott and his staff visited El Desierto, the ruins of a Carmelite mission situated in a mountain gorge some 15 miles from the capital. With an escort of dragoons to guard against guerrillas and robbers, they rode their horses over the green countryside, while their hosts traveled in carriages. When describing the trip to Mary, Robert spoke of the verdure, of the canal of "pure bright water" that skirted the road, and the magnificence of "the pine, hemlock, the silver (or balsam) fir, & others indigenous to this country, whose broad, glossy leaves contrasted well with the graceful feathery ones I have named." The seventeenth-century convent had been unoccupied for over a hundred years, and stood vine-shrouded and mysterious in a garden overgrown with trees and flowering shrubs. It appeared to Robert "a romantic spot."

The Mexicans saw to it that every comfort was provided for their guests, sending ahead carriages with cooks, waiters, and musicians, and a wagonload of cooking utensils, dishes, silver, glassware, and a table to seat fifty. By the time the party had gathered, the table was already set under a canvas shelter in the old garden, and an "excellent band" was playing. The guests found the table laden with delicacies and a variety of fine wines.

During the banquet, special musicians—three guitarists and two flautists—performed. The Alcalde and the councilmen proposed countless toasts, all friendly to the occupying army, and after the feast, made short speeches, expressing the hope that the Americans would remain until Mexico's problem with government and church were solved. When General Scott was called upon, he limited his remarks to the desire for a rapid peace settlement. After the table had been cleared, the band entertained for the remainder of the afternoon.

While the army was impatiently awaiting the signing of the treaty, American bands all over the city were nostalgically playing "Home, Sweet Home"; and the general officers at headquarters engaged in a little war of their own to pass away the time. There was dissension and bickering among themselves, and there were accusations against their chief and attempts to usurp his glory. Now that he had led a victorious army into the capital, the administration in Washington was eager to carp.

There are several opinions as to the origin of the quarrels, though the strongest suspicion falls on General Pillow, a former law partner of President Polk. Pillow included in his reports the claim that he initiated the movements at Contreras and Chapultepec, provoking a curt exchange of messages with General Scott and bringing about an immediate division of the forces—for and against their commander. Charges and countercharges were hurled with increasing choler, until finally at the boiling-over point, Scott clapped under arrest Pillow, Worth, and a Colonel Duncan to await court-martial.

The President ordered a court of inquiry to convene at Puebla, to investigate all charges, but taking a letter from Pillow as evidence against Scott, Polk shrewdly ordered the commander in chief to be tried first. At 3 P.M. on February 18, a special messenger who had made the trip from Washington in just twenty-three days arrived at headquarters with the order that relieved General Scott from the command and replaced him with Major General William Orlando Butler, whose military background consisted of thirty years of law practice. The messenger also brought a release from arrest for Worth, Pillow, and Duncan.

Besides being personally fond of General Scott, Lee held a high opinion of his military genius and lamented the quarrels that had brought him such unjust treatment. In a letter to his brother, Smith, now at home, he wrote:

> The great cause of our success was our leader. It was his stout heart that cast us on shore at Vera Cruz; his bold self-reliance that forced us through the pass at Cerro Gordo; his indomitable courage that, amid all the doubts and difficulties that surrounded us at Puebla, pressed forward to this Capital, & finally brought us within its gates, while others, who croaked all the way from Brazos, & advised delay at Puebla, finding themselves at last, contrary to their expectations, comfortably quartered within its gates, find fault with the way they came here. With all their knowledge I defy them to have done better . . . But to decide the matter upon an ex-parte statement of favourites, to suspend a successful general in command of an army in the heart of an enemy's country, to try and judge in the place of the accused, is to upset all discipline; to jeopardize the safety of the army & the honour of the country, & to violate justice. . . .

190

Lieutenant Hunt, stationed with his battery at Tacubaya, recalled Lee's distress at Scott's treatment. Often when returning from some mission in the western valley, Robert would stop at the hacienda where Hunt was quartered. He enjoyed the peace of the gardens and liked to watch the great numbers of hummingbirds that darted into the flowers. As the two sat and talked, Lee often mentioned his desire to heal the breach between Scott and his officers, and told of his efforts in that direction. In disgust, he spoke of the probability that the General would be "kicked off . . . and turned out as an old horse to die." Hunt regarded Lee as "a peacemaker by nature."

The foreign population in the capital regarded Scott's dismissal "the result of low and vulgar intrigue by inferior men," as one Englishman told Colonel Hitchcock. To express their regard for him, Mr. Drusini, a wealthy British merchant, gave a formal dinner in the General's honor, a party which was, in the opinion of Hitchcock, "in the highest degree *recherché*." Besides Scott and Hitchcock, the only other Americans invited were Nicholas Trist (also in disfavor with the administration now), General Smith, and Lee, which attests not only to Lee's intimacy with General Scott, but to his recognition as one of the army's most distinguished officers. Scott later acknowledged that his "success in Mexico was largely due to the skill, valor, and undaunted energy of Robert E. Lee," and spoke of him as "the very best soldier I ever saw in the field."

Mr. Drusini's other guests included Mr. Doyle, the British Minister, Mr. Thornton, Secretary of the British Legation, Dr. Martinez, an eminent physician, and Mr. Davidson, a millionaire agent for the Rothschilds. As they drank their after-dinner coffee in the drawing room, Mr. Thornton and Mr. Doyle sat with Lee and Hitchcock. They deplored General Scott's dismissal, and assured the Americans that it would be condemned in Europe.

Lee inspected the large art collection in the National Palace, with a little girl called Charlottelita, whom he described in a letter to his daughter, Agnes, as "a great favourite of mine. Her mother is a French lady & her father an Englishman. She is quite fair with blue eyes, long dark lashes, & has her hair

191

plaited down her back. She cannot speak English but has a very nimble little tongue & jabbers French at me." After they had looked at the paintings and inspected the "richly furnished rooms," where they admired the large mirrors, the chandeliers, and the walls "covered with crimson tapestry & ornamented with gilt fringes," they called on General Smith, and then picked flowers in the gardens. Another afternoon, with Charlottelita and her older sister, he visited the National Picture Gallery to see the fine collection of Old Masters.

In March, Lee and several other officers rode sixty-five miles to tour the silver mines of Real del Monte. To help pass away the time, the American officers founded the Aztec Club of which Robert became a member.

But underlying all diversions was the ever-present desire to return home, and mounting discontent over the treatment of Scott. Robert wrote to Mary that he would remain so long as his services were needed, "but I confess there is a change in my feelings now, & I should be happy if I could leave the country tomorrow without dishonour."

When Mr. Custis learned that Robert had been brevetted a lieutenant colonel, he wrote him a congratulatory letter. On April 8, 1848, Lee replied, voicing his disgust with the method of awarding brevets:

I cannot consider myself very highly complimented by the brevet rank of 2 grades. They are bestowed on two officers at Palo Alto, Duncan & May, for one single effort on the part of each. I have never seen an officer present at the engagement that thought they deserved more than one. Gen. Twiggs in an official letter to Gen. Scott which has fallen under my eye, & has been endorsed by General S—— recommended me for two brevets for the battle of Cerro Gordo, 17 & 18 of April. So that if I performed any services at Vera Cruz or at the battles around the capital, they will go for naught. The Secrys rule did not seem to prevent Lt. Fremont from being advanced 3 grades from a Lt. of Top. Engrs. to a Lt. Col. of Rifles, Johnston from a Lt. of Top. Engrs. to a Lt. Col. of Voltigeurs. . . . I presume however their services exceeded mine, which I know to be small. Only one of these however, had previously been in an engagement. There will be no doubt other examples of the same kind, when the list is published. . . . I do not mention this in the way of complaint, but that you may not think I am overwhelmed with gratitude & obligation. The treatment which Gen. Scott has received satisfies me what those may expect who have done their duty. It will be better for me to be classed with those who have failed.

Speaking of the large number of officers who had resigned in disgust and protest, he told his father-in-law: "I wish I was out of the Army myself. But my desire is rather to allay the excitement, than to foment it by my example—I send you the papers containing the proceedings of the court. You will see what a person Genl. Pillow is, & for whom Gen. Scott has been sacrificed."

Lee found himself unexpectedly involved in the proceedings of the Scott-Pillow inquiry when he was called to answer charges by Pillow that he had disobeyed the regulations by allowing *The Washington Union* to print a letter of his that contained an account of Contreras and Churubusco. Lee identified his letter, which had been written to Mrs. Totten, and explained how she had sent it to the engineer office to be read; Colonel Totten was absent and his assistant, ignorant of the rules, had given it to the newspaper. Lee stressed that the letter had been addressed to Mrs. Totten and not to engineer headquarters. This, and the fact that his account of the battles was both brief and impartial, absolved him from responsibility.

On March 31, and again on April 8, he appeared in court as a witness for the prosecution. To add to his disgust at having any part in the inquiry was the publication in *The New York Courier* of his role in the proceedings, and the statement, as he wrote in anger to Mrs. Fitzhugh, "that I had either furnished the data or offered myself as evidence for their truth, neither of which I did do, or had any knowledge of until I saw it in print. I consider it a great outrage."

By April 12, the United States had ratified the peace treaty signed on February 1 at Guadelupe Hidalgo, and the spirits of the occupation army were raised at the prospect of going home. Reflecting this mood, Robert replied to a letter from his cousin, Cassius:

"It seems that all in Alexa are progressing as usual, & that nothing will stop their marrying & being given in marriage. Tell Miss G—— she had better dismiss that young divine &

marry a soldier. There is some chance of the latter being shot, but it requires a particular dispensation of Providence to rid her of the former. . . ."

Just before General Scott started overland to Vera Cruz, he gave Colonel Hitchcock the key to his wine closet, asking him to share its contents with Lee and other close friends at his discretion. "I shall consult Lee about it," the Colonel decided.

When a courier arrived from Queretaro with news that the Mexican Chamber of Deputies had ratified the treaty, and that the Senate would probably do so by April 24, Lee was in high spirits, and relayed the good tidings to Markie: "We are all much exhilarated at the prospect of getting home again. So tell your sweetheart you will keep him waiting no longer but are ready to give him 'indemnification for the past & security for the future.' The sweet violets you enclosed arrived safely—Give much love to Cousin Britt, your GrdMother, Miss Lumb & Kate. . . ." He wrote in a similar vein to Smith, looking toward a joyful reunion with this dearly loved brother, and with "Sis Nanie & the boys."

On May 27, Lee was ordered to accompany the engineers to Vera Cruz. From there Robert boarded the steamer *Portland* for New Orleans. With him was Jim Connally, the mare, Grace Darling, and Jim's dog, Jack. "Santa Anna," a pure white "mustang pony" that Lee had bought for Rob, was to follow.

Since his favorite mount, Creole, did not accompany him, it can be presumed that his fear of being "obliged some day to give her too hard a ride while she is so young & break her down," must have been realized.

On June 14, he wrote to Mary that he was then ascending the Mississippi, and expected "to reach N. O. before day tomorrow." For the comfort of his mare—"she already having undergone so much suffering in my service"—he decided to take the river route as far as Wheeling. With his customary attention to detail, he asked Mary to be sure to have his summer clothes ("in the English trunk") taken out and "nicely washed &c. by my arrival."

194

⇻⇻ IV ⇺⇺

Mounting Frustration

1848 ⋆ 1855

IV. Mounting Frustration

At Wheeling, Robert left Jim Connally, the mare, Grace Darling, and the dog, Jack, "to take care of themselves" while he went on by stage. When he arrived in Washington, his one concern was to reach home as quickly as possible, and in hurrying to the nearest livery stable to hire a saddle horse, he missed the carriage sent for him.

In the cool hall at Arlington, all the family except one member had gathered to await his coming. Mary and her parents were talking with their house guest, Mrs. Lippitt, but listening all the while for the sound of wheels on the gravel. Every now and then, one of the children would run out onto the portico to look for the carriage, and the terrier, Spec, sensing the expectancy, followed to sniff the air and scan the distance.

Upstairs, young Rob and his mammy, Eliza, were doing battle over the wearing of the boy's favorite blue cotton blouse dotted all over with white diamonds. Admitting defeat, Eliza at length allowed the triumphant youth to wear it, but they had argued so long that she had to hurry with the curling of his golden ringlets.

When next the children ran outside, Spec startled them by suddenly barking; then with a whine he set off at a run down the drive toward a lone horseman who had just come into view. They hurried back into the hall to report Spec's behavior, and to say that not "Pa'a" but some man on horseback was approaching. Then in dashed Spec, barking and whining with joy, and then out again to jump and lick Robert's hand as he dismounted.

Down into the hall raced Rob to find his father, and everyone talking at once with tears and laughter in their voices. Mary was wanting to know, womanlike, why Robert had not come in the carriage. The younger children stood aside, staring in wonder at this bronzed smiling man, his dark eyes shining with tears, his black hair grizzled. There was a kiss, a tight

197

embrace, and a kind word for each one—Mary, Mother, Father, and the children—all grown beyond belief. Boo so tall and serious; Rooney, big and hearty; the Little Woman no longer *little;* Annie, gentle and shy; Agnes, quite the beauty; and little Milly, "so wonderfully sweet."

Suddenly looking about, Robert asked: "Where is my *little* boy?", and without waiting for an answer, he took up in his arms a small fellow with long golden curls. But it was not the little boy in the blue blouse with white diamonds—the little boy who stood aghast at what he saw—but young Armistead Lippitt, son of the house guest.

It was a slight understatement when the next day Lee wrote Smith: "It is not surprising that I am hardly recognizable to some of the young eyes around me & perfectly unknown to the youngest." In utmost truth he might have added that the second to the youngest was perfectly unknown to *him.*

For the Fourth of July, Smith and his family, Mrs. Fitzhugh, Cousin Brit, Markie, and the Lees from Alexandria came to Arlington. Mr. Custis' preparations were more extensive and elaborate than usual, for this was a dual celebration—in honor of the nation's independence and his son-in-law's safe return from the war, "preserved by a kind Providence from a thousand dangers."

Right after the holiday, Robert went to see his sister, Ann, taking Rob with him. Having injured her left hand, Mrs. Marshall was unable even to feed herself and was understandably in low spirits; but a visit with Robert, she always found, cheered her. While they were in Baltimore, the sailing ship carrying the pony, Santa Anna, came into port, and Lee and his son went to the docks to claim him. Rob remembered how his expectations were dashed when he first saw the unkempt, drooping little animal which had suffered from want of exercise and grooming on the long voyage. But it responded quickly to good care, and Rob was soon proudly receiving his first riding lessons from his father.

General Totten (he had been brevetted a brigadier for his service at Vera Cruz), allowed Lee just five days to reacquaint himself with his children before assigning him to "special duty" in the Washington office, and reappointing him to the Board of Engineers, then inspecting the Atlantic coast defenses. But when at home, as many hours as he could spare were spent with the children. A high jump had been set up in the yard, and it was remembered that he tried his skill with his older sons and their friends; that he boated with them on the river; joined their swimming parties; and helped them improve their horsemanship when they accompanied him on rides about the neighborhood, where he stopped to visit relatives and friends. He took great delight in petting the little ones, welcoming them to his bed each morning when, as they snuggled in his arms, he told them amusing or exciting stories. Whenever he entered or left the house, he never failed to call all the children to him, "kissing us—caressing us in his sweet way," one of them wrote, a custom he continued with his daughters all his life.

But there was one pleasure of their father's that appeared curious to the children: this was his fondness for having his hands and feet rubbed and tickled. On winter evenings as he sat before the fire, he would remove his slippers and place his feet in a child's lap in order to have them tickled, while two more children sat on either side of his chair, busily tickling his hands. As a reward, he would tell them "the most delightful stories." Occasionally they would become so absorbed in the tale they would forget their duty. Then their father would stop, and announce:

"No tickling, no story!"

One night, young Mary told the story of "The Lady of the Lake" in simple prose for the benefit of the younger children grouped about their father, "briskly tickling his hands and feet." Every so often he would interrupt her to recite line after line of the poem, "much to our disapproval—but to his great enjoyment," Rob recalled.

After an absence of three years, there was much to be learned concerning his relatives and friends, and many evenings were passed listening to Mary or her mother give detailed accounts. One of his favorites, "the beautiful Miss Mattie Mason," had married her brother-in-law Rhett, of Charleston, while Catherine Mason (she had been maid of honor at the Lees' wedding), had at last accepted the hand of a widower from Baltimore who had a family of grown-up children. Eliza Mackay Stiles was now in Vienna where her husband was the American chargé d'affaires, and she was painting with re- newed interest. Mary had written of Carter Lee's marriage to Lucy Penn Taylor, the daughter of George and Catherine Randolph Taylor, but weddings always called for more minute narration than space limitations of a letter allowed.

However, all the news was not pleasant, for there had been a number of deaths. The one that dealt the sharpest blow was Jack Mackay's. He had died on May 31, 1848, at his Savannah home. He was just forty-two. Mary had saved the sad letter from his family, recounting the details of his final illness and death.

Lee's brevet commissions were approved, and with the pub- lication of general orders on August 24, he was a colonel. He had received the final brevet on September 13, 1847, for his services at Chapultepec. In September, he was assigned the supervision of a fort to be built on a shoal in the Patapasco River, between Hawkins and Sollers Point, below Baltimore. On November 15, he went to Baltimore to accept the assign- ment, but left the same day to join the board of engineers who were ordered to inspect defenses at Boston, New Haven, and New York.

When Robert reached New Haven, he learned that one of his favorites, "sweet Miss Mary Anderson" of Savannah, was there visiting her relatives, the Gordons. She had been married for some years to Lee's West Point friend, Hugh Mercer, and they had named their latest-born for Robert. Delighted at the opportunity to see her again, he called at the Gordon house, only to learn that Mrs. Mercer was sick. However, as soon as she heard who was there, she asked that he come to her room. As Robert later described the scene to Hugh, he found her lying on her bed, trying to comfort herself with "*three* da- guerreotypes, five letters, and a hundred dollar note," while a doctor "as big as the side of a house," sat by the stove and dozed, though he opened his eyes in surprise when he overheard

Robert advise Mary to "dismiss the doctor & physic." In spite of her illness, he thought she was looking lovelier than ever.

After he had returned to his hotel room, he began to think about her loneliness, and he was strongly "tempted" as he told her, "to break my engagement with my military confederates this morn[r] & spend it with you." However, he resisted the temptation, and wrote her a letter instead, explaining:

But then came the thought of what service could I do you, the probability of my being more "plague than profit" & being unable to come to a satisfactory conclusion on this point before midnight I cut it short by embarking for New York. I hope however you are now better & trust you may soon be well. Can't you send me a little note to "Alexandria Virginia" assuring me of the fact? Tell my little namesake that I feel much flattered at his being called after me. I could wish him a better name & could give it too & would have to go no farther than his father's. . . . I send him with this a Christmas gift to remind him of me at the most important duties of his present life. . . .

When Robert returned to Baltimore, it was too late in the season to start any work at Sollers Point, so after passing a day with his sister, he hurried on to Arlington to reach there in time for Christmas.

In January, the Board of Engineers were sent to examine lands being reserved by the government as sites for future fortifications, and to recommend which ones should be kept and which released. The trip took them down through Alabama as far as Mobile, along both coasts of Florida, and then up to Savannah, where they spent two days. The first day Lee was so busy with his duties that he was unable to visit his friends, but the second morning he passed in making calls with Hugh Mercer, and took his noon dinner with the Mackays. Though Eliza was still in Vienna, Mary Anne, Margaret, Catherine, and Sarah were there, and their older brother, William, who since the tragic death of his wife and children in the explosion of the steamship *Pulaski* had been making his home with his mother.

Hugh Mercer found "Bob Lee" looking "remarkably well, and as young as ever he did, except that his hair is getting pretty well grizzled. I do not find him at all changed—he runs on just as he used to do—He made me laugh very heartily at some of his stories and laughed himself until the tears ran down his face. . . ."

At the end of March, he was back at Arlington with just a little over a day to pass with his family before taking up his duties at Sollers Point. Just before going he wrote a note to Markie:

The pain at leaving Arlington is much increased at my being unable to bid you adieu. My departure, coming so quickly upon my arrival causes many things to press upon my attention, & business drives entirely away pleasure. One of the pleasures I always antici-pate here, is the sight of you, Markie, & to forego it causes me great regret. . . . I preferred writing to detailing these messages to Cousin Brit, & had hoped time would have enabled me to have entered into detail, but the last sand in the Glass is nearly ex-hausted & I must be off.

That night he took the train to Baltimore, staying at the Exchange Hotel until he could find a house for his family.

The site for the fort had already been prepared the pre-vious season, so construction could now begin. This was, he admitted to Markie, an absorbing task, leaving him time for little else:

My thoughts are engrossed in driving piles & laying stone, & my imagination is exercised in the construction of cranes, Diving bells, steam Pile drivers &c. Poor subjects for correspondence with young ladies. If it was not for my heart Markie, I might as well be a pile or a stone myself laid quietly at the bottom of the river. But that has no hardness for you, & always returns warmth & softness when touched with a thought of you.

The heat was intolerable—too hot even for weddings. He advised that one young friend should wait until the autumn: "I think she is too feeble to encounter so much happiness till cooler weather, and there is nobody can eat cake & good things with the temperature at 100° but flies &c." Once again he was feeling "solitary," and had adopted two yellow kittens to keep him company. "There is however but little amusement in the evs. killing moskitoes & watching kittens playing with their tails."

At the end of July he was sick with a fever, doubtless contracted from the "moskitoes," and was forced to leave his post. Not wanting to expose the children, he accepted Mrs. Fitzhugh's thoughtful offer of a room at Ravensworth. But in his concern over the work he was back at Sollers by August 9, writing that day to Mary: "I think I am feeling stronger." During his absence the faithful Jim Connally had also come down with "the prevailing sickness."

Shortly after his return he was ordered to join the engineer board at Newport, Rhode Island, for consultation on the location of a new hospital and barrack at Fort Adams. Believing himself entirely recovered, he went on to Philadelphia where he suffered a relapse, though it was not severe enough to keep him from going on to New York. A day's rest at the Irving House in that city seemed to restore him, and he boarded the *Empire State*. But by the time he had reached Newport, he was sick again. He engaged a room at the Ocean House, went to bed, and called the doctor.

"My old friend Dr. Satterlee" came, he wrote home, and to Robert's relief he recommended that he stop all medication and see what complete rest and quiet would do. But two days in bed failed to reduce the fever, and Dr. Satterlee put him back on quinine. On August 18, he rode out with the engineers to look at Fort Adams, but he did not feel strong enough to get out of the carriage. Ten days later, he was back in bed, having been stricken while in church.

He had begun to find the confinement irksome, and the hotel much to his distaste. It was "large & noisy, having more than 300 visitors & with the exception of 3 or 4 they are peculiarly uninteresting to me. . . . I spend a stupid time here. Bore the young ladies of my acquaintance, fortunately for them I know but a few, & am bored in turn by other people," he complained.

Dr. Satterlee had stressed that he was not to return too soon to Sollers Point for the "bad atmosphere" would certainly bring back the fever. But Lee was determined that he could, and would, stay no longer at Newport. "I felt as if I could not get well there," he said later.

For some time he had wanted to see General Scott, so he proposed to the doctor that he continue his recuperation at West Point, where the General was then living. This was agreeable, provided he promised not to linger in New York.

"So I embarked aboard the 'Bay State,' fully charged with quinine & reached here very comfortably," he wrote Mary from his room in Cozzens's new hotel, about a mile below the Point. "I missed the fever yesterday & feel better today."

The visit with General Scott, who lived at the hotel, was enjoyable, and Lee improved steadily in the new environment. Among the subjects he and the General discussed was Custis' "unconquerable passion for Military life," and his desire to attend the Academy. Scott was far more sympathetic with this ambition than Lee, and offered to support Custis' application for admission when that time came.

On the last night of the annual cadet encampment, he and Scott rode up to the plain to watch the ceremonies. He found "the whole . . . illuminated & decked with evergreens, wreaths, transparencies, &c." They went into camp and shook hands and chatted with the officers and professors, and strolled around the parade ground where "the Genl. was recd. with deafening cheers." On the sixth day of his stay, Robert felt entirely restored, and parting with the General, went on down to New York where he had "a little private & public business to do." He reached Baltimore around the eighth of September, and hurried out to Sollers to inspect the work, which had been worrying him.

His next concern was to check the progress of the three-story brick house on Madison Street (three doors above Biddle) which his uncle, Williams Wickham, was building. Lee had agreed to rent it for his family and was disappointed to find that it was still not finished. The move was not made until some time after the New Year. The family found the house pleasant and comfortable, but Robert complained that his room was "hardly big enough to swing a cat in."

At this time, an unusual offer came to Lee. A delegation

from the Cuban junta, then organizing in New York, came to ask if he would consider commanding their proposed expedition to rid Cuba of Spanish control. It has been said that the committee first asked Senator Jefferson Davis of Mississippi, chairman of the Military Affairs Committee, to take command because of his acknowledged interest in Cuban affairs, but that he declined and suggested Lee. But Davis has written that the junta chose Lee because of his outstanding record in the Mexican War, which had distinguished him as one of the country's ablest soldiers. They were anxious for Lee's services, and offered a large sum of money to be paid on acceptance, and a handsome amount monthly which, added to the potential honors in case of success, made it a tempting proposal.

Lee thought it over, and then went to Washington to discuss a point of honor with Davis: as an officer of the United States Army, was he free to "accept a proposition for foreign service against a government with which the United States were at peace." The result of their talks, Davis wrote, "was his decision to decline."

Social life in Baltimore was active and pleasant. The Lees had many relatives and old friends there, and through Ann Marshall and her family they made new ones, the most notable being Jerome Napoleon Bonaparte, the son of Napoleon I's brother, Jerome. This Jerome had married a Roxbury, Massachusetts girl of beauty and wealth, Susan Mary Williams, and their eldest son, Jerome Napoleon, was a cadet at West Point. Robert was soon on intimate terms with them, writing during their absences those gay letters he enjoyed composing for an appreciative audience.

"The houses in town all give indication of the return of their occupants," he told Jerome, Sr. "Windows are open, brushes are flourishing, & dust flying. Yours still retains its closed impassiveness. . . . All the Belles of the city are said to be engaged, which has caused the belief in others of their sex, that the millenium is at hand. . . ."

In the fall of 1850, Jenny Lind came to the Front Street Theatre, an event Baltimoreans had been looking forward to for months. The Lees went with a group of friends. During the winter season, Robert regularly attended the concerts of the Germania Band.

On such occasions the children were allowed to stay up beyond their bedtime to see their parents off. As many times as they had seen their father in full uniform, they still felt a thrill of pride. He was always ready ahead of time and marveling at Mary's ability to be consistently late. When she finally appeared, there was always some further delay when she had to go back for her spectacles, her fan, handkerchief, or gloves.

The older children realized that no matter how long their mother took to dress, she was never chic. Robert was very style-conscious, and would often chide her about her indifference to fashion.

"Mrs. Lee, why don't you wear your dresses longer? I look at the pretty girls in town, and they all wear their dresses longer. If you don't lengthen yours, I shall have to walk with the pretty girls."

During the summer of 1851, a Virginian and his daughter came to the Hot Springs. As they were going up to their rooms, they met and spoke to a man so faultlessly dressed and so exceptionally handsome that the girl fairly held her breath. Pressing her father's arm, she whispered:

"Who is *he?*"

"That is Colonel Lee."

Walking along the upper porch they passed a plain, dark-haired woman seated in a rocking chair, reading a book. In a glance the girl noticed her calico dress, "low, unfashionable shoes," and blue cotton stockings. Her father spoke, and after they were out of hearing, whispered:

"*That* is Mrs. Lee."

Until Rob was old enough to attend Mr. Rollins' school on Mulberry Street, he went almost daily with his father to Sollers Point. Right after an early breakfast they took the omnibus to the wharf where a boat and two oarsmen were waiting to row them down the river. Lee did not take Rob to the shoal, but left him at Sollers in the care of a family with whom he took his noon dinner.

The boy was free to roam the wharves and fish, but his

206

chief delight lay in his father's companionship. Lee was nearly always bright and gay with his son, teasing and joking or telling him stories. Although this was usual, Lee could be "firm" on "all proper occasions," and demanded "the most implicit obedience." With his mother, Rob was often able to interpret her orders to suit himself, or circumvent them, he recalled, but "it was impossible to disobey my father."

Since young Custis was still determined to go to West Point, his father consented. On February 5, he wrote to General Scott for the letter of recommendation. Custis received his appointment and left Fairfax Institute on April 15 for a final visit with his grandparents. During the last week in May, he and his father left for West Point.

Custis had energy, ambition, and ability, and adjusted quickly to the routine, just as his father had done. The following April, Lee visited him and talked with his professors and instructors.

"I was much gratified at all I heard of you. . . . The commendations of your officers & teachers was to me the greatest pleasure I have ever experienced," he wrote after his return to Baltimore. He went into detail of that return home, knowing that Custis would be amused.

He had reached Baltimore before 5 A.M., he wrote;

day had broken, but I knew it was too early to expect admittance to the house at that hour, so I disposed of the trunk, & to wile away the time I walked leisurely up in the grey of the morning. I took the precaution to call by Williams' house & got his pass-key & let myself in, & had no difficulty in ascending to your mother's room. The door was locked & it took some little time to rouse her, but instead of admitting me or opening the door, she prevented my entrance by saying that Emma Randolph was in there. So we had to make our salutations in the passage, & I determined to go up & see the children. I found both Mary's, who has moved to the front room, third story, & Rooney's door locked. After some loud knocks, Mary's was opened, & allowing sufficient time for the opener to get under cover, I asked if I could enter. There was no answer, so I walked in & found Mary sound asleep, some person by her side, buried in bed with her head completely covered. I saw it was too long for any of the children & having succeeded in waking

Mary, she informed me that it was Cousin Cornelia Randolph. I had then to beat a retreat from there. I commenced applying at Rooney's door. After a little time it was opened, & stepping in there lay Rooney sound asleep in the middle of the bed, Mildred on one side of him & Rob crawling in on the other. Upon investigation I discovered that Rooney on coming up to bed had caught up the two little children from their room & put them into his bed, & fearful lest his mother when she came up might recapture them, had locked his door. I did not venture to examine farther into the house, so can't tell you what was going on in Cousin Brit's room all this time. I presume she was locked up, too. . . .

In May, at inspection during release from quarters, liquor was found in Custis' room. Although he and his two room-mates, Charles N. Turnbull and a lad by name of Wood, denied all knowledge of it, they were placed under arrest and threatened with dismissal. Custis wrote to his father at once, withholding nothing from him. This letter, he told his son, brought him

more pleasure than any that I now recollect having ever received. It has assured me of the confidence you feel in my love & affection, & with what frankness & candour you open to me all your thoughts. So long as I meet with such return from my children & see them strive to respond to my wishes & exertions for their good & happiness, I can meet with calmness & unconcern all else the world may have in store for me.

Though evidence was strong against the boys, Superintendent Henry Brewerton was convinced that the jug had either been placed in their room by others wishing to divert suspicion from themselves, or as a hollow form of prank. Instead of dismissal, each cadet received eight demerits.

Lee was relieved, and wrote in high spirits:

How is it with you, my dearest Mr. Boo? Times are pretty dull in B—— now, for Spec, the Parrot & myself. No Mim, no children, no Mrs. Bonaparte, no baby! Still we get along, & at Sollers we hammer on lustily. . . . I was delighted at the contradiction in your last letter of that *slanderous* report against the room of those fine cadets Lee, Wood & Turnbull. I could not believe it before, to the extent of the report. . . . Your letter did me good in other respects. It talked of being of the Colour Guard, of being relieved from the Post, of taking your ease in your own tent. That sounded well. It assured me of your being released from arrest, of being on duty again. . . . I was very sad before when I thought of you confined to your room, trailing to meals after the guard, and deprived of the relaxation and enjoyment of your comrades. It seemed unnatural. . . . But now things look right again, I am cheered up.

Rooney was at this time "excelling" in Greek and French at Mr. McNally's School, though his father admitted that in the latter language "his pronunciation is anything but pure Parisian." He was also, according to his father, "growing wonderfully. I do not know when he will stop if he goes on at this rate. His feet and hands are tremendous and his appetite startling." Confronted with those problems which almost every parent of an adolescent boy must face, Lee wrote:

There is a great deal of good & energy in him, if it only gets the right direction. I strive hard to fix his attention & desires on what is good, but he is still of that age when he cannot appreciate all its beauties. . . . His anxiety is still to go to West Point, & thinks there is no life like that of a dragoon. He thinks he might get through the Academy, though he would not stand as well as *Boo*. I tell him that he would get over two hundred demerits the first year, and that there would be an end to all his military aspirations.

He hoped to eventually dissuade Rooney from an army career.

"I can advise no young man to enter the Army," he wrote to Markie when she asked for advice concerning the future of her brother, Orton. "The same application, the same self denial, the same endurance in any other profession, will advance him faster & farther. Nothing but an unconquerable passion for Military life, would induce me to recommend the Military profession. Notwithstanding my experience & advice, all my sons desire to enter the service."

Young Mary was now sixteen, and to avoid confusion with her mother, was designated as "Daughter." Her father was amused at her budding interest in the opposite sex, and reported to Custis that when she and her girl companions took walks, which was nearly every afternoon, they never went into the country but always turned their steps toward town,

from which I infer that they are more attracted by sight-seeing than a desire for exercise and the beauties of nature. The confabs at the corners, too, are frequent & long, & their tongues try to cover their glances over their shoulders at interesting passers-by. I fear they are wicked things; tell Jerome [Bonaparte] and Lawrence [Williams] as soon as they come on, I shall take them in hand. I fear to tackle them alone. One old man against so many black eyes would be fearful odds.

During the spring of 1851, he began the underwater masonry on the fort, by then called "Fort Carroll." He found it "a work of great trouble," as he told Custis, but "I see my way . . . very clearly, & think I shall succeed in making as good a wall as if on dry land." He was using a diving bell—"a troublesome operation with awkward, timid men. They are getting somewhat tutored now, & I hope this month to do better. Besides I have overcome many of the difficulties, by contrivances & arrangements to meet them."

The project absorbed so much time and thought he did not even have leisure for personal letters. "You have not written to me for nearly four months," he chided Markie when he found an opportunity to write her, "and I believe it is equally long since I have written to you. On paper, Markie, I mean, on paper. But oh, what lengthy epistles have I indited to you in my mind! Had I any means to send them you would see how constantly I think of you."

In March, Eliza Stiles and her daughter, Mary Cowper, came for a visit. After a stay of more than two weeks, Robert had the further pleasure of escorting them to Arlington. He wrote Mrs. Custis that they would be taking the nine o'clock train on the morning of March 29, and would "reach Washington at 11 A.M. on *that day*. Can you send the carriage to meet us? Mrs. Stiles & her daughter have two trunks & a carpet bag, & though the trunks are large, I think the carriage, if *strong* ought to carry the whole party. If there should be any difficulty perhaps the market boat might bring over one trunk. . . ."

Congress adjourned that March without making any appropriations for the work on Fort Carroll. Construction would have to be suspended as soon as the balance from the previous appropriations was exhausted, but due to Lee's economy, this balance amounted to $40,600, enough, he estimated, to carry the project through the next year.

During the first days of autumn it was again excessively hot, so uncomfortable it precluded all desire to attend social functions.

"Between my engagements at Fort Carroll and at home, I have been nowhere," he wrote. In addition, "all our little people" came down with the whooping cough, though it was supposed they had already had it at Fort Hamilton.

"They have kept up a terrible barking for the last week or ten days, which does not seem to diminish."

That year, Christmas was spent at Arlington. For Custis, who would have to stay at West Point for the holidays, his father wrote a detailed account of their doings, describing everything from the excessive cold to the flirtations among the young people:

We came on last Wednesday morning. It was a bitter cold day, & we were kept waiting an hour in the depot at Baltimore for the cars, which were detained by the snow & frost on the rails. We found your Grandfather at the Washington depot, Daniel & the old carriage & horses, and young Daniel on the colt Mildred. Your Mother, Grandfather, Mary Eliza, the little people, & the baggage I thought load enough for the carriage, so Rooney & I took our feet in our hands & walked over. . . . The children were delighted in getting back, & passed the evening devising pleasure for the morrow. They were in upon us before day on Christmas morning, to overhaul their stockings. Mildred thinks she drew the prize in the shape of a beautiful new doll. . . . The cakes, candies, books, &c., were overlooked in the caresses she bestowed upon her. . . . Rooney got among his gifts a nice pair of boots, which he particularly wanted, & the girls I hope, were equally pleased with their presents, books, & trinkets.

The day after Christmas, Wallace and Edward Stiles, sons of Eliza's sister, Mary Anne, arrived. Mrs. Fitzhugh drove over, bringing with her, Minny Lloyd (her father, John Lloyd, had married Anne Harriotte Lee, daughter of Robert's Uncle Edmund Jennings Lee), and Lucretia Fitzhugh, so that with other guests identified just as "the twins," and Sarah Stuart, there was, as Lee told his son, "quite a tableful."

The young people have been assiduous in their attentions to each other, as their amusements have been necessarily indoors, [he went on] but the Beaux have successfully maintained their reserve so far, notwithstanding the captivating advances of the Belles. The first day they tried skating, but the ice was soft & rough, and it was abandoned in despair. They have not moved out of the house since. . . .

I need not describe to you our amusements, you have witnessed them so often, nor the turkey, cold ham, plum-pudding, mince pies, &c. at dinner. I hope you will enjoy . . . some equally good. . . . I had received no letter when I left Baltimore, nor shall I get any till I return, which will be, if nothing happens, tomorrow a week, 5th of January, 1852. You will then be in the midst of your examination. I shall be very anxious about you. Give me the earliest intelligence of your standing, & stand up before them boldly, manfully; do your best, & I shall be satisfied.

Fearing that Custis might procrastinate with his preparations for the all-important second-year examinations, he wrote him tactfully a few weeks after his return to Baltimore:

My dear Mr Boo, This is not my day for writing to you. It is your mother's turn and she claims the privilege. . . . I shall leave her to tell you of domestic events, & will jump to what is first in my mind, viz: that only four months have to *fly by*, you may say, before the June examinations & your furlough. Have you thought of that. . . . Why, Man, it will be upon you before you are aware. I must begin to prepare. I must get at my work & try to be through before that time. . . . You must prepare too. You must press forward in your studies. You must "crowd that boy Howard" [Oliver O.]. You must be No. 1. It is a fine number. Easily found & remembered. Simple & unique. Jump to it fellow. . . .

Custis apparently took the advice, and at the end of the June finals he stood in the "immortal section," and secured his long-awaited furlough.

On the twenty-seventh of May, General Totten sent Lee the following order:

You will prepare to transfer the operations now under your charge to Lieut. Whiting, in order that you may proceed to West Point towards the close of the month of August and on the 1st of September next relieve Capt. Brewerton of the Superintendency of the Military Academy, and of the command of the post of West Point, Capt. Brewerton to succeed to duty at Fort Carroll.

This was an honor that Lee received with little enthusiasm:

I learn with much regret the determination of the Secretary of War to assign me to that duty [he wrote Totten], and I fear I cannot realize his expectations in the management of an Institution requiring more skill & more experience than I command.

Although fully appreciating the honour of the station, and extremely reluctant to oppose my wishes to the orders of the Department, yet if I be allowed any option in the matter, I would respectfully ask that some other successor than myself be appointed to the present able Superintendent.

Not only did he sincerely believe himself lacking in skill but also he could not anticipate with any relish another confined and sedentary assignment. But his protest was believed to arise from his well-known modesty, and no serious attention was paid to it. When he learned that his appointment stood unchanged, he wrote wistfully to Jerome Bonaparte:

"Tell Mrs. B—— she has taken away a great part of my regret at leaving Baltimore by going away herself & diminished my reluctance to reach W.P. by placing herself there."

2

MARY and the children did not go with Robert when he left for the Academy on August 23, but returned joyously to Arlington to wait until the superintendent's house was ready for them. Unlike most women, Mary preferred to let her husband see to the arrangement of rooms and other domestic details, so she did not leave Arlington until the end of October. Their household furnishings were shipped on to the large pleasant two-story house, "a convenient house," so a daughter wrote on her arrival. It had "a fine garden with a pond in it & several meadows" and "quite a nice greenhouse with a splendid lemon tree in it."

In the absence of his family, Robert was again "solitary," but this time there was no faithful Spec to cheer him, for the little black-and-tan terrier had mysteriously disappeared during their last days in Baltimore. In lieu of the dog, he had "cajoled a kitten" to keep him company.

Although Custis was at the Academy, his father could visit him only during his free time on Saturdays. But he often watched his son from a distance as he drilled or marched with his corps, "when my eye is sure to distinguish him among his comrades & follow him over the plain."

This time when the family came, Annie and Agnes had stayed behind in Arlington with a governess-tutor. Daughter, Rob, and Milly were enrolled in the day school at the Point, but for Rooney, now in college preparatory years, the choice of a school presented a problem. Though the family believed he would "never do for any of the learned professions" and his grandmother thought him best suited for farming, his education was still a subject for much serious thought.

At the suggestion of Professors Mahan and Bailey, whose sons attended St. James' Academy, in Maryland, Lee considered that school, and another at Sing Sing, where Professors Bartlett and Church each had a son. The moderate tuition of the Maryland school appealed to Robert's frugality, but because of Rooney's disposition they decided to keep him nearer his father, so he was enrolled in a school in New York City.

Rooney had definite ideas about his future. He knew that a dragoon's life was the only one for him, and that he wanted to go to West Point. Tears would stream down his cheeks whenever his father reminded him "of the almost insurmountable difficulties to his procuring an app^t to W.P. & of my disapprobation of his application. I have however to give my consent to his making the attempt at the proper time."

214

Lee soon found that his duties made unrelenting demands on his patience and diplomacy in dealings with professors, instructors, tactical officers, the Secretary of War, the cadets, and with those parents whose sons were failing, or who requested special favors for them.

Nothing was too insignificant to be considered by him. Everything had to be read by him, debated, discussed when necessary, and either written about or acted on. His daily mail was staggering, and it is no wonder that he welcomed the sight of Markie's bold hand—"a relief to my eyes & a comfort to my heart"—in the stacks, and confessed that he often read her letters first, to hearten him for the day. He wished that she were his amanuensis:

"I should then have nothing to do but look at you Markie, which would soon restore my eyes."

The long hours (he reached his office at seven) passed in close work had soon affected his eyes.

His sense of order and innate artistic feeling prompted him, no matter where he was, to better his surroundings. By October, he had ready for approval a list of recommendations based on the sound fundamental principle that improvement brings increased efficiency, which in turn equals greater over-all economy. He saw the need for stables for the dragoon and artillery horses (then without shelter); for more horses (since only ten were fit for service); for new saddles; additional officers' quarters; more barracks; a tower clock; enlargement of the cadet hospital; improvement of the roads; and an increase in the water supply, which could be made by tapping Buttermilk Falls and enlarging the present reservoir. He requested two thousand dollars to build a new wharf, and a moderate additional sum to buy fencing to enclose the grounds; and he renewed the request made by the last board of visitors, that the unsafe and unsightly riding hall be replaced. Before the year's end, his recommendations had been approved.

A revision of Academy rules, the raising of academic standards, and the tightening up on discipline were his next undertakings. "The heads of the Academic Departments were relieved from teaching and made responsible for the instruction

215

of cadets." The hour of reveille was changed to conform to sunrise; except for those of the First Class about to graduate, cadets were not allowed to wear whiskers and they were prohibited from getting drunk either on or off limits.

The following spring Lee was proposing a new uniform dress cap. He recalled from his own cadet days that the cap was "heavy, harsh & uncomfortable to the head. The black patent leather crown when exposed to the hot sun in summer is particularly objectionable, causing headache, dizziness, &c."

Before his first year was out, he was convinced that his health was "failing fast," a theory in keeping with his belief that only an active outdoor life could insure good health. When working in mud and water up to his armpits at Cockspur Island, in the intense heat and cold on the Mississippi, and the "doses of heated granite" at the Rip Raps, his health was perfect. Even from Mexico, where pestilence was prevalent, he had written of himself:

"There are few men more hearty or more able to bear exposure & fatigue."

But once confined to an office, he began to speak of specific ailments and general decline. As soon as he was released, his customary good health was miraculously restored.

To secure proper exercise and relaxation, he rode Grace Darling five or ten miles every day; Rob usually jogged beside him on Santa Anna. Lee kept both their mounts at a steady trot, riding the dragoon seat with no posting and insisting over Rob's protests that the "hammering" was good for him.

Whenever he could, he accompanied his sons and their friends on their Saturday tramps over the hills and marshes in search of pheasant and woodcock, or fished with them for speckled trout in the mountain streams; and in the long summer evenings he took his daughters rowing across the river.

He gave swimming lessons to Rob and his best friend, Professor Guilford Bailey's son, and presented Rob with his first sled and ice skates, teaching him how to use both. He was not too preoccupied with his own work to watch his children's grades, sharing their triumphs and helping them over the hurdles.

To encourage Rob to be neat, Lee asked him to keep his room in the same order that was required of cadets, and even gave it a daily inspection until the tidiness became habitual.

There was a very congenial group of men on the faculty. Many of them were younger officers who had served with Lee in the Mexican War. They had organized a fencing, riding, and chess club, and a Shakespeare and Napoleon Club. Lee went to the meetings whenever he had time.

Evenings of whist were also popular, chiefly because of the presence of ladies, and there were many formal and informal parties and musical evenings at the professors' and officers' houses. The concert season for officers and cadets lasted through the winter. Each family subscribed a sum toward the salaries of the musicians and their leader, Mr. Apelles, who was an accomplished violinist and often gave solo performances.

Concerts for the officers were held in the library, but the cadets' were in the fencing hall which was, in the opinion of a Lee daughter, "much too small & the music very loud." She admitted, though, that it was "necessary to have it almost deafening to drown the noise made in the background by some cadets who appear to come for that purpose. Even those who accompany ladies, keep up a steady stream of conversation, hollowing in ones ears till they are half cracked."

The Hon. Governeur Kemble lived at Cold Springs, across the Hudson. For fifty years, his hospitality had been famed. In the days of Lee's cadetship, Colonel Thayer was his most frequent guest, and now Lee went each week to what one Academy professor called "meetings of the world's foremost intellects."

Dinners on these occasions were always "composed of many small dishes, besides fat turkeys and domestic fowls . . . the only objection . . . was the danger of eating too much. The wines were good, especially the port and sherry. Champagne wine he did not favor and only gave one glass unless it was specially called for. He disliked cigars also, but would pass his gold snuff-box around the table at the end of dinner."

The discussions which followed the meal

embraced every subject that claims the attention of civilized man— the policy of governments; the habitudes engendered by climate, race, and occupation; the laws and rites of various nations and ages; sculpture, history, politics . . . civil and military biography, poetry, and manners . . . such was the urbanity of the guests that everyone was allowed, without interruption, to state his opinions.

Lee inaugurated the pleasant custom of honoring each faculty bride with a ball. The newly married Mrs. Theophile M. D'Ormieulx, wife of the Principal Assistant Professor of French, remembered that when it was her turn, "We were most kindly received by Col. and Mrs. Lee, and I was taken in to supper by the Colonel himself.

"The table was covered with the Custis and Lee silver, superb candelabra, and four large silver wine-coolers which had been General Washington's, belonging to a set of six. . . ."

Speaking of "the kindly attentions of all the officers to the wives of their comrades," Mrs. D'Ormieulx wrote:

"A lady was rarely allowed to buffet alone in a snow storm, and I recall often meeting the Superintendent, Col. Lee, on my way to market of a bitter winter day, who would join me saying:

" 'Going to buy your little beefsteak, Mrs. D'Ormieulx, so am I, and will you allow me to offer you my arm?' "

There were four men at the Point to whom Lee was especially drawn. There were two Virginians, Major Robert S. Garnett, Commandant of Cadets, and Major George H. Thomas, Instructor of Artillery and Cavalry; a young man from Maine, Captain Seth Williams, the Academy's Adjutant, and Robert W. Weir, the handsome and talented Professor of Drawing.

Weir, who had studied art in Italy and was establishing a reputation as one of the important American painters of the century, persuaded Lee to sit for him.

The portrait, a spirited and pleasing likeness, was not finished until after Lee had left the Academy. When it was done, Weir presented it to Mary, who was critical of it.

Afraid that Mary's outspokenness might have caused her to criticize it in Weir's presence, and hurt him, Robert wrote to her from his new post in Texas:

I am truly sorry you are not altogether satisfied with Mr. Weir's portrait. . . . I hope you did not at least express your disappointment to him. He was very kind & earnest in his efforts, & desired success. I wished it as a present to you, but he would not accept any compensation & said he desired to present it himself & made such a point of it I had to yield.

[He explained further:] Much allowance . . . must be made for him, & it cannot be considered more than a sketch. He painted it at night, that being the only part of the day when I was not occupied, & the strong light shining in my eyes was so painful that I was obliged to keep them shut except when he wanted them.

As Superintendent, Lee had to entertain a great deal officially. On Tuesday, November 8, he gave a large dinner for his classmates who were holding a reunion. It was originally intended to be solely for men—a "he dinner" as Robert termed such gatherings—but with the arrival of a Virginia kinswoman, he persuaded Mary and her cousin to attend. The Lee daughters arranged the table, as they always did for these occasions. Agnes recalled how carefully this must be done since everything had to be "just right for Papa's scrutinizing eye."

A week later, there was a "grand dinner" to honor General Robles of the Mexican Army; and within a few days, another for General Scott. Christmas was celebrated by "a grand party to all of our cadet acquaintances." There were so many banquets that the children at last became "heartily sick" of them, though they felt certain that such events were "Pa's *delight*."

Rob remembered "how genial and bright" his father was on such occasions, and "how considerate of everybody's comfort of mind and body. He was always a great favorite with the ladies, especially the young ones. His fine presence, his gentle, courteous manners and kindly smile put them at once at ease with him."

When cadets from the Third and Fourth Class came to tea, or to the substantial Saturday suppers, many felt awkward in what must be an awesome presence. Then Lee would "address himself to the task of making them feel comfortable and at home." As the girls grew older, they helped entertain the cadets, but when they first came to the Point they were as ill at ease as the young men, and stayed upstairs or in the garden rather than enter a roomful of boys. Lee professed surprise at the large numbers of cadets who came to call, uninvited, on Saturdays, for he was certain they must find "the Supt. & his dame dull commodities in the interchange of social pleasure."

Cadet Lunsford Lomax, whose grandfather had fought in Lee's Legion, was a regular Saturday caller. He was particularly impressed with Lee's physical beauty and wrote his mother that he was the "handsomest man I have ever known, just like a marble model." Shortly after receiving this letter, Mrs. Lomax, who had not seen Robert for a number of years, met him again during the Christmas season at a reception at Colonel Cooper's Washington home. "I had forgotten that he was such a handsome man," she wrote in her diary that night. Recalling her son's description, she qualified it: "Handsome, yes, but not like marble. Colonel Lee is very human, kind, calm, and definite. The cadets are fortunate to have a superintendent to whom they can look up to with whole hearted admiration and respect—That means a great deal to youth."

Custis, Jerome Bonaparte, Jr., and John Pegram were also regular Saturday visitors, and often brought with them a lad who quickly ingratiated himself by his amiable ways, his humor, and his fine singing voice. His last name was Stuart, but he was known to his comrades as "Beauty" or by his first three initials, "J.E.B." Not too many years hence Lee would see much of this young man and come to value his particular talents.

Still another Saturday "regular" was Lee's nephew, Fitzhugh Lee or "Fitz," the eldest son of Smith Lee. He was regular, that is, when he was not under arrest or walking the post, for he was a carefree, hearty boy who stood low in scholarship but high in the estimate of his friends as a boon companion. He regarded some of the Academy regulations as made to be broken, thereby causing his Uncle Robert embarrassment. "I have not seen Fitz. to speak to him for almost six months until a few evenings ago," his Cousin Agnes wrote. "He is so full of mischief he is always getting into trouble." And later she reported: "Fitzhugh Lee, our first cousin . . . he got into a scrape poor fellow & his punishment is walking post & he is not allowed to visit." Twice the Superintendent had to recommend dismissal or court-martial when, in company with several other cadets, Fitz slipped off after taps to Benny Havens'. He was not dismissed, though this was not due to any interference on the part of his uncle, who treated his case with impartiality.

Custis, on the other hand, was paying strict attention to his studies, having worked his way up to the head of the class, where he was to stay. The family was very proud of him, particularly since he was several years younger than most of his classmates, and because, as his sister noted, "he was born and educated in Virginia where 'tis thought people are so lazy."

One day, Lee was pleased to receive a call from Major Thomas J. Jackson, a Virginian and West Pointer who had distinguished himself with the artillery in Contreras and Chapultepec. Later, he would be known to the world as "Stonewall" Jackson. He had recently returned from fighting the Seminoles, and had been offered a professorship in Natural and Experimental Philosophy at Virginia Military Institute. He wondered if Lee would recommend him. As they sat and talked, Robert was somewhat surprised and perhaps secretly amused to see Jackson suddenly lift one arm straight up in the air and hold it in this position for the rest of the interview. He did this, he explained, in order to allow the blood to run back into his body and so lighten the limb, for he was certain that one arm was unduly heavy, and one leg larger than the other. Regardless of such idiosyncrasies, of which Jackson had more than the usual share, Lee knew that he had ability, and was happy to recommend him.

Although Mary's health was never better than "fair," and

221

often much worse, she passed each pleasant morning at work in the garden. The first spring, she set out flowers from the greenhouse, and roots and cuttings from Arlington, so that by the next spring the garden was a profusion of lilies of the valley, tulips, and roses, a sight of which Robert talked in his personal letters. She took walks with the children to all the scenic spots, even climbing to the top of the Crow's Nest.

It was not unusual for her to have the house full of guests —her parents, Aunt Maria, the Talcotts, Smith Lee, and Markie—among them at least one charming young woman to whom Robert could play the gallant, and sigh when she left: "Now I have nothing bright to look at!" Mary had not often taken an active part in the social life on a post. But she did here. She gave Christmas and Valentine parties for the cadets, and held open house during the New Year, when "from morning till night the house was filled by officers & cadets; dinner was dispensed with by most of us while 'sweets' of all kinds supplied its place," Agnes wrote.

In 1853, Jefferson Davis became Secretary of War, replacing C. M. Conrad, who, in response to political pressure, had often reversed Lee's decisions on such important matters as cadet dismissal, thereby damaging the maintenance of discipline. Davis proved incorruptible, as well as understanding of Lee's problems, and gave him unquestioned support. The two men formed a friendship based on mutual admiration and respect. This remained staunch so long as Lee held the subordinate position, but with the coming of the Civil War, when his military reputation threatened to obscure Davis', relations became strained, and a break was averted only by Lee's refusal to quarrel.

Davis recognized Lee's administrative talents and his genius for organization, and was aware of the importance of his fine personal appearance and impressive manners, though he felt that Lee's noted fondness for young people was perhaps his foremost qualification. When Davis came to pay an official three-day visit during Lee's second year, he was surprised to note the number of gray hairs on the Superintendent's head. When he mentioned it, Lee "confessed that the cadets did exceedingly worry him, and then it was perceptible that his sympathy with young people was rather an impediment than a qualification for the superintendency," Davis felt. Though he found the Superintendent somewhat worn, the Academy showed great improvement, and Davis was enthusiastic in his praise of Lee's vision and energy.

This fondness for young people was manifested by a paternal interest in each cadet. He watched carefully over his progress and grades by means of the weekly reports, and discussed any problems with the instructors, or with the boy himself. Whenever he felt that a lad might be helped over a fit of idleness by receiving an encouraging word or a bit of tactful advice from home, he made this suggestion to parents. If a cadet were ill, Lee did not allow the parents to be kept in suspense about their son's condition but wrote frequent and sympathetic letters, assuring them that the boy was receiving the best of care.

He took personal pride in those cadets who were in the "immortal section," and invited them to tea or supper as an acknowledgment of his appreciation of their hard work. He was never happier than when he could say to a parent, as he did to one beaming mother as he held her hand: "Never worry about your boy, dear lady. He is a very promising young man." But in those boys who piled up demerits through indolence or delinquency, he took even more of an interest.

He did not encourage spies and talebearers to augment his regular channels of discovering erring cadets. One afternoon when he and Rob were riding up a wooded glen far beyond Academy limits, they came on three cadets who, at sight of them, hurdled a wall beside the road and took to the forest. Lee rode along in silence for some time before he asked Rob:

"Did you know those young men? But no; if you did, don't say so. I wish boys would do what is right, it would be so much easier for all parties!"

He said no more, and he made no effort to find out who they were.

When it was certain that a boy must be dismissed because of his inability to do the work, Lee often suggested to his parents that he be allowed to resign before the examinations, to spare him the mortification of failure. Whenever he could, he included in these letters some encouraging word concerning the young man's good character or his efforts to succeed.

He considered dismissal of cadets "the most unpleasant office I am called on to perform," and the time of the June examinations was "a wearisome & painful season" because "some of my young friends will have to leave us." It distressed him that they had not listened to his warnings. After signing the last orders, he always took personal leave of each one, wishing him success and happiness in the future.

He felt that many cases of dismissal might be prevented if the system of reckoning demerits were changed from a twelve-month basis to six months. Being thoroughly conversant with the reasoning of boys, he knew that if the cadet were to face the count every six months, he would be less likely to procrastinate his reforming. His suggestion was approved, and the soundness of his reasoning was soon proved: at the end of the first six months after its inauguration, only two Fourth-Class cadets had chalked up more than the maximum one hundred demerits.

Since one erring cadet later achieved international renown in the art world, his case is of interest. He was James McNeill Whistler, the son of the distinguished West Point graduate, George Washington Whistler who, after graduation, taught drawing at the Academy, and then resigned to lay out many of the country's first railroads; and at the invitation of the Tsar, became superintending engineer for the railroad from St. Petersburg to Moscow. His brilliant, witty son chafed at the limited field of study, at the food, the clothes, the drill, discipline, and the lack of humor. Once, when reported for an absence from parade, his defense was:

"If I was absent without your knowledge or permission, sir, how did you know I was absent?"

When he could not give the date for the Battle of Buena Vista, the history professor by way of admonition asked:

"What would you do if, as a West Point man, you were asked this question at a dinner party, and could not answer?"

224

"Do?" Whistler replied indignantly. "Why, I should refuse to associate with people who would talk of such things at dinner!"

At the end of his third year, June, 1854, he was asked during finals to define silicon.

"A gas," said Jimmy.

For deficiency in chemistry, a general indifference to other subjects (with consequent low grades), and a few infractions of rules which added up to 135 demerits, Lee had to recommend dismissal. Whistler appealed, asking for re-examination in chemistry, but after a careful review of the case, Lee decided the appeal was unjustified. Years later, after Whistler had become a famous painter, he was one day talking about his cadetship.

"Had silicon been a gas, I would have been a major general!" he remarked drily.

Rumor that Lee was "dissatisfied" with his post had reached his friend Jerome Bonaparte, who made the mistake of mentioning it to him. "I am not *dissatisfied*," Robert replied in annoyance.

Nor has any soldier cause to be while endeavouring to perform his duty. That duty may not be pleasant to him, & there may be circumstances attending it, distasteful & impalatable, but while assigned to its performance, he has no right to be dissatisfied, much less express it. . . . I have more at heart the prosperity of the Academy than my own pleasure, while under my charge I shall administer it to the best of my ability. But when called upon, shall relinquish that charge with more cheerfulness than I felt reluctance in undertaking it.

In April, 1853, the family was overwhelmed with grief at the unexpected death of Mrs. Custis—"one day in the garden with her flowers, the next with her God," as Robert explained its suddenness to Markie, then in London. She had wakened with a headache, but suspecting nothing unusual, had gone shopping with her granddaughters to Alexandria. The next morning the headache was worse, and the doctor was called, though he found nothing to cause alarm. But when he came back on Saturday, her condition caused him to "look very grave" and "Mama was written and telegraphed for," Agnes wrote in her journal. When it was apparent to her that she was dying, her chief concern was for her daughter:

"How terribly she will be shocked when she hears this," she said.

Then turning to Annie, who was weeping unrestrainedly at her bedside, she asked: "How can you cry so?"

Both granddaughters then climbed on her bed and she took them in her arms, and talked lovingly to them while her husband knelt beside the bed, imploring God to spare her.

That night Agnes entered in her diary: "My darling Grandmama has passed away from this earth! O I can't believe it! . . . Poor Grandpa is almost heartbroken."

For many years, Robert had been signing his letters to Mrs. Custis "your devoted son," and now the loss of this woman whom he acknowledged was to him "all that a mother could be" was overwhelming.

I have no language to express what I feel, or words to tell what I suffer. The blow was so sudden & crushing, that I yet shudder at the shock & feel as if I had been arrested in the course of life & had no power to resume my onward march . . . But well as I know the happiness it has brought to her, I feel the anguish it has left to me. May God give me the necessary strength.

Almost a year later, he was still grieving over what he called his "irreparable loss."

Since boyhood, Robert had taken Sunday worship and daily prayer as a matter of course, though religion was incompatible with the irrepressible flow of animal spirits in his young manhood. But the impact of Mrs. Custis' sudden death caused him to think seriously about religion for the first time, hoping to find consolation for his loss, and on July 17, he joined his daughters Mary and Annie and was confirmed by Bishop John Johns in Christ Church, Alexandria.

Being a man of emotion, he accepted religion without question. His interpretation was simple and literal. His deity participated closely in human affairs. "His was a practical, every-day religion, which supported him all through his life," one of his sons wrote, "enabled him to bear with equanimity every reverse of fortune, and to accept her gifts without undue elation."

226

As soon as Mary received the telegram, she left for Arlington, but did not arrive in time to see her mother alive. The household was in turmoil, and her father in a state of collapse, but to everyone's surprise, she assumed immediate charge and proved capable of carrying the whole burden alone. On the day of her coming, she conducted morning worship, forgotten in the confusion, and after breakfast walked over the grounds to select a site for the grave, chosing a secluded spot in a grove close to the house. She nursed her father, who developed pneumonia, and kept so busy that she was unable to think about her own sorrow. Robert's duties at the Point prevented him from coming to the funeral. He did not join her until July 6, and was amazed to find that she had borne up so well.

That fall, when they were ready to return to West Point, they persuaded Mr. Custis to come with them, though he was reluctant to leave his beloved home and "Tom Tita," the great orange cat who was his constant attendant. New scenes and interests soon cheered him, but Robert, well knowing the old gentleman's belief that his affairs demanded his unremitting attention, feared he would not stay satisfied for long. To divert his mind, they kept him busy. When Rooney, who had failed to get his appointment to the Military Academy, left for Harvard College, his father went with him and took Mr. Custis along. After they had settled Rooney, they went on to see Niagara Falls; and when they returned, Mary met them in New York City and took her father to see the Crystal Palace, attended the theater with him, and visited friends. But just as soon as the Major had his fill of the metropolis, he found that "business" required him to return to Arlington at once.

Knowing that his spirits would soon droop again and his health suffer, Robert felt it was Mary's place to go to her father. Yet, her presence was also necessary for the welfare of the children who, as he wrote, "require more care than my duties permit me to bestow." While they were seeking a solution, Markie, who had recently returned from Europe, offered to stay at Arlington and care for Mr. Custis, "supplying to him the place of his only daughter."

Washington Irving was among the distinguished guests who attended the examinations (for the public was allowed to be present), witnessed the grand review in honor of the board of visitors, dined with Lee, and watched the graduation exercises for the class of 1854 which saw Custis Lee as No. 1 man. General Scott, his daughter, son-in-law, and a large party of friends also came to the ceremonies, arriving unheralded at the Superintendent's house.

After Lee had escorted the General and his party over the grounds and through the buildings, and ordered a salute fired in his honor, he left them to rest until dinner, and returned to his office to finish the letter he had been writing to Markie when interrupted by Scott's coming. He was worried, he told her, about the short notice to the servants, and the menu. "But for an Arlington ham, & some of my Shanghai chickens, which I had proposed for my solitary dinner, I should doubt whether their hunger could be appeased, as ten additional guests will have to be provided for. But having given all the required directions, I will wait with patience & *hope* for their execution."

This board of visitors had nothing but praise for the Superintendent: "The board cannot conclude this report," they wrote in summing up, "without bearing testimony to the eminent qualifications of the superintendent for the honorable and distinguished post assigned to him by the government. Services conspicuous in the field, and when our country was engaged in a war with a foreign nation, have lost none of their luster in the exalted position he so worthily fills."

They had two suggestions. In order to include important subjects then omitted from the curriculum, and to allow time for new appointees to take remedial instruction, they advised that the course be extended an additional year. They also recommended that Spanish be offered. Jefferson Davis approved both suggestions, and they were introduced the following semester.

Custis Lee had "a violent chill" which kept him from taking part in the last hop, the last parade, from watching the fireworks, and receiving in person his diploma and the honors of being No. 1 man. In the judgment of his sister, Agnes, he missed little by not hearing the graduation address by

Senator James Asheton Bayard: "It was the longest, most uninteresting thing about 'unlimited extension', etc. Stupid to a degree." But she considered the music at the parade, "beautiful—'Home Sweet Home' went to many a heart," and the fireworks display which was ended by setting fire to two tar barrels and rolling them into Execution Hollow, was a "grand sight."

After guard mount, the graduates came to the Superintendent's house to say good-by. They were all "in the highest spirits," Agnes remembered, "& amused themselves & us with the variety of their citizens dress."

At the end of summer neither Agnes, Annie, nor Mildred could bear to think of leaving Arlington. They asked to be allowed to stay with a governess, but their father did not approve, this time. "We have expostulated, and begged and reasoned & Papa is inexorable," Agnes complained on the eve of their departure. The afternoon before going, the girls tearfully visited "each loved haunt" for the final time, and called on the servants, bringing a parting gift to each.

Robert left home on a Saturday morning. "We were soon whirling in the express train to Baltimore," Agnes wrote, for they planned to pass several days with Ann Marshall in her new home on Culloch Street. With Robert went Daughter, who had an infected foot and had to use crutches; Rob, Rooney, Annie, Agnes, and the dog, "Tip." Their mother, grandfather, and Mildred were coming later.

They found Mrs. Marshall "well, for her, and walking all about the house." After visits with the Bonapartes, the McKims, and other Baltimore friends, they boarded the train for New York. Their party excited much sympathy and attention, for Rooney and his father were carrying Daughter, Annie was toting the crutches, Rob had Tip in his arms, and Agnes was loaded down with four "large and heavy cloaks." She remembered with amusement that "whenever we had to change cars, the conductor would scream 'Jack' or 'Bill' to come & help a lady who couldn't walk. Instantly two or three great men would rush up & lift us, cloaks, crutches, dog, & people up or down whether we would or no."

The year 1855 proved a busy one for Lee: Congress granted the necessary appropriations for the new riding hall and clock tower, for additions to the officers' quarters, and the cadet hospital. Seeking still further improvements, he had included in his annual estimates an application for funds to build a gashouse to provide light for cadet barracks, to construct houses for the unmarried officers (he had previously forwarded plans), and to enlarge the professors' dwellings.

Regardless of the press of work, he kept up his personal correspondence and included in his busy schedule some theater-going and visiting in New York. Whenever he went to the city, he was nearly always charged with some errand for Mary, his daughters, or even Markie. On one occasion when Markie had given him a dollar to buy some embroidery thread, he said to her afterwards: "I did not discover until too late to count, that I had only expended half the money you gave me to make the purchase. I asked for eight twists, & found they were charged on the bill at 50¢. I still . . . have another half dollar to expend for you. This comes of your having insisted on my taking the money. I am so poor an accountant I make mistakes under such circumstances."

Ever since 1853, the Secretary of War had been urging Congress to strengthen its regular armed forces for frontier duty, since Indian troubles were constant. But it took the massacre of Lieutenant John L. Grattan (who had graduated from West Point in 1853) and thirty of his men, by the Sioux Indians near Fort Laramie, to prod Congress to act. On March 3, 1855, four new regiments—two cavalry and two infantry— were created specifically for frontier duty. Jefferson Davis was perhaps aware that Lee was restive in his present post, and appointed him lieutenant colonel of the Second Cavalry under the command of Colonel Albert Sidney Johnston. The First Cavalry was commanded by Colonel E. V. Sumner, and Joe Johnston was its lieutenant colonel.

On March 5, as Agnes was walking along the snowy path toward home, Cadet Stockton waved a newspaper and called to her:

"Oh, Miss Lee, Miss Lee, do you know your father is Lieutenant Colonel in one of the new regiments?"

She thanked him, and in her words, "sprang on to tell the news first at home but Dr. Cayler was just informing Mama so I ran upstairs to be first there."

The family's initial reaction was favorable. They were pleased at the thought of promotion (for Lee was still only a captain of engineers with the brevet rank of colonel), and a return to Arlington. But Arlington lost its appeal when it was remembered that "Pa'a" would be going far off to "those Western wilds."

Robert was delighted to be able to leave the superintendency, and pleased at the prospect of promotion, but the idea of separation from the corps in which he had served for more than twenty years was a sad one.

My *future plans* form the constant subject of my thoughts [he told Markie]. Personal consideration or convenience would not induce me to sever my connexion with my Corps, or to separate myself from my family. And the thought that my presence may be of some importance to the latter, or necessary to my children is bitter in the extreme. Still in a military point of view I have no other course, & when I am obliged to act differently, it will be time for me to quit the service. My trust is in the mercy & wisdom of a kind Providence who ordereth all things for our own good. . . .

The change from my present confined & sedentary life, to one more free & active, will certainly be more agreeable to my feelings & serviceable to my health. But my happiness can never be advanced by separation from my wife, children, & friends—You know how painful it will be to part from you. But I shall not anticipate that it will be for long.

By staying in the engineer corps there was little chance for Lee to advance beyond his present rank in time of peace, but in the army the picture was different. There were "some forty or fifty officers mostly in higher commissions, rendered non-effective by infirmities of age, by wounds or chronic diseases," who must be replaced. Lee's champion, General Scott, had recently said to William Preston:

"I tell you, that if I were on my death-bed tomorrow, and the President of the United States should tell me that a great battle was to be fought for the liberty or slavery of the country, and asked my judgment as to the ability of a commander, I would say with my dying breath, 'Let it be *Robert E. Lee!*'" It was obvious that Scott would do anything within his power to help Lee, and since he had been restored to favor and promoted to lieutenant general, he was able to do so.

On March 15, Robert wrote his letter of acceptance to General Totten. It had been a difficult decision: "In thus severing my connexion with the Corps of Engineers, I cannot express the pain I feel in parting from its Officers, or my grateful sense of your constant kindness and consideration. My best exertions have been devoted to its service, and my warmest feelings will be cherished for its memory."

Jefferson Davis was particularly pleased at Lee's acceptance, for having long admired "his bold, graceful horsemanship," he felt that "the son of Light-Horse Harry Lee now seemed to be in his proper element."

The physical inroads upon his health were far less than he imagined. Only his eyes had really suffered, and during the last year he had reluctantly taken to wearing spectacles. His equanimity, however, had not escaped unscathed. The tedious and demanding work had taken its toll, and it was observed how often during those final months his neck and head would give a twitch or jerk, which was a certain sign that his patience was at an end. When complimenting a friend upon his ability to keep his temper imperturbable during stress and confinement, he opined significantly: "What a blessing it would be if it could only be possessed by the Supt. of the Mil. Acady!"

On Saturday of the week before the Lees left the Point, the cadets serenaded them, playing among other pieces "Home, Sweet Home," and "Carry Me Back to Ole Virginy." The next Wednesday, about nine in the evening, the band gave them "a splendid serenade."

All throughout Passion Week, they were packing, and selling off all furnishings but those in the library and parlor. On the Saturday prior to their departure, the cadets called to say good-by. It proved a trying time for several young men who had lost their hearts to the Superintendent's vivacious, black-eyed daughters, and there were many sighs, and tender pressures of the hand at the final good-by, and invitations on the part of the girls to stop at Arlington during the summer furlough.

The next day was Easter Sunday, and though it was raining hard, the Lees went to church. Throughout the service Agnes sat gazing "sadly for the last time on Mr. Weir's beautiful picture above the altar."

Monday it was still "pouring rain," but since everything was packed and all arrangements for departure made, the family—which included Agnes, Annie, Mildred, Rob (again carrying the dog), Daughter (still unable to wear her shoe for her foot had "not responded to leeches & blisters"), and their cousin, Helen Peter, boarded the omnibus. They found the wharf "crowded with umbrellas shielding officers & some ladies come to bid a 'last, long farewell.' "

Though parting with these loyal friends was hard, and tears glistened in Robert's eyes as he shook each hand, as soon as they had left the landing he had felt his heart "leaping" at the thought of returning to Arlington, "where my affections & attachments are more strongly placed than at any other place in the World."

⇢⟫ V ⟪⇠

Exile to the "Desert of Dulness"

1855 ⋆ 1857

V. Exile to the "Desert of Dulness"

THE TRIP to New York was a pleasant one. The adults in the party enjoyed the company of Judge and Mrs. Wayne, who had been visiting at the Point, and the younger children were kept amused by Jimmy Cayler, the son of Dr. John M. Cayler, the post surgeon.

In New York City, the Lees stopped over one day with Mrs. Cook, a friend from Fort Hamilton days. In spite of the continuing rain, they went to Mr. Cozzens' house to look at his fine collection of paintings of West Point, and visited the Academy of Design. Their parents turned back, but the girls found the downpour no deterrent to going on to the Crystal Palace, where they were especially "impressed with the statuary and paintings." The following day they left for Baltimore, their party joined by Mrs. Winfield Scott and a pretty young bride, Mrs. Henry Halleck.

At French Town, they took the steamer to Baltimore. The children found this exciting as it was their first trip on the Chesapeake Bay, and the entire family "ate with relish the delicious supper of fresh perch." After landing in Baltimore at eleven P.M., they drove directly to Mrs. Marshall's, two carriages being necessary to hold them all. "The four chicks being considered models of propriety were put in one carriage alone." Mrs. Marshall was "looking very badly," in the opinion of Agnes. "One foot is sprained & she only uses one arm a little. She hasn't been out of bed since October."

There was little excuse for gaiety there, but right next door lived Cousin Anne Carter, who had a large and jolly family, augmented considerably by "crowds of cousins now staying with them." Among these visiting cousins was Charlotte Wickham of Shirley. The Lee girls thought her "very pretty and sweet" and "liked her very much." Shortly she was to capture Rooney's heart.

They dined with the Bonapartes, and had a short visit with

the McKims, then left for Washington—all except Daughter, who had decided to stay with her aunt. The Arlington carriage was at the station to meet them. "We soon jumped into our carriage," Agnes wrote, "& after putting Pa down at the War Office started for home." Though the pace was "brisk," to her "it seemed an age before we dashed around the garden fence" and up to the door where she "sprang out on the steps" to "kiss Grandpa & Cousin Markie."

There was little leisure for Robert to enjoy Markie's bright presence, or spring on the verdant hill, for each weekday he rode into Washington to finish his accounts. During those hours passed at home he found much to demand serious thought. Mr. Custis was now seventy-five, and called on him for help with his complicated accounts, which involved proceeds, expenditures, and losses on his three estates, a mill on Four Mile Run, Smith's Island, and property in Washington and Alexandria. Earlier this year, Lee had written him: "I am as much horrified as you are at the results of the settlement of Mr. Nelson's [an overseer] accounts. . . . I did not expect so large a balance against you. . . . I think you had better put the accounts in the hands of a regular accountant & get his decision on them. I should like very much to examine them myself, but there is no hope of my being able to do so before summer." But Mr. Custis had waited for Robert's return.

In addition to these financial problems, the Arlington house and outbuildings were badly in need of repair, for the Major, always indifferent to such matters and inclined to indolence, had since his wife's death become even more inattentive to these details. Robert could not order repairs, he could only suggest and urge them. The only ones his father-in-law approved were the installation of a furnace to heat the whole house, and completion of the unfinished "Big Room," making it into the drawing room that was originally planned.

Robert drew up minute plans for both projects, ordering the marble mantelpieces and facings for the twin fireplaces in the drawing room, and a crystal chandelier for the ceiling. He worked on these details up to the day before his departure for Louisville to take temporary command of the Second Cavalry.

That day, among other letters, he wrote to Robert E. Launitz of New York City, enclosing a sketch for the monument to be placed on Mrs. Custis' grave. He wanted it made "of the best monumental marble of full size & dimensions & to be perfect in every respect, the base being of granite. It is desired that the wreath contain some *lilies* of the *valley* & *heartsease* if practicable. On the plinth the name Mary L. Custis to be in raised letters;" on the reverse of the shaft, the words: "Blessed are the pure in heart for they shall see God."

He left for his post on Wednesday, April 18, taking with him the mare, Grace Darling, and sanguinely expecting to be back in one month. He had been at Louisville only a short time when he was ordered to Jefferson Barracks, Missouri, to take temporary command of Regimental Headquarters. There his time was spent in organizing and instructing recruits, and his temper was often tried by the inefficiency of the establishment, and the slowness with which his requisitions for clothing and supplies were treated. In a letter he described the state of one recruit, whose condition was typical, and how he handled the problem:

Yesterday at muster, I found one of the late arrivals in a dirty, tattered shirt & pants, with a white hat & shoes. . . . I asked him why he did not put on clean clothes. He said he had none. I asked if he could not wash & mend those. He said he had nothing else to put on. I then told him immediately after muster to go down to the river, wash his clothes, & sit on the bank & watch the passing steamboats till they dried, then mend them. This morning at inspection he looked as proud as possible, stood in the position of a soldier with his little fingers on the seams of his pants, his beaver cocked back & his toes sticking through his shoes, but his skin & solitary two garments were clean. He grinned happily at my compliments.

Whenever Robert was separated from his loved ones, he sought comfort in the company of small animals. At Jefferson Barracks he adopted a "fine puss" that had been "educated" by Colonel Sumner's daughter, though for Lee's taste, puss was "too fond of getting up on my lap & on my bed." But he was pleased that the cat followed him about the house where he was quartered, and amused when it stood "at the door in an attitude of defiance at all passing dogs."

Toward the end of September, he was temporarily detached from his regiment and detailed to serve as a member of a court-martial convening in Fort Leavenworth to hear charges brought against several officers at that post. When the court adjourned, instead of being sent back to his regiment, he was ordered to Fort Riley in western Kansas, for the trial of an assistant surgeon charged with deserting his post during a fatal epidemic that had claimed fifty-nine lives—among them a friend of Mary's, Mrs. Lewis Armistead.

He was greatly depressed by the testimony, and wrote a gloomy letter recounting all the unhappy details of these sudden deaths which often followed just a few hours after being stricken. He closed with the pessimistic reflection: "A soldier has a hard life & but little consideration."

From Fort Riley, he replied on November 8 to a letter from Mary in which she had complained about his distant assignment. He asked her to "take a happier view of things & not be dissatisfied because they do not accord more nearly with your views & wishes. We rarely know what is good for us & rarely see things as they really exist, so clouded is our vision by narrow selfishness, & often complain of what we ought not & blame others when the fault is on ourselves."

Before he had left home, they had decided to build a summerhouse. Now he urged her to go on with it and not wait for him to return (which she wanted to do), for he was certain that the rumor she had heard—that he would be ordered back to Washington for the winter—was groundless.

When finished with the trial at Fort Riley, he was ordered to attend another at Carlisle Barracks, Pennsylvania, and when that court adjourned, he took the long overland journey to West Point for yet one more court-martial. He considered this duty "tedious," though he was looking forward to returning to Arlington where he would await further orders.

When he reached home, he found Mary still fretting at their separation; yet when he suggested that she, Daughter, and Milly go with him wherever he should be ordered, she refused to leave her father. Her whimsicality seemed more pronounced than ever, and he hoped he could attribute it to the absence of their children, of whom she professed herself "bereft," for Annie and Agnes were at boarding school in Staunton; Rob was at Mr. Lippitt's "for one more term," Custis, on duty in Savannah (and staying with the Mackays); and Rooney, still at Harvard.

News of Rooney was not encouraging. Never of a studious disposition, he had found that college life offered many more diverting occupations than a strict application to books, and like his Uncle Carter Lee, he was soon exceeding his quarterly allowance and running deeply into debt. As his father described him: "He is a cheerful, affectionate fellow but I think is easily satisfied as to his daily amount of study & learning."

Rooney had become the most popular and prominent man in his class, for attributes that were more social than academic. He pulled the stroke oar on the crew, his classmate Horace Porter remembering that he was "the best oarsman I have ever seen." Tall (he was 6 feet 2 inches in his stocking feet), "largely built, handsome, genial, with liberal Virginia openness toward all he liked, he had also the Virginia habit of command and took leadership as his natural habit," his friend, Henry Adams, grandson of John Quincy Adams, described him.

Though his father was tolerant of indolence—"idleness is so agreeable to us all, that we must not blame too much the young for enjoying it"—he was continually on the alert for signs of undue waywardness in his sons, ever mindful of their inheritance. For a number of years Rooney's "careless & reckless disposition" had worried him. At this time, he was powerless to do more than write him tactfully. He knew he could expect little firmness from Mary toward this favorite son whose failings she excused and whose debts she paid from her private income.

On February 12, Lee left for San Antonio. Before taking the steamer, he stopped to see his sister, Ann, finding there was now fear that her lungs were afflicted.

The overland trip from Lavaca to San Antonio, Robert wrote, was most of the way knee deep in mud:

"With my breeches rolled up to the top of my boots I

plunged through regardless of its depth—followed by my faithful Achates Mr. Radziminski," a lieutenant in the Second Cavalry.

During the period of inactivity following his arrival in San Antonio on March 6, there was time for reflection. He doubted the wisdom of accepting a command that stationed him so far from the supervision of his family's interests. But as had been his practice for some time, he turned to his religion, reading the Bible and prayer book "to draw much comfort from their holy precepts & merciful promises."

The officers stationed at the garrison welcomed him warmly. He wrote Mary that he dined with a different family each day, and often took tea and supper with them as well. He was especially friendly with Major Robert H. Chilton, whose wife had been Laura Mason of Alexandria, and he enjoyed playing with their little girls, Emma and Laura. Still, he looked on his fortnight's stay in San Antonio as "a tedious time."

As soon as he received his orders to take command of four companies of cavalry stationed at Camp Cooper on the Clear Fork of the Brazos River, he hired for his cook and factotum a Frenchman who had served Colonel Hardee and was well recommended by him. Also, he wrote home, he had added to his "personal property some camp chairs, tables, a little crockery & some cooking utensils . . . being unwilling to go into the wilderness entirely unfurnished with the means of extending aid or hospitality to my friends. For myself, unless I can have things very nice, I care little for expedients."

His sense of economy was outraged at having to pay the same price for "common white crockery" as he had for French china bought in Baltimore. Lest he be suspected of extravagance, he wrote:

"I only got however 1 doz. plates, 4 dishes, 2 vegetables, ½ doz. cups & saucers, teapot, sugar, &c. I get very tired of *tin*, when used constantly."

On March 21, he said good-by to his friends, mounted Grace Darling, and took the road north to Fort Mason, 110 miles beyond. With him went the Frenchman and Lieutenant

Radziminski, who had, at Lee's suggestion, provided for the trip "a boiled ham, hard bread, a bottle of molasses, & one of extract of coffee"—little, he admitted, to strain the talents of his cook.

When he reached Fort Mason, Colonel Albert Sidney Johnston invited him to stay at his house until all arrangements were made for the trip to Camp Cooper.

Johnston was also a West Pointer of marked ability. Since his graduation three years before Lee, he had had a varied and interesting career both in and out of the army. He had served in the Black Hawk War against the Sac Indians, had been Secretary of War for the Republic of Texas, Inspector General on Butler's staff during the Mexican War, and a farmer on the Brazos River. In 1849, he had returned to the army as paymaster, staying in that post until selected by Jefferson Davis for his present command.

Lee accepted Johnston's offer, and on meeting Mrs. Eliza Johnston for the first time, was well impressed with her:

A very sweet & pretty woman, [he told Mary]. Is intelligent & well adapted to her position & life. She employs herself in teaching her children . . . 2 boys and a girl, & while superintending the preparation of their lessons, occupies herself in painting the birds & flowers of the country. She has much talent & is very satisfied & is anxiously looking forward to the time of arrival of spring flowers.

There is no doubt that Robert was thinking of his own lonely existence, and attempting to analyze Mary's disposition, wondering why, if so attractive and refined a woman as Eliza Johnston was "satisfied" and "well adapted to her position & life," Mary could not adapt herself, too. He admired another officer's wife, Mrs. Richard Johnson, also "*au fait* with camp life." He took tea with her twice, and was impressed with her management. "Though her living room was a canvass porch, her kitchen a tent, & her servants few, everything was nice," he took pains to tell Mary.

He now undertook the additional duties of housekeeper, and in his memorandum book for this period are found recipes for baked ham, "Good Biscuit," "Home-Made Drinks for the

Fields," and such helpful suggestions as "How To Clean Paint."

He was still gravely concerned over Rooney's disposition to incur debts, and wrote Mary from Fort Mason:

I doubt whether he knows his own indebtedness, & if he did, & it was all cancelled whether he would remain so. He inherits much of that disposition from both branches of his family, & does not seem to strive to overcome it, or to restrict his wishes to his circumstances. Those who live long enough will see how it will end, & I pray & trust it will end right [he concluded gloomily].

Mrs. Johnston was doubtless well impressed with Lee, but when he declined to stay at Fort Mason and testify in a court-martial then sitting on a slander case, she was vexed, and wrote in her diary for March 31 that he had first "humed and ha'd" before refusing to testify to the complaining witness' character as a gentleman. "A mean act in my opinion when he knows the mans reputation as well as he does. I suppose he feared to become unpopular." She had apparently forgotten that except for two weeks passed at Jefferson Barracks, Lee had been absent from his command until now, and knew little or nothing about the officer on trial.

On the thirtieth, Lee turned his horse's head "due North," as he wrote Eliza Stiles, and set out on the road to Camp Cooper, taking with him an escort of seven men and eight wagons. He had been told that such items as eggs "were not among the luxuries" in the wilderness, so he bought a few hens which he carried in a coop fastened behind his wagon. At the end of each day's march he let them out to feed, and was rewarded, he told his daughter, "with a considerable number of eggs" on the two hundred-mile journey.

He reached Camp Cooper on April 9, and was pleased to find that, unlike the part of Texas he knew, this country was fertile and rolling, well watered, lightly timbered, and contained large herds of deer, antelope, and thousands of wild horses. It was a paradise for hunters (there were several experts in each company), who were eager to bring in fresh meat for the mess; and it offered similar opportunities for foragers familiar with plant lore who returned with bunches of lamb's quarters and plantain for salad (excellent with bits of young pork, Robert wrote Eliza). There were also many predatory animals: spotted panthers, some as large as Bengal tigers; tawny, maneless lions; and a variety of small wildcats. To complete the picture of primitive wilderness, there was a bountiful supply of rattlesnakes, and Indian camps were just down the river.

Lee did not look at the red man through the eyes of a Longfellow or a Cooper; in fact, he found "the whole race extremely uninteresting." He explained his attitude in a letter to Eliza Stiles:

"We are on the best of terms with our neighbours the Camanches, & I am happy to believe that there is no love lost between us. I see more of them than I desire, & when I can be of no service take little interest in them."

When he first saw Chief Catumseh, "whom the Government is endeavouring to humanize," he wrote: "It will be uphill work, I fear."

The Indian was dressed in the shreds of a greasy coat of checked cotton, dirty corduroy leggings, and a battered "sixpenny straw hat." He took Lee in his embrace, and according to Robert, there followed "a long talk very tedious on his part, very sententious on mine. I hailed him as a friend as long as his conduct & that of the tribe deserved it, but would meet him as an enemy the first moment he failed to keep his word. The rest of the tribe (about a thousand, it is said) live north of us, & are hostile."

He found Catumseh's six wives, who wandered in and out of the army camp at will, distasteful to his sight, "their paint & ornaments rendering them more hideous than nature made them."

Not all his relations with the Indians were strained. When he was asked to prescribe for the sick head chief of the Southern Comanches, Ila-tem-a-se, who "wanted a big *medicine man*," he was amused that he had been chosen. He sent Eliza a colorful and spirited description of his call:

His lodges are only 2 miles below us, & when I presented myself before them on my big horse Bald Eagle, attended by an orderly dragoon, the explosion among curs, children & women, was tremendous. The medicine men rushed at me, made significant signs that I must disrobe before presenting myself before the august patient. I patiently sat on my horse till I ascertained what garment they considered most inimical to the practice of the healing art, which I learned to be the cravat. Then alighting, unbuttoning my coat & slipping off the noxious article, I displayed to their admiring eyes a blue check shirt, & was greeted by a general approving *humph*. The charm was fully developed, & I walked boldly in. The lodge was carpeted with Buffaloe robes. The sick man was stretched on his couch with his wives & servitors around him. His shield, bows and quiver were suspended outside, near which stood his favourite horse ready to be slain, to bear the spirit of his master to the far hunting ground. I thought him labouring under an attack of pleurisy—administered a loaf of bread & some sugar, of which I knew him to be very fond & which I carried with me, & told him, I would send a man to complete his cure. So in the evg the Dr. rode down with his steward and drugs & cupped him pretty freely, which I hope will restore him. . . .

Camp Cooper was a settlement entirely under canvas. Characteristically, Lee began to improve it even though he had been ordered to search the area for a better campsite. He sent fatigue parties to the oak groves north of the Clear Fork to cut logs and to quarry stone, and with these materials he set the men to building a kitchen, bakehouse, guardhouse, stables, and storehouses. When these projects were started, he turned his attention to making his own encampment as homelike as possible, planting a plot to vegetables, and tending to the needs of his hens, who had become very tame.

This morning I found an egg at my tent door, & a few minutes since another hen seems desirous of presenting me with another. After walking around my chair & peering up at my writing, she hopped upon my bed, but disliking such intimacy I rose to dislodge her when she skimmed across my table, upsetting my ink & rendering my letter so illegible that I have been obliged to write this one, & have consequently been more hurried than would otherwise have been.

When his rows and hills of cabbage, corn, and beans began to sprout, he had to fence the garden against the depredations of the hens, for whom he had already attacked the problem of a snakeproof dwelling. Hampered by the want of boards, he cleverly overcame this deficiency by setting up a "house of twigs" which he described in a letter to Annie:

I planted four posts in the ground & bored holes in each, three feet from the ground, in which I inserted poles for the floor, & around which were woven the branches that formed it. . . . The sides & top were formed in the same way, & the whole is covered with branches with their leaves on, which makes a shady house but furnishes little protection against rain. Soldier hens, however must learn not to mind rain. I converted the coop they came in, into nests.

He had been trying, he told his daughter, to find a cat, asking at every ranch in the area, but since coyotes and snakes destroyed all the vermin, cats were not needed, and it was impossible to find one. In the absence of a cat, he had adopted a rattlesnake for whose meals he captured frogs.

Here in the wilderness, he found the leisure to answer Eliza Stiles's last letter which, as he told her,

I have carried with me on all my wanderings. Have read it & reread it, & each perusal has brought me fresh & pleasant thoughts. Had I transferred to paper all the contemplated replies that occurred on these occasions you would have been overwhelmed. . . . I must tell you however I am encamped on a branch of the Brazos, many degrees West of you, though but a little South. I wish it was the Etowah, & that we were tributaries to the Alabama. I might then hope to see you. Here I have none.

[After describing his Comanche neighbors, he continued:] But I shall speak no more of this wild country. I wish to talk of you, your mother, sisters & all from Broughton St. I suppose this will find you at Etowah, enjoying your own home & the society of Mr. S., the boys & dear May Stiles [her daughter]. . . . I am glad to hear that Custis makes himself agreeable to your good mother. I hope she finds an improvement in the rising generation, & is thus cheered by the prospect of the advancement of mankind, for whose benefit she has done so much. I confess when I was with her, I was so taken up with her daughters, that I could make myself agreeable to no one. They were blessed creatures! . . . I suppose I am sent here for my sins. It is all right. I like the wilderness, & the

247

vicissitudes of camp life are no hardship to one. . . . Tell Mr. S. when he becomes Secry of War he must bring me in. . . . I hope you will all be together in Cass this summer & that I could be with you. Remember me to all & believe me always,

Yours,
R E Lee

In June, there came a welcome respite from the monotony of camp life when Lee took command of an expedition to find Chief Sahnaco, whose hostile tribes were raiding the settlements above San Antonio. He took with him four companies of cavalry, and several Delaware Indian scouts and a guide, Jim Shaw. But as he wrote to a friend, Sahnaco had

received notice of our movements from the Indians in our vicinity, scattered his people, & fled to the North. We divided also, in pursuit, & thus traversed 1600 miles of the most barren & least inviting country I have ever seen. It forms part of the high salt plains lying below New Mexico. Has but little water, grass or game, no trees, & as hot as a scorching sun on arid plains, can make it. The water is salt, brackish, bitter & sweet by turns, stagnant & tepid, at times even the mules refuse to drink it.

We caught as many Indians as bears, but the chief offender escaped out of the Dept. beyond which I was prohibited from going. On reaching Wichita I halted. . . . We lost no men & but few horses, but were not compensated for our labours.

The "Glorious Fourth" was celebrated by a thirty-mile march. As he wrote Mary:

"The sun was fiery hot, the atmosphere like the blast of a hot-air furnace, the water salt—still my feelings for my country were as ardent, my faith in her future as true, & my hopes for her advancement as unabated as they would have been under better circumstances."

By July 22, he was back at Camp Cooper, and wrote home that in spite of the hardships of those forty days, he had "enjoyed good health." Only the sedentary life prompted complaints.

Camp Cooper was sweltering unrelieved from an extended drought that wasted Lee's vegetable plot, and brought much sickness to the men.

A particularly promising young officer whom he had noted was Lieutenant George McGaw Dick, a West Point graduate in the class of 1855, and son of the Pennsylvania Congressman, John Dick. During Lee's absence young Dick had taken sick with what was diagnosed as "inflammation of the intestines," but he was now considered convalescent, and felt well enough to sit up and write letters home.

But on July 30, he had a relapse. The next night he died. His last words, as if to lessen the grief he saw on the faces of those gathered about his bed, were: "I am going to a better world." When he left the room, Lee returned to his tent and wrote to the boy's parents.

As he told Eliza Stiles several days later: "It is sad to see a young soldier die, & heart rending to announce it to his parents. May God support the living. The dead I trust are happy."

In the midst of the heat and sickness a new adjutant arrived with his "little wife, 2 children & a niece about 14. . . . I took them into my tent until I got some place to put them in," Robert described their coming. "Such a time they had of it. It furnished them little else but a shade from the sun & a narrow bed for the children to sleep on."

He satisfied the youngsters with molasses and bread until dinner time, and refreshed their parents with wine and water. After tea, he had two tents pitched for them on the riverbank, and divided with them his supply of eggs and butter, brought that morning from a settlement down the river.

He described the wife as "quite a pretty little woman from New York," but her oldest boy provoked the comment: "People do not know the misery they entail on their children & society by bringing them up badly," a reflection that caused him to ask: "And yet what have I done?" He then cautioned Mary about Rob, with advice that was an echo of Light-Horse Harry Lee's counsel to Carter:

Let him never touch a novel. They print beauty more charming than nature, & describe happiness that never exists. They will teach him to sigh after that which has no reality, to despise the little good that is granted us in this world & to expect more than is given. Instil into him industry & frugality & teach him to be

249

prudent before he is liberal & to be just before he is generous. He must study human nature, more by experience than by precept, learn to guard himself & his actions, & not to be deceived by the low, the cunning, & the envious.

Several letters from home brought unpleasant news. Mary had been sick for a month, and her "rheumatism" had spread from her right hand, up her arm to her shoulder, the pain causing many of her nights to be sleepless. She was going to try the waters at the White Sulphur Springs. Robert knew from this decision that her suffering must be acute for, as he told her, "you are always so loath to do anything for yourself."

Over the past year, Rooney had been sick with "intermittant fever." He was anxious to quit school for a while, and in May wrote his mother that he thought he should take a leave of absence. He obtained the approval of the faculty and his physician, Dr. Johnson, who wrote Mary that she need not be alarmed, as this was merely "a matter of precaution."

But Robert regretted the action, for as he wrote: "It has broken into one of the best years of his education from which I had hoped much & in which he seemed to be improving." He gave Rooney the option of "either finishing his collegiate studies at Cambridge or the Virginia University, or giving up altogether."

Now Rooney wrote his father that he had decided to return to Harvard that fall. But Lee held grave doubts about his future:

Although anxious & ambitious for his improvement, education, & usefulness in life, I have no desire for his nominal standing when he wants the real [he told Mary]. It is the substance not the show I desire from him. If he cannot obtain the former, I wish him to abandon the chase of the latter. He has to make his bread in the world for I cannot always aid him, & must therefore make up his mind as to what the end & means of obtaining it. All I can do for him, he can rely on. It is time he began thinking of something besides running about amusing himself. I wish him to do so at once.

250

But the letter that brought the worst news came from Edward Vernon Childe in Paris, announcing the death of his wife, Mildred, Robert's younger sister. "Though separated from her for years," Lee wrote, "I was little prepared for this sudden & harsh severance. Nor can I realize that she, so loved in youth, so dear to me in mature years, has preceded me in that long journey on which we are all hurrying." Two weeks later when writing home, he spoke of the shock this news must have been to "poor sister Ann. . . . It shook a stronger frame than hers & brings at every recurrence of the thought, scalding tears & sad reflections."

But the depressing tidings were offset by a delightful letter from Miss Cornelia Van Rensselaer, one of Robert's New York "sweethearts," and a cheerful one from Custis, who was "living in clover" at No. 75 Broughton Street. He described his work on Forts Jackson and Pulaski, and gave welcome news of the Mackay family and their never-failing hospitality which, he felt, might be his only danger: that he would be "killed by kindness."

But the letter that brought the most pleasure was a long and spirited one from Eliza Stiles, giving the latest news of her mother, sisters, and her own family. She also spoke of the possibility of her husband being made Secretary of War, in which case, she playfully promised Robert many indulgences.

When he answered her letter, he mentioned the rapidity with which her children were growing up: "Another daughter on the verge of womanhood! I hope she is as sweet as her predecessors. Henry to be married too! And you realizing the pleasure of grandchildren. Of this last I know nothing." His next words are perhaps significant when it is considered that only two of his sons married, and none of his daughters:

"I know it will require a tussle for any one to get my children from me, & beyond that I do not wish to know."

In discussing the possibility of Mr. Stiles becoming Secretary of War, he had this to say:

As you promise me such fine times . . . I shall be more anxious for it than ever. Do not let it be too long, or I shall be too

251

old to be benefitted by it. Unless they give me some position which will enable me to bestow some care upon my family, I fear I shall be obliged to resign. Though fully endorsing the ancient sentiment, *dulce et decorum est pro patri mori*, a man's wife & children have some claims upon him.

It was in keeping with these pleasant thoughts of Savannah and the carefree days spent there that Inspector-General Joseph K. F. Mansfield, whom Lee had first met at Cockspur, should arrive.

"I pitched him a tent by the side of mine & set him a plate at my table. He is a capital officer & a good man & I have enjoyed much the pleasure of his company," he told Mary.

Mary's next letter spoke of her "continued indisposition & suffering," and her "helpless state." To his further distress, she told him that the check he had sent Rooney to pay off all his debts had missed him, since he had left for Cambridge ahead of schedule in order to spend a week with his Aunt Ann. Robert's patience was easily exhausted with this son, and he complained: "I fear all his affairs will be as loosely managed. He seems only to have time or thought for running about." What was yet Rooney's secret was his love for Charlotte Wickham, still staying at the Carter house next door to Mrs. Marshall.

On August 14, a courier brought Robert orders to attend a court-martial at Ringgold Barracks, near Comargo on the Rio Grande—"almost the farthest place they could send me," he reflected dismally. He had just finished a letter to Eliza Stiles when his orders came, and he added a postscript to tell her of his destination. "Truly there is no rest for the wicked," he concluded.

In her last letter, Mary had written about a new brigadiership that had been created, and the petition that had been widely circulated and signed, requesting President Pierce to give Lee the appointment on the basis of his outstanding service in peacetime, and his pre-eminent distinctions in the field. Both she and her father counted on it being given to him. But Robert was too familiar with the workings of the political machine that gave undeserved promotion through favoritism and nepotism to hold such illusions. When Eliza Stiles had spoken of her son wishing to enter the army, he had written her to urge him to choose some other profession:

"It is a hard life & he can never rise to any military eminence by serving in the army. He must rise *out* of it, & then come in a Major Gen¹. That is worth having, as a man may hope to accomplish something."

The day before he left for Ringgold, he answered Mary's letter. Touching on the possibility of promotion, he said:

"As to the brigadiership, I have never had the least expectation of receiving it. I had thought it would be conferred on General Smith for political reasons,"—a prediction that was shortly fulfilled.

2

LEE'S mood was far from light as he set out at dawn the next morning on the 730-mile ride to Ringgold Barracks to attend the trial of that doughty Indian fighter and loyal soldier, Major Giles B. Porter. At Fort Mason, his friend Major George H. Thomas joined him, for he had also been ordered to the trial. Robert found his company "a great comfort" on the journey, which took twenty-seven days. They met but one delay when they were detained for a day by high water. "I . . . had to swim my mules and get the wagon over by hand," he told Mary. "My mare took me very comfortably, but all my wardrobe, from my socks up to my plume, was immersed in muddy water." The letter had to be brief, he explained, for he was suffering from "a stiff finger, caused by a puncture from a Spanish bayonet, while pitching my tent on the road, which struck the joint."

Soon after his arrival at Ringgold, he received another depressing letter from Mary whose stay at the White Sulphur and Warm Springs had brought no relief. She talked also of Rooney's doings, a subject that never failed to irritate his father, so that in his reply he revived the discussion of the missing check. "He thinks entirely of his own pleasures & not of what is proper to be done," he complained once again.

But there was diversion in the company of a number of army friends who had also been ordered to the court, among them the president, Colonel Carlos Waite. Robert greatly admired Mrs. Waite's fine cat, "Jim Nooks," whom she took everywhere on a leash, and fed him (according to Robert), on "coffee & cream for breakfast, pound cake for lunch, buttered toast for tea, & Mexican rats, taken raw, for supper. I have been trying to persuade her to let me take him to Camp Cooper, but she says she cannot part from him."

The trial proved to be exceptionally tedious, since Porter had for his counsel "two Texan lawyers, a Judge Bigelow & a Colonel Bowers, very shrewd men, accustomed to the tricks & stratagems of special pleadings, which if of no other avail, absorb time & stave off questions." But what concerned Lee more than the proceedings was "the state of my man Johnson, who has fever. I hope it will prove a slight case for his sake & my own, for, though he is a poor cook, he is all I have, & neither the Major [Thomas] nor I can stand these long & interesting sessions of the court without eating."

At the end of October, the court adjourned to Fort Brown, near the mouth of the Rio Grande. The trip was made on the steamer *Ranchero*, whose captain, Mr. King, Lee enjoyed talking with. At Fort Brown, Robert was in direct contact with the outside world for the first time in many months, for steamers from New Orleans called regularly at nearby Brownsville, bringing mail, newspapers, and general intelligence from the "States."

"The steamer brought the President's message to Cong: & the reports of the various heads of the Depts. . . . so that we are now assured that the Govt: is in operation & the Union in existence; not that we had any fears to the contrary, but it is satisfactory to have the facts to go on. They restrain supposition & conjecture, confirm faith, & bring contentment," he wrote in good spirits.

But neither the news from home nor the country at large

was cheering. Mary was now using crutches, her father's accounts showed declining income and mounting debts, and the younger children were all sick. Rooney continued to be a source of concern to his father: "He gives me many anxious days, sleepless nights, & adds more than years to the gray hairs in my head."

The flame of sectional hatred was being fanned to alarming proportions by the unreasoning fire-eaters and impractical idealists of the North and South. But Lee

was much pleased with the President's message & the report of the Secy of War, the only two documents that have reached us entire. The views of the Pres. of the systematic & progressive efforts of certain people at the North to interfere & change the domestic institutions of the South, are truthfully & faithfully expressed. The consequence of their plans & purposes are clearly set forth, & they must also be aware that their object is both unlawful & entirely foreign to them & to their duty; for which they are irresponsible & unaccountable; & can be accomplished by *them* through the agency of a civil & servile war.

In this enlightened age, there are few I believe, but what will acknowledge, that slavery as an institution, is a moral & political evil in any country. It is useless to expatiate on its disadvantages. . . . While we see the course of the final abolition of human slavery is onward, & we give it the aid of our prayers & all justifiable means in our power, we must leave the progress as well as the result in his hands who sees the end, who chooses to work by slow influences, & with whom two thousand years are but a single day. Although the abolitionist must know this & must see that he has neither the right or power of operating except by moral means & suasion, & if he means well to the slave, he must not create angry feelings in the master. . . . Still I fear he will persevere in his evil course. Is it not strange that the descendants of those pilgrim fathers who crossed the Atlantic to preserve their own freedom of opinion, have always proved themselves intolerant of the spiritual liberty of others? . . .

Porter's trial dragged on. For exercise and relaxation, Robert took daily walks along the banks of the Rio Grande, observing the wild flowers and the many birds and animals he came on in these rambles "through the chaparral." "The birds of the

Rio Grande form a constant source of interest & are as numerous as they are beautiful in plumage," he wrote Mary. "I wish I could get for you the roots of some of the luxuriant vines that cover everything, or the seeds of the innumerable flowers."

One afternoon, he met a Mexican shepherd tending an unusual breed of sheep. The herder told him that they were called "Obispo (which translated means *Bishop*) & that their flesh was very good. Tell your father," he instructed, for Mr. Custis had always raised sheep at Arlington, and had bred a hardy strain of fine-wooled animals known as "Arlington Improved." In 1803, he had inaugurated an agricultural fair at which the finest sheep and homespun in the country were exhibited. This was a novel idea and was immediately so popular that it became a traditional event that he held each year on his birthday, April 30. On that day "the great of the land" gathered in General Washington's war tent, set up near Arlington's famed spring, described as "gushing forth fountains of living water," to watch the awarding of prizes and the ceremonies and festivities.

Another day, Lee walked over the bridge into Matamoros, finding the little Mexican village "neat," "though much out at the elbow." He enjoyed most "the orange trees loaded with unripe fruit," and the oleander in full bloom. In town he called on "an old acquaintance of mine whom I have not seen since the Mexican War, *Dominguez*, the famous guerilla chief and captain of the Spy Company that engaged in our service."

He was amused at the arrival of a colonel, minus his wife, who, it was rumored, had left him. "He will have here to make love to the Mexicanas, for I know of no one else he can devote himself to," he observed drily.

But generally he found little to entertain or interest him, and he was easily annoyed and depressed. He complained about the Episcopal minister who possessed, he felt, "a strong proclivity to High Churchism, of which I am not fond. Waiving more serious objections I think it unsuited to our people, institutions, & not calculated to extend episcopacy among the masses—therefore impolitic."

As Christmas drew near, his thoughts naturally turned to

the family who would gather "around the hearth at dear Arlington. . . . Though absent, my heart will be in the midst of you, & I shall enjoy in imagination & memory all that is going on." Instead of walking along the river, he visited the shops in town, seeking presents for the children at the garrison. The stock was scanty, but he was able to find "a beautiful little Dutch doll for little Emma Jones—one of those crying babies that can open & shut their eyes, turn their head, &c. For the other two girls, Puss Shirley & Mary Seawall, I found handsome french teapots to match cups given by Mrs. Waite, then by means of knives & books I satisfied the boys." To Jeannie Dawson, nearing fourteen, he gave a prayer book.

On Christmas Day he first distributed his gifts to the children, then attended church, though he was critical of the Reverend Passmore's sermon on the birth of the Saviour: "It was not as simply or as touchingly told as in the Bible."

With Major Thomas and his wife and small daughter, he dined at two o'clock on "roast turkey & plum pudding." He brought the little girl the present of "a pretty singing bird."

Christmas night he spent in his room, reading over with great interest back copies of the *Alexandria Gazette* that had been forwarded to him. "Besides the usual good reading matter, I was interested in the relation of local affairs, & inferred from the quiet & ordinary course of events, that all in the neighbourhood was going on well."

New Year's Day was celebrated at the garrison and in Brownsville with all the "forms and ceremonies" of large cities: "The ladies were attired in their best with cheerful boards spread for exhausted visitors. Their small & limited houses, compressed everything in one room. The army ladies could make little exhibition," though there was "cake, wine, & plenty of smiles for all comers."

When he called on the Dawsons, Jeannie had a present for him. "She had worked me a watch case . . . the only New Year's gift I received." In town, he went to see Mrs. Passmore, the rector's wife, and Mrs. Moses, whose husband was agent for the quartermaster department. Then, because "I had often wished to pay my respects to Mrs. King, wife of the captain of the Steamer Ranchero . . . who has been very civil to me on many occasions," he stopped at her "nice cottage." Her table was spread with bowls of sweet oranges from her own trees, "& many other things tempting to the eye, but I tasted nothing." By midafternoon his calls were finished, and he took his customary walk through the chaparral.

January ended, but Porter's trial continued. "I hope all this mass of testimony will be of service to him," Robert commented. "He will at least have the satisfaction that Dr. Chapman . . . used to assure his patients, that if they did die, they should die hard."

With the coming of the second week in February, there was still no sign of the end of the trial, and he complained: "My time passes very monotonously," finding his chief diversion in his daily walks. Returning from one of these "rambles" he wrote: "The spring seems to have opened in earnest. The trees are putting forth their young leaves. The birds are building their nests, & the cattle cropping the young grass. The air is fragrant with the sweet odour of the acacia, & chaparral is bright with the early flowers. The path of my evening walk is lined with the running verbena . . . the purple & the pink."

One afternoon, he met a Mexican carrying in his serape a wild kitten—"a noble specimen of the Rio Grande wild cat—spotted all over with large spots like a leopard." Lee wanted to buy it to take back with him to Camp Cooper, but the man explained that it was already sold to a resident of Brownsville. However, he promised to get Lee another, and several days later brought him an even larger specimen.

By this time, everything was trying to Lee's patience. He complained of Rooney's silence (he was "Fitzhugh" when his father was annoyed with him): "I have not heard from him since his first arrival at Cambridge. He does not seem to think it necessary to write me now." The neighboring children were "uproarious," and as he listened to their noise, was subjected to their impudence, and observed their "indifferent or incompetent mother" ignoring their behavior, he decided that he was an advocate of

Infant Schools where children can be gathered together under well-trained instructors, & taught to practice politeness, gentleness, courtesy, & regard for the rights of others. These may be realized to a certain extent in well regulated families, but among a large number of pupils, with a variety of dispositions, an actual world of infant intercourse & infant business, when each child brings its stock of selfish animalism, to aggravate that of its playmates, the necessity & advantage of *self-denial* & *self-controul*, can be forcibly exemplified & their exercise confirmed into habit.

By March 7, the court had adjourned *sine die*, and Lee was free to return to San Antonio. Reluctantly, he left his wild cat behind, for it had already "grown as large as a small-sized dog, had to be caged, & would strike at anything that came within its reach. His cage had to be strong & consequently heavy, so I could not bring it. He would pounce on a kid as Tom Tita would on a mouse, & would whistle like a tiger when you approached him."

From the courtroom, he went directly to the *Ranchero*, and "immediately upon landing I saddled up & took across the Prairie." But when he reported to headquarters in San Antonio he was displeased to find that there were orders for him to proceed to Indianola, Texas, for further court-martial duty. He had ten days before he was scheduled to leave, and spent much of this time in fruitless efforts to find another cook and orderly since the ones he had told him they would not return to Camp Cooper as it was "too dreary."

He also went to see Dr. McCormick—"considered a very skilful physician"—to describe Mary's symptoms and see if he could not prescribe for her. The doctor wrote out a prescription and also made up some pills which he sent by a friend just then leaving for Washington. When they reached her, Mary took the pills, but finding they did not agree with her, administered them to the servant, Uncle George, also suffering from "rheumatism"; she reported that they brought the old man relief.

Lee was cheered by letters from all the children including "the old Roon," temporarily restored to favor, and in high spirits he wrote to his daughter about a cat he had seen "dressed up for company. . . . He had two holes bored in each ear, & in each were two bows of pink & blue ribbon. His round face set in pink & blue, looked like a big owl in a full blooming ivy bush."

"After a tedious passage in the stagecoach with nine fellow sufferers," he reached Indianola, going by way of Gonzales and Lavaca. While the stage was changing mules in Lavaca, he called on Mr. and Mrs. Monod, the French couple with whom he had passed the night when on his way to join General Wool's army. At their house he saw "cats as is cats," describing his visit to Milly:

Mr. Monod received me with all the shrugs of his nation, & the entrance of Madame was foreshadowed by the coming of her stately cats, with visages grave & tails erect, who preceded, surrounded, & followed her . . . in her train she pointed out Aglai, her favourite eleven years ago when I visited her. They are of the French breed & education, & when the claret & water was poured out for my refreshment, they jumped on the table for a sit-to. If I can persuade the mail stage to give a place to one of that distinguished family, I will take it to Camp Cooper, provided Madame can trust her pet into such barbarous country & Indian society.

He stayed at the Casimir House during the trial, which lasted ten days. After his return to San Antonio, he again devoted considerable time to finding suitable servants. On April 7, he wrote that he had at last discovered a cook

that promises some comfort. . . . He is clean & respectable & I wish for nothing more for myself, but I like to have something good for my friends & companions even in the wilderness. When you have to give $20 a month you are led to expect some return, though $25 a month failed to induce one who was said to be better, to leave town. I shall give him a trial in the plains tonight, though if he proves incompetent I shall have no means of replacing him.

Wistfully he told of dining a few days before with Major and Mrs. McDowell, whose French cook had "produced elegant Charlotte Russe, macaroons, & a variety of cake."

By April 12, he had reached Fort Mason where he was

recd with the usual kindness by all officers, which I everywhere meet with. There are only three ladies at the Post, Mrs. Thomas,

Mrs. Smith (wife of Dr. Charles) & Mrs. Johnson, wife of Capt. J. I could only take supper with one, though asked by all. . . . I supped with Mrs. Johnson, breakfasted & dined with Mrs. Thomas today, & am to take tea with Mrs. Smith. The supper last night was so good, so much to my taste, venison steak, biscuit & butter, that I had little appetite for my breakfast this morg. though waffles, eggs & wild turkey were three dishes that it presented, & when dinner of wild turkey, tomatoes, fresh peas, snap beans & potatoes, was followed by plum pudding, jellies & preserve peaches, I despaired of eating any of Mrs. Smith's supper. But I shall take to the road at daylight tomorrow which I hope will produce a favourable reaction. . . . The kindness I always receive from my brother officers, & the sincerity & cordiality with which it is accompanied, make me very much ashamed of my meagre hospitality.

On April 19, he wrote: "After an absence of seven months I have returned to my Texas home." During this time he had traveled some two thousand miles. He found his "valuables in better condition than I had anticipated," for though his tent, which he described as "dilapidated," had frequently blown over in storms, it had always risen again, but not without some breakage to his precious white crockery. By this date, his German cook, Kremer, having been tried, did not come up to his hopes, "though my expectations ought not to have elevated him higher than the reality. But what would this life be without hope?" he asked. "I hope to get back to you again; to find you well; every thing prospering. The children wise, good & happy!"

He could not seem to escape court-martial duty. A week after his arrival at Camp Cooper, trial was set for Lieutenant Robert N. Eagle, Second Cavalry, charged with a minor infraction. Much to his distaste, Lee was appointed president of the court. Major Thomas had been ordered to the trial, and Robert was concerned about the comfort of Mrs. Thomas, who came with her husband. "The Major can fare as I do, but I fear she will fare badly, for my man Kremer is both awkward & unskilled. I can, however, give them plenty of bread & beef, but with the exception of preserved vegetables, fruits, &c., can give very little else. I sent yesterday to the settlements below &

got a few eggs, some butter & one old hen. I shall not *reflect* upon *her*."

During his long absence, his own hens had been left in the care of his washerwoman, but as he told Milly: "No one will attend to your business as well as you will yourself," and when he returned he found them all gone.

Shelter for Mrs. Thomas posed something of a problem, too, for the day they came, Lee had worn his white linen coat, and the thermometer in his tent, with the walls raised and a fine breeze blowing, had registered 89°. That night he went to sleep without a blanket, but shortly after midnight a norther came roaring down the valley of the Clear Fork, making it necessary for him to get up and put on all his blankets, and when he arose in the morning he found: "Fires & overcoats are in fashion again."

Summer brought its usual scourge of fevers and dysentery, which caused much suffering among the little children in camp. Robert was deeply grieved when "a bright little boy, an only child" died. In the absence of a chaplain, his parents asked Lee to read the funeral service. Two weeks later, another child died. "He was as handsome a little boy as I ever saw—the son of one of the sergeants, about a year old; I was admiring his appearance the day before he was taken ill. His father came to me, the tears flowing down his cheeks, & asked me to read the funeral service over his body, which I did at the grave for the second time in my life. I hope I shall not be called on again."

Regardless of the heat, Lee was spending almost every day in the saddle—"from 8 A.M. till 5½ P.M."—getting the "full benefit" of the fiery sun while searching up and down the river for a better campsite. He always took with him a number of the younger officers, several of whom left records of the feeling of awe and affection with which he was universally regarded by his men, because of his integrity, impartiality, and paternal interest.

"Fighting is the easiest part of a soldier's duty," he once told a friend. "It is the watching, waiting, labouring, starving, freezing, wilting, exposure & privations that is so wearing to the body & trying to the mind. It is in this state that discipline tells; & attention night & day on the part of the off^r so necessary. His eye & thoughts must be continually on his men. Their wants anticipated & comforts provided." It was this vigilance, this "attention night & day" with his "eye & thoughts" continually on his men, that so endeared Lee to them.

One young soldier's frank reaction to his impartiality amused Lee, and he told the story to friends after his return to Virginia. The young cavalryman was not guilty of any serious offence, but still he was visibly shaken when he appeared before Lee. Seeking to reassure him, Robert said kindly:

"You shall have justice." Swallowing hard, the boy responded:

"That is what I am afraid of, sir!"

On May 22, 1857, Mary wrote: "Gen: Scott has been kind enough without consulting us to obtain for Rooney an appointment in the 6th Infantry of 2nd Lieut." The appointment had been made on the recommendation of his two uncles, Judge Marshall, and Edward Vernon Childe, who since Mildred's death had been living in Baltimore.

On July 5, Robert replied to her:

Your information of Rooney's appointment in the army, was entirely unexpected. I had been preparing the way for it, should he desire it, upon graduating next year. If he does desire to enter the army, however, perhaps it is as well now as then. . . . If he enters now he will gain one year rank, which may be a fair offset to the additional information he might gain by continuing at college.

From Cambridge, Rooney wrote his mother that if the family did not approve, he would refuse the appointment. However, he was still feeling "as full of military ardour as ever I did," though he admitted that he would have preferred a commission in the calvary. When he received his father's permission, he hurried over to ask his friend Henry Adams to write his official letter of acceptance.

When Robert came to thank General Scott for the favor, he indulged in a bit of humor at the expense of this errant son:

As he failed to get an appt to West Point, & had entered College, I had hoped he would have graduated, & have made a useful citizen. But as you (used to) say "boys are only fit to be shot," & he seems to have had from his infancy an ardent desire for this high privilege; perhaps the sooner it is done the better. He is accordingly in great glee that he will now be able to offer so shining a mark in his person as a 2nd Lt. of Infy. . . .

On July 17, he received another summons for court-martial duty, at nearby Fort Mason, this time. As he rode Grace Darling down the road past the groves of cottonwood and elm and the Indian lodges, he had no way of knowing that he would not return. But just after the trial began, an express brought him orders to report immediately to San Antonio to take temporary command of the Second Cavalry, for Colonel A. S. Johnston had been ordered to Washington. Lee sent a message to Camp Cooper, asking that his trunk and personal effects be forwarded to San Antonio. He arrived there himself on the twenty-seventh, and took over the command the next day.

When he learned that Johnston's assignment was to Utah, to quell the Mormon troubles, he wrote to his friend that he presumed, then, he would not be taking Mrs. Johnston with him to Salt Lake, as he understood that "wives there were a drug on the market."

But this little sally was not indicative of elated spirits, for, as he told Mrs. Fitzhugh in a letter written from what he termed "a desert of dulness," though he had a house and

other comforts I have been sometime without, I fear I am not more satisfied than when destitute of them. In truth the wilderness of Texas is more agreeable to me than its cities, & the only advantage I enjoy in my present sojourn, is the facility it affords for communicating with my friends.

I can think of nothing that would interest you in this paradise of the Texans. It is as far as I can judge as good as any of their cities, but the only thing attractive to me is the river . . . the country beyond is naked prairie, parched, crisp & destitute of vegetation. . . . I can tell you nothing of the society of the place, as I have so far confined myself to my army acquaintances. I see much of Major & Mrs. Chilton whom you know, & their nice little children.

In San Antonio, he felt the absence of the challenge that had imparted some interest to his life at Camp Cooper, and he missed the long days passed in the saddle. "Now that I am not obliged to ride, I never mount a horse," he observed dispiritedly. With the less active life, he was more aware of his loneliness and longing for his children. "It is grievous to me at all times to be so far from all I hold so dear," he said. In writing to his "Precious Annie," who had been ill, his mood was bright, but an underlying sadness was evident:

Perhaps it is only the sight of your venerable Papa that is wanting? If so I think two of you girls had better come out to him. Pack up your trunk, come to New Orleans, & take the steamer to Indianola. Two strong minded American women can easily wend their way here. I will promise a cordial welcome & respectable shelter, while I remain here, & then a pony & a blanket apiece to accompany me in the plains. . . . I do not enjoy San Antonio. Indeed I have been nowhere or seen no person, except the officers on the station, & I think I feel more lonely than at Camp Cooper, for there I expected nothing & solitude seems more consonant to my feelings & temperament.

Mary now wrote to him about Rooney's engagement to Charlotte Wickham of Shirley. "I cannot say that your *news* surprized me . . . as did the *lady*," he replied. "The event I was prepared for, but not the object. Charlotte is a sweet, amiable child, but I fear is ill calculated in health or from education to follow the drum over our Prairies. I hope you have told her of the hardships of a soldier's life, & the privations to which she will be exposed in a marching Reg.t" He reminded Mary that "both her father & mother were constitutionally feeble," and had died young. "However, if their plans are to wait three years, both may change their minds a half a dozen times before then. They are both mere children." He intimated facetiously that he had found for his son the ideal woman, who was obviously in the market for a husband:

There is a kind of widow here I was going to recommend to Rooney. She seems to be a strong-minded woman, with the benefit of Texas habits. I was invited to her house to a musical party, but declined. About a week afterwards I thought it incumbent on me to return the compliment by a call. I found the house & made myself as agreeable as I could for about 5 minutes, & when I rose to depart she took me out in her garden to see her corn & potatoes by *starlight*. But she had waked the wrong passenger. I told her I had no knowledge of horticulture, & took no interest in agriculture in Texas. I have not seen her since. . . . She would take care of a man finely. Those are the kind of women tell *Chass* [Charlotte] a man wants in the army.

But Charlotte was dear to him, and he wrote her a warm and tender letter of congratulation, welcoming her prospectively to the immediate family.

On October 21, a telegram brought the news of Mr. Custis' death—news that Robert admitted was "as unexpected as it was afflicting." In Mary's letter that followed, she recounted the details: an attack of influenza developed into pneumonia. Shortly after midnight on October 12, "we were all summoned to take leave of him at his request while he knew us." He talked of his son-in-law, of his favorite grandson, Custis; told Mary she "must make the best of Rooney's marriage, talked with us for a short time, then asked for Mr. Dana," the rector of Alexandria's Christ Church.

Lee made immediate application for a leave of absence, based on "the imperative necessity of my presence at home in consequence of the disabled condition of my wife." Orders for court-martial duty in early November were canceled and he prepared to turn over the command to Major Thomas. He settled his accounts, paid off his factotum, and placed his mare in reliable hands. When word was received from Washington that he had been granted a two-month furlough, his trunk was packed and he was ready to leave.

Where his future course lay was once again a matter for deliberation. As he wrote to Albert Sidney Johnston on the day of his departure:

"I can see that I have at last to decide the question I have staved off for twenty years, whether I am to continue in the army all my life, or to leave it now."

⇻ VI ⇺

Storm Clouds Gather

1857 ★ 1861

VI. Storm Clouds Gather

WHEN LEE first considered resigning from the army, around the time that Andrew Talcott entered the field of private engineering, he had earnestly wrestled with the question. But as the years passed and the service won its place in his affections, and he feared he would not find so much friendship elsewhere, this debate with himself, though sincere, became a form that merely possessed the semblance of a struggle. At this time, as much as he regretted having left the engineer corps, and as much as he disliked Texas, there would be no doubt that he would return to the Second Cavalry as soon as conditions at Arlington allowed. But as he traveled homeward, thoughts about his future were foremost in his mind, and he even considered the possibility of Mary and the girls accompanying him to his post, believing that with both parents gone, there would be less to bind Mary to Arlington (he did not know yet that she would cling to it because of the *graves* of her parents).

The possibility of their coming with him would be contingent on Mary's health, for it was difficult to judge from her letters whether her "disabled condition" was temporary or not. Heretofore, though her symptoms were often alarming, she had always recovered her "fair" state of health and been able to carry on.

But as he thought about Mary's temperament and her inability to adapt herself to radical changes of environment, he feared that she would be more than ever discontent and disposed to fits of nervousness, making life on the remote frontier less bearable than it was normally.

As soon as he saw her face, drawn with pain and lined and aged beyond her forty-nine years, and her ankles and feet so swollen she could not move without crutches, he was certain that she would never be able to go with him. Yet this did not stop him from engaging in the sham battle with himself over his future. When he asked Mrs. Fitzhugh a week after his arrival:

"Dear Cousin Anna what can I do—I fear Mary will never be well enough to accompy me in my wandering life, & it seems cruel to leave her," he already knew the answer.

For a long time, he had known that the mansion and out-buildings were badly in need of repair, but not until the day after his arrival when he closely inspected the property did he realize that "everything is in ruins & will have to be rebuilt." He was depressed further by Mary's condition, and his sense of loss, for as he wrote: "I miss every moment him that always rec^d me with the kindness & affection of a father, & I grieve to find his chair empty & his place vacant—The grass is already green over his grave—May God have mercy upon us all."

The elegance of the newly completed drawing room must have contrasted strangely with the general picture of neglect and decay. Right after it was finished, Agnes described it in her journal:

The carpenters, the mason, the plasterers, the painters have left at last & lo! the change they have wrought. The white walls adorned with fine pictures in gilded frames, the marble mantels, white bolts & woodwork, the dark walnut doors, the register of the furnace— everything combined denotes a change. . . . We have sent for our furniture at W.[est] P.[oint], then velvet & marble will fill this apartment, parisian clocks will tinkle their silvery bells from the mantels, crystal chandeliers on golden brackets will shed their soft light from the walls, handsome cases with well-bound & titled books, & rare curiosities will display their treasures. . . . The hall has been rewashed & pictures nicely hung. Sister is making frames ornamented with leather for Grandpa's pictures; hung up high they look very well. Our old parlours are now the dining-room.

Mr. Custis had left his property to be distributed among his grandchildren, though Mary received a life estate in Arlington, adjacent lands in Alexandria and Fairfax County, and the mill on Four Mile Run. The family plate she had the privilege of dividing among the children, but "the Mount Vernon plate, together with every article I possess relating to Washington, that came from Mount Vernon, is to remain with my daughter at Arlington House during said daughter's life, and at her death to go to my eldest grandson, George Washington Custis Lee, he taking my name and arms, and to descend from him entire and unchanged to my latest posterity." The White House plantation of four thousand acres in New Kent County was left to Rooney, and Romancock of a like acreage, in King William County, to Rob. Each granddaughter received the sum of ten thousand dollars to be paid out of the sale of Smith's Island and lands in Richmond, Westmoreland, and Stafford Counties; any balance was to be made up by proceeds from the White House and Romancock farms. To his son-in-law, he left one lot in "square 21, in Washington City."

After the legacies were paid, all Custis slaves, 196 in number, of which 63 were on the home estate, were to be "emancipated in such manner as my executors may determine . . . in not exceeding five years from the time of my decease."

Since the three other executors failed to qualify, Lee had to act alone. After he had visited the White House and Romancock where conditions were worse than at Arlington, he wrote: "I would prefer relinquishing to the boys the property at once, with its responsibilities. They are young & might make something of it."

At the White House, the overseer had ignored orders, received in 1855, to build new Negro quarters, a barn, and corn houses; he had failed to account for the wheat crop of that year, had rendered no accounts at all for the next year, and had departed before the arrival of his successor, leaving no inventory of property, and many debts, over a thousand dollars of which were presented to Lee upon his arrival.

At Romancock, the mill that was supposed to supply the farm with bread was "at a standstill"; the barn, corn houses, and fences were down, "& the overseers house was in such a bad state, that he could not keep his family in it." Further, the fields were badly impoverished by overplanting.

As he explained to Custis, now stationed in San Francisco working on the construction of Fort Point: "It would be an easy matter, as you are aware, to put things in order if the means were available, but without the means & debts pressing, the progress will be slow." Mr. Custis had left "upwards of $10,000 in debts." He estimated that it would require about $10,000 to put Arlington in order with hired labor, and a similar amount for the two other estates, since there was no mansion at Romancock. During his first three months at home, he spent $831 to strengthen the beams of the Arlington house, and $700 for implements, lime, and guano for all three farms. But he attacked this newest challenge with his usual energy and efficiency, and prepared for the coming winter by having the worst leaks in the roofs patched, and the supply of coal hauled in.

In riding about the farms, he found it a nuisance to dismount to open gates, so he devised a latch that could be opened without getting off the horse. He took a sketch to Mr. Schneider, the blacksmith, and asked him to make a dozen.

"Well, Colonel, I will make one. If that pleases you, I will make eleven more." After Lee had tried the first one he went back to Mr. Schneider and said:

"Make the eleven. It is the very thing I want, and could not be improved."

In January he was writing to Custis:

I wish I could give you cheering accounts of my progress in my business & arrangement of your Grandfather's Estate. Debts are pouring on me, not in large amounts, but sufficient to absorb my available funds. So far I have paid all that have been presented by tradesmen & merchants. I fear I shall not be able to touch Mrs. Nelsons & Mr. Conrads. I have made arrangements to rent out the mill for $400, but shall have to put it in repair, which will absorb two years rent. . . . The old miller . . . claims nearly $1000, or 6 years wages. Mr. Daly also claims 2 years wages. I have not been able to procure a manager for Arlington. I wish to get if possible a respectable single man, whom I can put in the North wing of the House, & who would be a protection to the establishment & a relief to your mother in my absence. I fear I shall not succeed. The accommodation is so poor on the farm that it deters respectable men with families from engaging. The inability to procure an overseer for Arlington has kept me a close prisoner.

It is obvious from this reference to his absence that he had already made up his mind to return to his post. But he did not acknowledge it. Instead, he said that his decision need not be made until the expiration of his leave, which had been extended at his request to the autumn of 1858.

It had been many years since Robert and Smith had spent Christmas together. This year, Smith was stationed in Washington, serving on court-martial duty, so he and Sis Nanie and the younger boys came to Arlington. Robert's brother-in-law, Edward Vernon Childe and his daughter, Mary Custis (or Marie), also passed the holidays with them. Shortly after the New Year, Childe and his daughter returned to Baltimore, and on January 15, Robert took Agnes to their house where she was "to stay with Mary Childe & take lessons in various branches."

Agnes viewed the move with conflicting sensations, for though she would be near her "dear Aunt Ann," and she enjoyed the company of her cousin Mary, who was "so kind & gay," she hated to leave "dear dear Arlington my home of joy & sadness—I cannot bear to leave it & Papa & Mama—& all of them," she wrote.

Robert went to see his sister. This was his first visit with her since his return from Texas, and he found her "comfortable" and "as cheerful as usual," though still confined to her bed. Charlotte Wickham, Rooney's affianced, was now living in Baltimore in order to study music and painting, for which she had considerable talent. Robert thought he had never seen her looking so well and radiant.

He ordered a load of lime and guano to be sent to Romancock and the White House, and at the end of his first week went there to start the repairs and prepare the fields for sowing. He paid all bills as they were presented, and made up an inventory. Then he returned to Arlington to supervise the work in progress there, admitting that he felt "more familiar with the military operations of a campaign than the details of a farm."

Frequent delays due to rainy weather and illness among his laborers and mechanics made it seem as though the work would never be done:

I can see little prospect of fulfilling the provisions of your Grdfather's will within the space of five years, which seems to be the time within which he expected it to be accomplished & his people liberated [he wrote dispiritedly to Custis, in February]. The Sec. has been kind enough to extend my leave of absence till the Fall. I hope by that time to get things in a more satisfactory condition. In the meantime you must think the matter over & decide what you prefer doing. If you wished to resign & take this place, & Rooney to get married & settle down at the White House, there would be no necessity for my leaving the Army. In a pecuniary point of view I would not advise your resignation. . . . If you could pick up in California some bags of gold, or marry some nice young woman with enough for both, you might then resign if you felt disposed, & live the life of a country gentleman. Without that you would progress slowly. I am *thinking* aloud for your benefit, as I wish you to view the subject in all its bearings. I had thought myself of applying for your appt in any new Regts that might be raised this winter, if I saw any chance of success. . . . The service in the Engineer Corps is preferable to that in the Regts. No place is without its drawbacks. . . . A Captaincy in the Engrs. in time of peace, in responsibility, dignity & usefulness, would rank with a field officer of the line. In time of war it might be different. . . .

But before Custis had received this letter, he had decided to deed his rights and title to Arlington, the mill, and personal property, to his father, and sent the deed on to him. He followed it with a letter to his mother: "I trust that Pa' will not refuse my interest in Arlington, for my sake, if not his own—I can never have any interest separate from my dear Father & Mother. . . ."

When Lee received his son's letter with the deed, he was deeply impressed by "the filial feelings of love & consideration, as well as your tender solicitude for me, of which however I required no proof." He was equally touched by Custis' generosity & disinterestedness." He replied at once to thank him, though he felt obliged to refuse:

It is not from any unwillingness to receive from you a gift, you may think proper to bestow, or to be indebted to you for any benefit, great or small [he explained carefully], but simply because it would not be right for me to do so. Your dear Grdfather distributed his property as he thought best, & it is proper that it should remain as he bestowed it. It will not prevent me from improving it to the best of my ability, or of making it as comfortable a home for your mother & sisters & yourself as I can. I only wish I could do more than I shall have in my power to do.

[Ever mindful of unnecessary expense, he continued:] I wish you had recd my previous letter . . . in time to have saved you the trouble of executing the deed. . . . And indeed I also regret the expense you incurred, which I fear in that country is considerable, as I wish you to save *all* your money & invest in some safe & lucrative way, that you may build up old Arlington & make it all we would wish to see it. The necessity I daily have for money has I fear made me parsimonious.

This desire to scrupulously carry out Mr. Custis' wishes was only one reason for Lee's refusal. Although he was testing it under the most adverse conditions, he had reached the decision that he was temperamentally unsuited for the life of a farmer. To accept Custis' offer would mean resignation from the service, something he obviously did not want to do.

Rooney had by this time returned from duty in Texas, determined to resign from the army, get married, and live at the White House. But orders that were sending his regiment on active duty in Utah suspended these plans for the time, since he knew that it would be a reflection on his reputation if he resigned on the eve of the troops taking to the field. His father supported his decision. When Rooney left for Governor's Island to await transportation to Fort Leavenworth, Robert felt "pained" at parting with him, and wrote in low spirits to a friend:

"If I could only have my children around me, I could be happy." Yet he would never take the step to make this possible.

Though he was on leave, he was not exempt from court-martial duty. On April 26, he left for Newport Barracks in Kentucky, to attend the trial of General Twiggs. To his gratification, it was brief, and he was back at Arlington by Tuesday, May 4. On his way home, he stopped in Baltimore to see his sister, passing a part of Sunday and all day Monday with her. She was "very feeble" and "more distressed than usual." He found Agnes and his niece Mary Childe so engrossed with wedding preparations and festivities "that were in full blast," as he termed it, they had little time to devote to their father and uncle. "There was a great rage for matrimony in B—— & the fever seemed to be infectious. It made me anxious to extricate Agnes. Weddings, Brides, Bridal presents, Parties, &c. formed the chief topic of interest. Those that had passed away were flat & unprofitable, but those in the future caused much excitement," he told his Cousin Anna right after his return.

He both approved and urged marriage for his sons, for he could then easily acquire more daughters to bring him pleasure. But marriage for his girls was something else. He never encouraged them to marry, and admitted that it would require "a tussle" to get them from him. "He was apt to be critical on the subject of our young men visitors & admirers," one of his daughters remembered. Just now, he had reason to extricate Agnes before she succumbed to the fever.

As a child, Markie's brother Orton had formed a strong attachment for Agnes, and with maturity, this had ripened into love. He spent much of his time at Arlington, and Markie remembered that whenever he was there, the question "Where are Agnes and Orton?" always arose, for they were in the habit of taking their horses for long rides over the countryside, or going for walks in the grove. Although Orton was extremely handsome, brilliant, and had an engaging personality, he was sadly lacking in self-control, was disposed to recklessness, and had of late developed an overfondness for liquor.

Robert would have liked nothing better than to have stayed in Baltimore long enough to attend several of the weddings to which he was invited, but when he learned that there was a possibility of his regiment being ordered to Kansas for active duty, he said to a friend:

"I must join it!" and hastened back to Arlington to finish as much work as possible "in anticipation of an abrupt summons away." The summons did not come.

Mary's reluctance to appear in her crippled state at social functions limited Robert's participation in the Washington season to a degree, and he wrote almost enviously of Smith's ability to circulate so freely: "Thursday night at Lady Napier's grand party. Friday night a Senatorial dinner at Mr. Cockrane's (on gold). Last night I really forget where, but another dinner." But her condition did not preclude festivities at home. Three of their daughters had reached an age where social activities formed one of their chief interests, and Daughter was old enough to have suitors. Milly remembered well the great number of army officers who called on young Mary, and strolled with her in the garden.

Whenever there were women house guests, it was Lee's custom to go into the garden before breakfast and pick roses. Then he would lay a dewy rose beside each lady's plate—full blooms for the older ones, buds for the girls, and a tiny bud for Milly.

The gatherings of young people at Arlington did much to liven his spirits. When with them, he set aside his problems and became witty and gay. Once, on coming into the hall, he found Annie and her friend Kathrine Stiles of Savannah, weeping in each other's arms at parting. He told them brightly:

"No tears at Arlington! No tears!"—a rule he did his best to enforce.

During the spring, he tried to find the metes and bounds of the Arlington property and the mill tract, in order to have it surveyed and marked, for he found neighbors trespassing with fences and buildings. In vain, he went through all Mr. Custis' mass of papers, and had the Fairfax County records searched for clues; he admitted momentary frustration but not defeat. Constant rains brought to a halt the repair work on all three plantations. But there was one note of encouragement: the crops of oats and corn promised a good harvest, proving the wisdom of having revitalized the soil.

He found his ailing family a trial that absorbed almost as much thought as the farms. It was still so difficult for Mary to walk, he began to advocate early in the year (knowing how long it would take her to make up her mind where to go) that she devote the summer to seeking relief at the ocean and the spas. He had watched the effect of cold baths throughout the winter ("a fearful experiment," it seemed to him), and was convinced that they had reduced the swelling in her feet and

277

ankles. Therefore, he urged a month of sea bathing before trying the hot springs.

Daughter, who had also been sick, had passed several weeks with Aunt Maria Fitzhugh, hoping that the change might bring about her cure. But when she came home her father found her "still feeble in appetite & strength," and greatly to his annoyance, "as knowing & opinionative as her Aunt Anne, so all the experience of others is lost to her."

His gentle Annie was "by no means strong" either, and he planned for her to go to Cedar Grove "where I know she will enjoy herself, & perhaps may be benefitted." The only "hearty woman" in the house was "Precious Life," as he now called Mildred—"for you are truly precious to me, & more than life."

"She is much exercised with her chickens, & they by her," he joked. "I see for them no prospect of peace but the frying pan."

In addition to supervising the restoration of the three farms, and the health of his "womankind," he was working to have Custis transferred to the Engineer Headquarters in Washington so that he could live at home as "a protection & comfort" for his mother and sisters, and see how he "would like to become a farmer."

At this time, Lee's admirers were advocating his appointment to the brigadiership left vacant by the recent death of General Persifor F. Smith. James M. Porter of Pennsylvania, a one-time nominee for Secretary of War and a founder of Lafayette College in Easton, wrote to President Buchanan:

Col. Lee is one of the most accomplished and best educated officers in the Army. . . . He is a highly finished gentleman in his manner and deportment and one of the best educated men, both in a military point of view and as a general scholar, that we have in this country. . . . He is in the prime and vigor of life, and admirably adapted for the command of our forces.

Although he did not receive the appointment, the petition was an indication that he was by no means forgotten, as he was often tempted to believe, and that his reputation had spread beyond the limits of the Army, where presently General Scott's infirmities were prompting much talk of Lee as his most logical successor.

A Mr. Moore was finally hired as overseer for Arlington, but he had no sooner moved into his quarters than he fell sick, delaying the departure for the Hot Springs until almost the middle of August. With her customary thoughtfulness, Aunt Maria invited Agnes, Rob, and Mildred to stay with her at Ravensworth during their parents' absence (Annie was going with Charlotte Wickham to the Alum Springs), since none of the children "inclined to the *Hot*," as their father wrote, Rob in particular "begging" that he might not "have to suffer again."

The terms of Mr. Custis' will were subject to several interpretations, particularly the part regarding the emancipation of his slaves, so Lee petitioned the Circuit Court of Virginia for a legal construction. When the court failed to act on the will by October 22, 1858, it became necessary for Robert to ask for an extension of his leave, which was granted until May, 1859. When the November term also adjourned without any action on the will, he was greatly disappointed, and complained:

"I never proceeded so slowly before in anything I have undertaken. . . ."

His cousin Anna Fitzhugh was aware of the drain on his personal funds, and sent Robert a check for one thousand dollars, a gift he graciously accepted—not for his present operations, as he explained, but "to be applied by me hereafter. . . . From my heart I thank you for this, & the many kindnesses you have always bestowed upon me. I feel them sensibly & appreciate them most highly. Too sensibly & too highly for my limited language to express." He explained to her the system he had evolved that allowed him to finish the present work without having to call on her gift:

As I limited from the outset my operations to my finances, & have advanced them according to my means, they have not borne so heavily upon me, & I have been enabled to meet their costs as I have progressed. . . . Everything so far is paid for. . . . I counted the cost before commencing. I have not been led astray in my progress by the desire to accomplish all I might think necessary. I have had a strict regard for economy both in my plans & progress.

279

Just before leaving for West Point on December 13 to attend a court of inquiry ordered to investigate a complaint about Professor Mahan's methods of teaching engineering, Lee wrote a note to Andrew Talcott, promising him a visit on the way home. It was supposed that the inquiry would take no more than three days, but when twice that number had passed and the end was still not in sight, he wrote Talcott again, doubting the possibility of a visit. To reach Arlington in time for Christmas, he feared he would have to go directly. After sending "much love" to the Beautiful Talcott, he included a special message for another favorite:

"Tell Mollie Gray not to get married till I get down. I want to make a last appeal to her sense of justice & truth—before I return to Texas alone."

He described the inquiry which deprived him of a visit with the Talcotts and Mollie Gray, as "extremely unpleasant & irksome," for it was also keeping him from supervising the work at home. But he found one indemnification for the inconvenience and privations. While passing through New York, he met Rooney's colonel, Charles A. May, and was "highly gratified at the encomiums he passed upon your soldiership, zeal, & devotion to your duty," he wrote the now "precious Roon," who had joined Custis at the Presidio in San Francisco.

This reunion of his sons, he told Rooney, was the most rewarding event of the year: "Hold on to him as long as you can. Kiss him for me & sleep with him every night. He must do the same to you & charge it to my account. God grant that it could be my good fortune to be with you both! I am glad that you stood the march so well, & are so robust & bearded. I always thought & said there was stuff in you for a good soldier."

Custis' health was now a cause for concern, for he was suffering acutely from what he believed was rheumatism, which seemed to increase rather than lessen with time. His father was "alarmed" at the news, and urged him to see Dr. McCormick, now also stationed in San Francisco. He hoped the physician might decide that the coastal climate was unfavorable, and get Custis transferred to Washington.

Toward the end of January, 1859, Lee was asked to serve

on a board of cavalry officers meeting each day in Washington from ten until three o'clock, to decide on a uniform style of horse equipage. After six or seven weeks of deliberation, one of the items adopted was the cossack saddle which George B. McClellan had brought back from an inspection tour of European methods and equipment—the saddle that would later bear his name. These meetings were time-consuming, and Lee was further annoyed by a heavy cold. The state of the roads after the weeks of incessant rain was the worst he had ever seen them, and made his daily rides a trial. There was some compensation, he admitted, and this was the pleasure of seeing Smith every day, for he also was serving on a board that met in the same building.

Rooney and Charlotte decided not to wait any longer to be married. Rooney sent in his resignation, and by January 30, was back home on leave. Since Mary was still unwilling to appear publicly, she did not go with Robert and the girls to Shirley for the March wedding. Until the repairs on the White House were finished, Rooney and Charlotte stayed at Arlington.

By the end of May, Robert's troubles at home were increased by the lengthening sick list. Charlotte had taken a bad cold and was under the doctor's care. Markie arrived for a visit but soon became "a Martyr to Neuralgia." Agnes's eyes had troubled her all winter and spring, and since they showed no improvement, her father took her to the doctors, who were in agreement that rheumatism was the cause and were "treating it accordingly." Among his other patients there was little to cheer him. Annie was "still far from strong," and Mary's condition had grown worse since his return from Texas; he had begun to despair that she would ever "be entirely relieved."

He was made to "feel very uneasy" when Edward Childe wrote him about Ann Marshall's threatened blindness. "The probability is as afflicting to her as the reality which she believes will occur," Robert wrote. He went to Baltimore to see her, finding her condition "poor."

"You see what a suffering set we are," he wrote Custis, whose "rheumatic attack" showed no improvement.

In spite of these constant demands, or perhaps because of

281

them, he was planning to return by the middle of June to his regiment, feeling free to leave Mary, for Custis' application for transfer to Washington had been made. But as the time drew near, the transfer still had not been approved, the court had not yet acted on the will, and the work at Arlington was far behind schedule, so Robert applied for an additional four-month leave. He was still greatly distressed that it had taken so long to do so little.

You must not have your mind exalted by Rooney's account of the improvements at this place [he warned Custis]. They are very meagre & only serve to ameliorate matters that formerly were very rough & ugly. I have not the means to do what I should like. . . . I have been able to do nothing to the grounds around the house, except to clean up on the hill, & have been obliged to limit myself to what is most essential, & promises something for man & beast to eat, & to furnish shelter & protection. You will find things, therefore, I fear rough & unsightly, as much as I desire to polish up your mother's habitation, & to prepare for you an acceptable home.

During the summer, Lee had his first personal encounter with the extravagances and inaccuracies of the abolitionist mind and pen, when the *New York Tribune* (and later the *New York Times*), printed two unsigned letters which accused him of keeping Mr. Custis' emancipated slaves in bondage by a ruse. They stated that the slaves had been freed on Mr. Custis' death, but Lee had deluded them into believing that they must wait five years for freedom. They accused him also of making even the aged people toil "from daylight to dark" on rations he had ordered cut to "half a peck of unsifted meal a week for each person, without even their fish allowance." Each writer also told of the capture of three Arlington slaves who, according to one correspondent, had "run away," while the other stated that in the innocent belief that their five-year period of waiting had expired, they had decided "to leave for the North." Both letters were in agreement on the point that when the slaves were brought back to Arlington, Lee had them whipped, and when "the brute in human form" refused to administer thirty-nine lashes to the one woman slave, Lee stripped her and applied the whip himself.

282

Two slaves, a man and a woman, had actually run away, and when they were brought back to Arlington, Lee hired them out in lower Virginia, an action dictated by the simple economic expedient that the demand for Negro help was small in northern Virginia. To have whipped a slave would have been as abhorrent to Lee as to his accusers. After the slaves had returned, a faithful and trusted servant told the Lees that for many months two abolitionists (perhaps the authors of the scurrilous letters) had been working among the Arlington slaves, urging them to run away, and inciting them to murder and armed rebellion. This was a common practice in the border states. "We were preserved I say by the *special* mercy of God," Mary wrote Eliza Stiles.

But as Lee had always done, he chose to ignore the slanders. "The *N. Y. Tribune* has attacked me for my treatment of your Grandfather's slaves, but I shall not reply. He has left me an unpleasant legacy," he said to Custis.

In August, Mary decided to try the healing waters of the Capon Springs. Agnes was going with her in the hope she might be cured of her eye trouble. Robert escorted them and, as was his practice, stayed on several days to see that they were satisfied, and then went home. He passed several evenings pleasantly with Custis' classmate, "Jeb" Stuart, a lieutenant in the First Calvary, spending his furlough in his native Virginia.

Early in October, Lee served on a court-martial meeting in New York, and was rewarded by a visit with the Talcotts. While he was in New York (which was now Army headquarters), General Scott, that "true & warm friend," as Robert described him, offered him the post of confidential secretary. Lee weighed its advantages, which were considerable since it offered the opportunity of staying with his family.

"If Colonel Lee accepts, what will they say, General, if all the staff are Southerners?" an aide asked Scott.

"If the Southern rascals have so much merit, how can we fail to advance them!"

But Lee refused because he foresaw another sedentary assignment, and because, at the moment, frontier duty seemed preferable to the trials and problems of home.

In his refusal "he was lavish in his thanks and terms of admiration for his old chief," a staff officer wrote, and Scott, knowing his man, was not offended. The post was filled by that other able and learned officer, Erasmus D. Keyes.

When Lee returned to Arlington, he devoted all his thoughts to pressing forward the work, for he was determined to rejoin his regiment without another extension of leave, little knowing that in a few days he would be called on to play an important role in what became the prologue to the nation's greatest tragedy.

2

MONDAY morning, October 17, 1859, was crisp and clear. Among the golden leaves in the grove at Arlington there were already many scarlet ones. The dogwood was in full berry, and the fallen seeds of the magnolia lay like crimson jewels on the brown earth. Persimmons were sweetening, and seckel pears glistened between the thinning leaves. All were portents of another winter that would find the work unfinished. Still, Lee could not justify another application for an extension of his leave. His departure for Texas was made easier by assurances from General Totten that Custis' transfer to Washington would soon be approved.

As he looked over his accounts and records that morning, he noted with satisfaction that the most pressing repairs and improvements had been managed by strict economy. He decided now to make up a list for Custis' use, enumerating the most important remaining tasks: Completion of repairs on the mill; a floodgate in the causeway across the creek; opening of the ditch through the swamp to drain it for health reasons; building of hay barracks north and south of the lane to the barnyard; fencing the pasture; removal of the pigpens from behind the kitchen to the ravine north of the icehouse; clearing brush, thinning trees, and removal of stumps.

His notations were interrupted at this point by the unexpected arrival of Jeb Stuart. He was delighted to see him, though it was evident, when Stuart handed him a sealed message from the War Department, that he had not come on a social call.

The letter ordered Lee to report at once to John Floyd, the Secretary of War. Without even taking time to change into his uniform, Lee rode with Stuart to the Secretary's office. Floyd told them about an insurrection at Harpers Ferry.

At eleven o'clock the previous night, a man known to his neighbors as Isaac Smith, a prospector, had entered town with a band of nineteen or more armed men. They had seized the United States Arsenal from its single watchman, had secured a number of hostages, and taken over the sleeping village. It was now under the rule of these raiders, whose avowed purpose was to free the slaves.

The Department was uncertain how many troops would be needed to quell the insurgents but had already ordered to the scene a detachment of marines from the Washington navy yard and a body of troops from Fort Monroe. Floyd asked Lee to take command of all forces, including the Maryland and Virginia Militia, already on its way to the Ferry; he asked Stuart to act as his aide.

They hurried to the railway station, stopping only long enough to send a message to Mary. They missed the 3:30 P.M. train that was carrying the marines, but a dispatcher, learning of their problem, gave them the use of a locomotive. A telegram was then sent to the train ahead ordering the marines to leave it at Sandy Hook and wait there for Lee's arrival. Then he and Stuart climbed into the cab with the engineer and fireman. Although it was ten-thirty that night when the engine carrying the two officers screeched to a stop at the little station, Lee marched the waiting marines to Harpers Ferry, a mile and a half away.

During the day, hundreds of armed citizens and the two companies of militia had reached the town. After a desultory exchange of fire with the raiders, and several casualties on both sides, Smith and his survivors and thirteen hostages took refuge in the fire-engine house at the Armory. If the militia had had proper leadership, the whole affair would have been over by the time Lee arrived.

As soon as he learned the number of raiders, Lee posted

marines around the engine house to prevent escape in the dark and telegraphed to Baltimore that the soldiers from Fort Monroe should proceed no further, for he would not need them. Then he made plans for an assault on the engine house at dawn. "But for fear of sacrificing the lives of some of the gentlemen held by them as prisoners in a midnight assault, I should have ordered the attack at once," he wrote in his report.

Around two A.M., he explained his plan to Stuart. He would demand surrender of the whole party at "first dawn" but, fully expecting Smith to refuse, he would have ready a storming party of picked men who would, at a given signal, take the place with the bayonet in order to save the hostages (among whom were several Negro slaves who had refused to accept freedom from their masters' captors).

Before dawn, Lee offered the honor of storming the engine-house first of all to Colonel Shriver of the Frederick, Maryland, volunteers. Shriver promptly declined:

"These men here have wives and children at home. I will not expose them to such risks. You are paid for this kind of work!"

Lee then turned to Colonel Baylor of the Virginia Militia, who, if he had other inclinations, was forced to refuse in order not to cast reflection on Shriver. He then asked Lieutenant Israel Green of the marines if he wished the honor of "taking those men out," and Green removed his hat, bowed, and thanked him for the opportunity. Lee next asked Green to pick twelve men, and when they had been chosen, he personally instructed each one to use only the bayonet.

Around seven o'clock that morning, all was ready. Stuart, armed with a white flag, walked to the enginehouse doors, while some two thousand people looked on. When he told Smith that he had a communication for him from Colonel Lee, the door opened four inches, Smith placed his body against the crack, and training his cocked carbine on Stuart, took the paper. One look at Smith and Stuart recognized him:

"He was old *Osawatomie Brown* who had given us so much trouble in Kansas."

After reading the demands for his surrender, John Brown declared he would surrender only if he and his party were allowed to escape. Several hostages then begged Stuart to ask Lee to come and reason with Brown, but Jeb assured them that the Colonel would never accede to any terms but those he had offered. Then one hostage shouted in defiance:

"Never mind us, fire!" And Lee, standing on a slight eminence a few feet from the enginehouse, heard the words and recognized the speaker as his old friend, Colonel Lewis W. Washington, a grandnephew of George Washington. Robert shook his head, and turning to Lieutenant Green, who stood beside him, remarked:

"The old revolutionary blood does tell!"

It had been agreed that in case of a refusal of the terms, Stuart would step back from the door and wave his hat. He now did this, and at the signal, three of Green's men attacked the doors with sledge hammers. But when the doors did not yield, Green, seeing a forty-foot ladder lying on the ground, ordered the marines to use this as a battering-ram. At the second blow, the door was shattered and the defenders began to fire wildly. Green slipped through the hole unharmed, his men following, though not without injury and one fatality.

By now, Lee had approached the door, within range of raider Edwin Copoc's rifle. Copoc took aim at him, but just as he was about to pull the trigger, Mr. Graham, a hostage, knocked the muzzle aside, causing the bullet to fly harmlessly in the air. It is possible that in that crowded day Lee never learned how narrowly he had escaped death from gunfire, for the second time in his life.

Three minutes after Jeb Stuart had waved his hat, the affray was over, and Brown, bleeding profusely, was carried out. None of the hostages was injured—only dishevelled, hungry, and thirsty. A young officer standing at the door admired "the coolness and nonchalance" of Colonel Washington, who, as he walked quietly away from the fort, took from his pocket a pair of dark green kid gloves and began to pull them on, quite as though he were starting out on an afternoon stroll. He was shortly surrounded by a group of excited friends who, after finding that he was unharmed, invited him to "take something" with them at the Wager House. With a smile he replied:

"Thank you, I will. It seems a month since I've had one."

A mob immediately swarmed forward to demand the captives, but Lee, with that firmness which allowed no question of his authority, declared that he would protect them. "His orders, conveyed in mild language, were instantly obeyed, and his motives universally understood." He treated the "rioters," as he called them, with kindliness, having Brown and his wounded compatriot, Aaron Stevens, carried to the paymaster's office where cots were set up and a surgeon called. Brown's wounds were found to be superficial, and after they were dressed he was left to rest.

During the afternoon, Virginia's Governor Wise, Senator James M. Mason, Colonel Washington, and several other dignitaries came to talk with Brown. But before Lee allowed them in the room, he first asked Brown and Stevens if their presence would cause either one pain or annoyance. Brown replied that he was "glad to make himself and his motives clearly understood." During the interview, Lee took no other part than to write down the names of Brown's men as they were mentioned.

After the colloquy, Lee sent two parties into Maryland to search Brown's farmhouse, and to hunt for other members of his band. A large store of weapons and ammunition—one hundred Sharpe's carbines, one hundred belt revolvers, five hundred spears, and fifteen hundred pikes—were found stored in a schoolhouse a short distance from Harpers Ferry. At the farmhouse there were many papers, the most important of which Lee forwarded to the Secretary of War, at the same time asking orders as to the disposition of the prisoners. When he received orders that Brown and his men were to be held in the custody of the United States Marshal and the county sheriff, Lieutenant Green and an escort of marines took them to Charlestown, the county seat.

Lee disbanded the militia and upon Green's return was completing his report, intending to start for Washington that evening. But at nine P.M. he was brought word that about sunset a body of raiders had descended from the mountains, entered the quiet hamlet of Pleasant Valley, five miles away, and murdered an entire family. Though always doubtful of rumor, Lee hurried to the village with Stuart, Green, and twenty-five marines, finding the town as peaceful as its name, and the "murdered" family tranquilly sleeping. They then returned to the Ferry, reaching there in time to take the 1:15 A.M. train to the capital. From the train, Lee went directly to the war secretary's office, presenting him both a written and verbal report. It was nearly noon before he could at last turn wearily homeward.

John Brown's trial was set for October 25, and the entire North was aroused at what it considered "undue speed." Governor Wise's mail was flooded with threatening and abusive letters, and rescue of Brown by force or subterfuge was darkly hinted. But when Brown refused rescue, the abolitionists who had backed him financially and morally began preparing the way, from the pulpit, the rostrum, and the press, for his martyrdom.

On the evening of October 26, Bronson Alcott, William Ellery Channing, Franklin Benjamin Sanborn, and Henry David Thoreau met at the home of Ralph Waldo Emerson. Recording the meeting in his journal, Alcott wrote:

We discussed the matter at length, I defending the deed, under the circumstances, and the *Man*. His rescue would be difficult, even if he would consent to be taken. And the spectacle of a martyrdom such as his must needs be, will be of greater service to the country, and to the coming of a righteous rule, than years of agitation by the Press, or the voices of partisans, North and South. 'Twas a bold stroke, this of his, for justice universal. . . .

Perhaps Brown, with his zealot's eye, glimpsed martyrdom, too, and sensing a greater service to the cause by his death, preferred it to rescue.

If Lee saw any portents in Brown's act, he failed to record them. His sole comment was included in his final report:

"The result proves that the plan was the attempt of a fanatic or a madman."

He was not alone in this judgment, for many of Brown's most enthusiastic supporters were shocked by his sudden and unexpected raid, and some questioned his sanity.

289

Brown's execution was set for December 2, and Governor Wise, apprehensive of mob violence, ordered to Charlestown the Virginia and Maryland militia and a body of cadets from the Virginia Military Institute, one of whose commanders was Professor Thomas J. Jackson. Wise convinced President Buchanan that he should send Lee with some troops to Harpers Ferry to prevent seizure of the arsenal.

Once again, Lee's orders to return to his regiment were suspended as he left Washington with four companies of artillerymen from Fort Monroe. He was kept busy most of November 30, posting his sentinels and pickets, and securing quarters and meals for his men. He professed to be sorely disappointed that "no charming women have insisted on taking care of me," as he declared they always did Smith Lee. "I am left to my own resources."

The day of Brown's hanging passed quietly at Charlestown and Harpers Ferry. But at both towns there was a significant gathering of men in the Federal and State forces. Here were commanders and men in the ranks, now of one purpose and allegiance, who would shortly be spilling each other's blood on this very soil, the severing of their allegiance hastened by the hysteria arising from this one man's hanging. In the company of militia from Richmond, there stood a young man who would prove an enemy to both North and South—the actor, John Wilkes Booth.

The forces at work to divide the country commenced their work with renewed ardor that very day. In Concord, Massachusetts, Bronson Alcott planned a "Martyr Service," which was held at two P.M. in the town hall. The throngs that overflowed the meeting house were moved to tears by the readings of Thoreau, Emerson, and Alcott. Sanborn's "dirge," composed for the occasion, was sung by the congregation. This was typical of meetings and services held all over the North, though they were more numerous in New England, where the seed of radical abolitionism grew rankest. Fearful of reprisal, it was not until December 12 that Lee and his troops were ordered to leave Harpers Ferry.

Winter had come to Arlington, and the year's work was

almost at an end. Once again, Lee made ready to return to his regiment, and once again his orders were suspended—this time so that he might testify before a United States Senate hearing on the "Harpers Ferry Conspiracy." He was also asked to attend meetings of the Military Committee of Virginia's General Assembly, called for the purpose of arming the State, for the people were apprehensive not only of retaliation but of a slave uprising.

On February 8, he received orders to take temporary command of the Department of Texas, with headquarters in San Antonio, and left Arlington before dawn on the tenth.

"As long as this journey has been before me, & as often as it has been delayed, still I find when it does come, it is not the less sorrowful or hard to bear," he told his Cousin Anna in a farewell letter.

But he was relieved that Custis and Rooney were "both on the spot, & able to attend to the general welfare." He had hoped to escort Mary as far as Richmond on her way to the White House, where she wanted to be present for the birth of their first grandchild, but as might be foreseen, she was not ready and he was unable to wait for her.

Lee registered at Mrs. Philip's Hotel, facing the plaza in San Antonio, on February 21. The next day he was writing Annie of his distress at being so far away, and his "longing desire" to see her again.

"I know it is useless to indulge these feelings," he told her, "yet they arise unbidden, & will not stay repressed. They steal on me in the business hours of the day & the waking hours of the night & seem to hover around me working or sleeping."

Since his appointment as commander of the department was, as he termed it, "accidental," and would last only until a higher ranking officer was sent to fill it, he was in a quandary to "know where to fix myself or whether to fix myself at all. Things look so uncertain."

Of his duties, he wrote home: "I have not much work to do but many vexatious reports to listen to & small means to correct & improve. In addition to Indian alarms & depredations, we have the fillibustering reports & Mexican aggressions to scruti-

291

nize & discuss. The latter come so thick & various, that it is difficult to sift the chaff from the grain."

His most irksome problem was Juan Nepomuceno Cortina (occasionally Cortinas), a Mexican soldier and brigand who for the last ten years had been making border raids, and by slipping across the river after each foray, managed to evade Texas authorities. On the night of December 5, however, Cortina and his band had been defeated by United States troops, with the help of the Texas Rangers at Brownsville, and since then the bandit had remained quiet. But reports began to come to Lee now that Cortina had gathered a few followers again and was making raids into the small settlements along the Rio Grande. There were so many contradictory accounts concerning him, and so much talk of Indian depredations in that area, that Lee decided to investigate for himself. With a small body of cavalry, he rode out to Eagle Pass which Cortina was supposedly approaching.

On arriving there, Lee found the report "all flam & clap trap," so he wrote a daughter. From Eagle Pass he marched along the left bank of the river toward Laredo, all of it "wretched country" where the only persons he saw were "a few miserable Mexicans, driving their oxen," and the only wildlife, "a few mustangs, rattlesnakes, deer, antelope, & one turkey." When he reached Laredo, he encountered what was to become a familiar story in this search for Cortina: the brigand had not come to Laredo, but was rumored to be nearing the next settlement farther down the river.

Since his baggage wagon got stuck in the mud, Lee bivouacked in a vacant room in the old quarters at the fort, and wrote Annie from his cheerless surroundings. The room was damp, and he would be glad to get on with his march toward Rio Grande City. The movement would be a repetition "of what has preceded," he told her. "Reveille at 4 a.m. March at 5½. Encamp about 2 p.m. Graze horses till dark. Tattoo at 8 p.m." But he preferred this active life to staying in San Antonio, was "quite comfortable" in his tent, and satisfied with his rations which consisted of "a nice boiled ham, coffee, rice, eggs, tomatoes & molasses." Before he left San Antonio, some army wives had given him a large sponge cake and a pound cake, but "that has in a measure disappeared, for cake cannot travel with cavalry long." Wistfully he added: "If I had one of my daughters to keep house for me I would be set up."

When he reached Ringgold Barracks, he made a careful search of the lower Rio Grande valley, again finding everything quiet. On his return to the Barracks, he received a jubilant letter from Rooney, announcing the birth of a son. "That anxiously expected little boy!" Robert replied:

I sincerely congratulate you & my darling daughter at this prosperous advent. . . . You must kiss his dear mother for me, & offer her my warmest thanks for this promising scion to my scattered house, who will, I hope, resuscitate its name & fame. Tell her I have thought much of her & long to see you both, & your little treasure. . . . Your Mama must have rejoiced at another *baby* in the house, & had all her former feelings brought back afresh. I never could see the infantine beauties that she did, but I will be able to appreciate him by the time I see him.

Major John S. Ford of the Texas Rangers called on Lee while he was at Ringgold. He wanted him to know that his men were encamped some forty miles below, and though they had seen nothing of Cortina either, they were willing to cooperate with the cavalry if he should appear. Ford was greatly impressed by Lee's presence, finding him dignified without hauteur, grand without pride, "in keeping with the noble simplicity characterizing a true republican. . . . To approach him was to feel yourself in the presence of a man of superior intellect, possessing the capacity to accomplish great ends, and the gift of controlling and leading men."

When Lee came to Fort Brown, after thoroughly scouring the country along the way, he found further reports concerning the brigand.

The last authentic accounts I could get concerning Cortinas, was that with his wife, children & 2 men he was making his way in Mexican Ox carts into the interior & was 135 miles off. The Mexican Authorities with whom I have been holding a sharp correspondence *said* they had sent an express to the authorities to arrest him. Still I do not expect it to be done & do not like to enter in blind pursuit after a man so far in the interior, with broken down horses. It is the food for them that stops me more than anything else. . . . If it was prairie in a grass country in which horses could live, I would try him.

While at Fort Brown, Robert learned of his friend Joe Johnston's appointment to the post of quartermaster general, recently vacated by the death of Thomas Jessup; it carried with it the rank of brevet brigadier general. Johnston had always been aggressive and never averse to angling for promotion. As early as 1846, Lee had observed this characteristic and remarked on it good-naturedly to Jack Mackay. Recently, Johnston had been on detached duty in Washington, working on a special assignment, which because of its importance would have earned him promotion in line with his years of service. But he had overplayed his hand this time, finding himself highly unpopular. Since he was a cousin of Secretary of War Floyd, his appointment was so obvious an example of nepotism that it caused much resentment, particularly among officers who ranked him.

Lee's family shared the resentment and made caustic comments on Joe's promotion. In a letter to Custis, Robert said:

My friend Col. Joe Johnston is a good soldier & worthy man & desires all advancement when it can be done without injustice to others. I think it must be evident to him that it never was the intention of Congress to advance him to the position assigned him by the Secy. It was not so recognized before, & in proportion to his services he has been advanced beyond any one in the Army, & has thrown more discontent than ever on the system of favouritism in making brevets.

As much as Lee desired advancement, he knew that he was incapable of ever seeking it or playing for favors. As one fellow officer observed: "He never intrigued for promotion or award." As he now looked back over his life, it appeared to him to be a failure, though he believed he saw its error:

"A divided heart I have too long had, & a divided life too long led." This, he felt, accounted for "the small progress I have made on either hand, my professional & civil career." He realized that his life had always been torn between inclination and obligation, that in every important step, due to some outside force or to one from within, obligation had been the governing factor and had thwarted his inclinations. He had stood by and watched other men take the bold strides that led them to success, unable to follow their example. He had looked on while others less deserving received promotion and glory, while he remained relatively unnoticed. He observed other men basking in the love and devotion of their wives and children and their close friends, while he remained solitary.

He foresaw a life of loneliness on remote posts, a life shorn of the company of his children, the comforts of a home, and the intimate friendships he needed. He must have thought, too, about the void of marriage to a woman incapable of happiness anywhere but in her childhood home; a woman who clung not to her husband, but to her parents, and now that they were gone, to the memory of them.

Believing that a man may manifest and communicate his joy but should conceal and smother his grief, he kept these melancholy conclusions to himself, although a few references to his "past errors," "the error of my ways," and the acknowledgment that he had too long had a divided heart and life escaped him, giving the clue to his mood.

He was convinced that he could expect little cooperation from the Mexican officials toward the capture of Cortina, and so felt free to return to San Antonio. He had his wagons greased, the mules foraged, and a stock of provisions packed. For his own fare he took a boiled ham, roasted coffee, eggs, and potatoes, and "kind Mrs. Gilliam" presented him with a large cake. But the day before he was to start, word was received that Cortina had returned, the report being "so straight" that he laid a plan to take the Mexican by surprise. He sent two detachments across the river to make the capture, but the wily Cortina escaped because, Lee felt certain, he had been warned in advance. He was keenly disappointed, for it meant that the entire expedition had, as he said, "accomplished but little." This was, however, the last time he was called on to look for the man he now termed "that myth Cortinas."

He found San Antonio sweltering, and sought escape from the heat by swimming in the river. "The thermometer has been ranging up to a hundred degrees for nearly three weeks, occasionally exceeding it," he reported to Agnes. "If any of your friends are preparing to personate salamanders, send them out."

A week later, in spite of the unbroken heat wave, his mood was still bright when he proposed to Annie that "Leo," an Arlington feline, and "the ornament of the establishment," be given as a wedding present to their cousin, Mary Carter. This act would be "handsome on the occasion" and "creditable to the family. See if you can't get Custis' consent. There will be a void in the hearts of the family I know, which might possibly be filled by Tom." He then urged his daughter to "eat plenty of strawberries for me . . . & raspberries with cold cream. We do not indulge in such trivial amusements here, & ice is abhorrent to our taste, toned down & softened with tepid water."

He had been suffering for some time with what he judged was rheumatism: "It is uncomfortable . . . in its present stage but more to be apprehended as the harbinger of future evil," he feared. "I hope it may pass away, for being in the right arm, makes it more objectionable for a soldier . . . if heat can drive it away, I am in a prosperous way."

He was still living at the hotel. Since his future was so uncertain, he did not think it "right to incur the expense" of establishing himself but in a "temporary manner. I therefore . . . suffer all the annoyances that a person of my unfortunate temperament must undergo in such an establishment, in such a country, & such a population." Major Chilton was being reassigned to Virginia, and Robert regretted the loss of his company and that of his wife and daughters. After the departure of little Emma and Laura, he sent this message home: "Tell Mildred I have not a soul now in all Texas even to give me a kiss." And to Mildred, who was at boarding school in Winchester pining for home and her pet cat, he wrote:

"I have no little girls here now to play with, & expect that I am more lonely even than you are without Tom. You have other kittens about you but I have not."

He took an active interest in the completion of St. Mark's Episcopal Church in San Antonio, and asked Mary if any of her "rich friends" could spare a thousand dollars or two for a good cause. But his chief interest lay in the progress at Arlington, and much of his time was spent in thought about it. In long letters to Custis, he discussed crops, soil, improvements, accounts, and investments. The survey of the estate had finally been made, and he was glad to learn that there was more property than they had thought. The mill was bringing in some revenue, and it was apparent from all reports that Custis was admirably managing two occupations at once.

He was also greatly pleased to find that Rooney had with such ease turned his sword into a ploughshare, and had made a good crop at the White House. He was also furthering the improvements on his farm by a strict attention to economy, a faculty his father admitted he was amazed to find in this son. Still, he could not resist giving Rooney advice in a vein that was strongly reminiscent of Light-Horse Harry's in letters to Carter. Though Robert's language was less eloquent and classical, it carried the same burden:

I am glad to hear your mechanics are all paid off, & that you have managed so well for your purposes. As you have commenced, I hope you will continue, never to exceed your means. It will save much anxiety & mortification, & enable you to maintain your independence of character & feeling. It is easier to make our wishes conform to our means than to make our means conform to our wishes. In fact, we want but little. Our happiness depends upon our independence, the success of our operations, prosperity of our plans, health, contentment, & the esteem of our friends, all of which my dear son, I hope you may enjoy to the full.

Mary had written that the publishers of her father's *Recollections* were planning to issue a new edition. Lee had with him a copy that he read "at occasional times," and had made notations of the errors he had found. He sent this memorandum to her along with a newspaper clipping about the artist, "little Jimmy Whistler," as he called him. Familiar with his schoolboy failings, he commented: "I wish indeed that he may succeed in his career. He certainly has talent, if he could acquire application."

He was relieved to learn that Rob had decided on a civil career, and had enrolled for the fall semester at the University of Virginia. The prospect of the education of both Rob and Mildred being "advanced as far as the opportunities admit," pleased him. "The education of a man or woman is never complete till they die," he told Mary. "There is always before them much to learn & more to do. Our hardest lesson is self-knowledge, & it is one that is perhaps never accomplished."

By the end of September, the worst heat was over and there came the welcome rains: "The thirsty earth is laughing with delight," Robert wrote. "How good is God! Nature is smiling again, & man encouraged."

His heart was lightened and he was even able to joke about his inability to push himself for advancement: "Tell my friends to give me all the promotion they can," he suggested facetiously. He pretended to be alarmed at the possibility of Agnes, who was visiting in the North, being "captured" by the abolitionists—"especially if she has been expressing any opinions inimical to their theories."

The arrival of two detachments of recruits brought some interest to the "desert of dulness," for among the officers who accompanied them were four wives, two of whom were brides. Major Brooks, in command of one of the detachments, had an independent wife who both amused and baffled Robert.

One blustery Saturday morning in late November, she accompanied her husband into town from their camp, and while the Major was adjusting his papers, Lee invited her into his office to warm herself. He found her young, refined, and pretty, and attractively dressed in a stylish "travelling costume." Nothing would have pleased him more than to have had her company for an hour or two, had he been able to penetrate her reserve. Try as he would, she remained aloof. When he suggested that rather than expose her dainty self to the rigors of camp life in winter, she take a room at what he termed "the crack Hotel of the City," she dismissed the advice curtly.

When later he asked her to take dinner with him that day and she refused coldly, he was puzzled at his inability to overcome her apathy.

"She adhered to her husband," he wrote drily. Mrs. Brooks' frigidity prompted him to pun:

"I did not see or hear anything of any little streams or rivulets & hesitated to ask."

3

WHEN General Twiggs arrived on December 13, 1860, to take over the command of the Department of Texas, he told Lee at their first meeting that he believed the Union was in danger of being dissolved in just a matter of weeks. Robert, however, took a more sanguine view.

If I thought so, I would not take the trouble to go to Mason but return to you now [he told Custis]. I hope . . . the wisdom & patriotism of the country will devise some way of saving it. . . . The three propositions of the President are eminently just, & are in accordance with the Constitution, & ought to be cheerfully assented to by all the States. But I do not think the Northern & Western States will agree to them. It is, however, my only hope for the preservation of the Union, & I will cling to it to the last. . . . I am not pleased with the course of the "Cotton States," as they term themselves. In addition to their selfish, dictatorial bearing, the threats they throw out against the "Border States" as they call them, if they will not join them, argue little for the benefit. While I wish to do what is right, I am unwilling to do what is wrong, either at the bidding of the South or the North. One of their plans seems to be the renewal of the slave trade. That I am opposed to on every ground.

That afternoon, Charles Anderson, a Kentuckian with strong Union sympathies, called on Lee to show him a copy of General Scott's "Views," which the General had sent with the request that Anderson show it to Twiggs and Lee, and others at his discretion. In this treatise, Scott proposed measures to prevent war, but in the event of their failure, he gave suggestions for strategy.

When Anderson came back to pick up the pamphlet, he brought with him Dr. Willis Edwards. As soon as they were seated, Anderson recalled that Lee addressed him earnestly:

"My friend, I must make one request of you, and that is that you will not suffer these *Views* to get into the newspapers." He was fearful, he explained, that the suggested methods of warfare might be taken out of context and printed as proof of the federal government's manifest aggressiveness. Anderson agreed to keep the pamphlet from the press.

During a discussion of the national crisis, Lee maintained his usual reluctance to take sides: "Somebody is surely grievously at fault, probably both factions," was his only comment. However, when Dr. Edwards brought up the problem of a man's first loyalty, Lee had a definite opinion which he did not hesitate to state. He had been taught to believe, and did believe, that his first allegiance was to Virginia, Anderson remembered him saying.

On December 18, he left San Antonio to take command of Fort Mason. He took along servants, wagons, horses, and mules, and in his satchel, a copy of Edward Everett's *Life of George Washington*, which Custis had sent him by General Twiggs' aide, Major Nicholls. He looked forward to life at Fort Mason since he preferred Texas wilderness to its cities. "My personal comforts will be less there," he wrote his son, "& I will have to exchange the protection of a house for the shelter of a tent. But I shall not mind that . . . except so far as it will take me further from you all, & render communication with you more distant & precarious. But God's will be done!"

There was need for this unwavering faith, for the next day, while he was on the road, South Carolina seceded from the Union. "God defend us from civil war!" was the prayer of all but the most fanatic minds, South and North. The festivities incident to Christmas were curtailed throughout the land by the uncertainty of the future, and even at Fort Mason, Lee found "the officers & men of the Regiment . . . much exercised as to their future. All are looking for what is to turn up, & are consequently at a loss how to make their arrangements." There was concern over the possibility of Texas following

South Carolina's steps. For this contingency Lee made plans to fortify the post to protect United States property.

Events that would lead up to the ultimate schism now came in rapid succession: the day after Christmas, Major Robert Anderson (a brother of Lee's friend, Charles) spiked the guns at Fort Moultrie in Charleston's harbor and moved his garrison to the more easily defended Fort Sumter. On January 17, Senator Crittenden's peace resolutions were tabled, thus ending almost the last hope of reconciliation. Like other reasonable persons, Lee had hoped for their success since they were, as he said, "fair & just." He felt that they should have received the "cheerful assent & support of every patriot."

"Madness, literary frenzy, seems to possess our Countrymen," a Virginia intellectual observed. "The incredible fatuity of the South—incredible if it were not exhibited before our eyes—finds its parallel in an equal fatuity at the North." Of this frenzy and fatuity Lee made this statement, highly significant in view of his later actions:

The proceedings of the Southern States in sequestering the public property within their reach or as it is pompously termed, Capturing the U. S. Forts, arsenals, &c., &c., whenever there is nobody to defend them, I fear will not calm the angry feelings existing in the country, & except in self defense, I think unnecessary. I therefore conclude that those States on no condition will adhere to the Union. . . . If the bond of the Union can only be maintained by the sword & bayonet, instead of brotherly love & friendship, & if strife & civil war are to take the place of mutual aid & commerce, its existence loses all interest with me. . . . I can however do nothing but trust in the wisdom & patriotism of the Nation & to the overruling providence of a merciful God. I am particularly anxious that Virginia should keep right, as she was chiefly instrumental in the formation & inauguration of the Constitution. So I could wish that she might be able to maintain it to save the Union. . . .

As he read the biography of Washington, he was even more deeply impressed with the nation's fatuity: "How his spirit would be grieved to see the wreck of his mighty labours!" he wrote Mary on January 23, 1861.

301

I will not however, permit myself to believe till all ground for hope is gone that the work of his noble deeds will be destroyed, & that his precious advice & virtuous example will so soon be forgotten by his countrymen. As far as I can judge from the papers, we are between a state of anarchy & civil war. . . . I fear that mankind will not for years be sufficiently christianized to bear the absence of restraint & force. I see that four States have declared themselves out of the Union; four more will apparently follow their example. Then, if the Border States are brought into the gulf of revolution, one half the country will be arrayed against the other. I must try & be patient & await the end, for I can do nothing to hasten or retard it.

Rooney had written to his father about the baby's christening, performed at nearby St. Peter's Church by the family friend, Mr. Dana (the rector of Alexandria's Christ Church) who was visiting them at the White House. The child was named Robert Edward. On January 23, the delighted grandfather replied, and asked that "the dear little fellow" be taught to "love his Grand Papa, to bear with his failings & avoid his errors."

Rooney had also written at length about the state of the country, and his father, in this same letter, once again reaffirmed his strong love for the Union, and his contempt for succession:

As an American citizen I take great pride in my country, her prosperity & institutions & would defend any State if her rights were invaded. But I can anticipate no greater calamity for the country than the dissolution of the Union. . . . I hope therefore all Constitutional means will be exhausted, before there is resort to force. Secession is nothing but revolution. The framers of our Constitution never exhausted so much labour, wisdom & forebearance in its formation & surrounded it with so many guards & securities, if it was intended to be broken by every member of the confederacy at will. It was intended for perpetual union . . . It is idle to talk of secession. . . . In 1808 when the New England States resisted Mr. Jeffersons Imbargo Law & the Hartford Convention assembled, secession was termed treason by a Virga statesman. What can it be now? . . .

He expressed similar sentiments to Markie. He had heard from home that Custis and Orton Williams were each looking forward to a captaincy in the army of the Southern Republic. "The subject recalls my grief at the condition of our country. God alone can save us from our folly, selfishness & short sightedness. The last accounts seem to show that we have barely escaped anarchy to be plunged into civil war." His next words are important:

I wish to live under no other government, & there is no sacrifice I am not ready to make for the preservation of the Union save honour. If a disruption takes place, I shall go back in sorrow to my people & share the misery of my native State, & save in her defence there will be one less soldier in the world than now. I wish for no other flag than the "Star Spangled Banner" & no other air than "Hail Columbia."

But events were never too serious to prevent Robert from enjoying the presence of a pretty young woman, and such a being arrived at Fort Mason on the evening of January 22 in the form of the bride of Lieutenant William W. Lowe, adjutant of the regiment. Lee invited them to breakfast, and for this special occasion his servant "adorned the table with the equipage of my mess chest. It is the first time I have had it all out." In describing the event to Markie, he asked:

"What is your conception of a bridal breakfast in the Comanche country? The most important accompaniment is a fine appetite. The lady's I am sorry to say was timid, her swain's bold & soldierly, & he attacked the beef steak, hashed turkey & boiled eggs fearlessly. They dine [with me] again tomorrow."

On February 1, the Texas Convention passed an ordinance of secession by a vote of 166 to 7. Though it called for a general referendum, there was little doubt as to the result. Lee now became restive and hoped for the removal of Federal troops before Texas left the Union. "I certainly shall not want to stay," he remarked.

On February 6, an express from San Antonio brought an unexpected summons for him. By direct order of the War Department, he was relieved from duty with the Second Cavalry, and requested to report to General Scott in Washington not later than April 1.

Lee could not be certain of the meaning of this summons, but he probably strongly suspected that the wily old chieftain was hoping to keep him loyal to the Union, and wished to enlist his services before Virginia made her decision. Sensing that there would be no return to Texas, Robert prepared to take all his possessions.

On February 13, he was ready to leave. A group of his closest associates stood by to see him off. As he prepared to climb into the ambulance that was carrying his belongings, Captain Richard M. Johnson asked the question that was foremost in the mind of everyone there:

"Colonel, do you intend to go South or remain North?"

"I shall never bear arms against the Union, but it may be necessary for me to carry a musket in defence of my native State, Virginia," he replied enigmatically. As the ambulance started off, he turned to wave, calling back:

"Good-by! God bless you!"

At noon, his driver stopped at a favorite resting place for travelers—a spring shaded by a group of splendid oaks. Here, Lee met one of his officers, Captain George Cosby, returning from San Antonio. Since Cosby was about to eat his lunch, Lee suggested that they eat together. The Captain expressed surprise at seeing his commander here, and Lee told him about General Scott's message. Cosby knew of Scott's "exalted" opinion of Lee, and told him that he suspected Scott wanted his help in planning a campaign against the South.

Lee feared that Cosby was right, and told him that if this was what Scott wanted, he would decline, and resign from the service. However, he was hopeful that Virginia would not act on impulse, Cosby remembered him saying, but

would act as she had in the past, and would exhaust every means consistent with honor to avert civil war. That, if she failed and determined to secede, he would offer his services. That he had been taught that his first allegiance was due his mother State; that he fervently hoped that some agreement would be reached to avoid such a terrible war; and there was no personal sacrifice he would not make to save his beloved country from such a dreadful calamity; but under no circumstances could he ever bare his sword against Virginia's sons.

As he spoke, tears filled his eyes, and he turned aside to avoid displaying his emotions.

When, that afternoon, the ambulance turned into San Antonio's usually quiet streets, Lee saw that they were crowded with armed men on whose shirts he observed a red insignia. Guards were posted at every important corner, and the plaza had the appearance of a military camp. As his vehicle stopped in front of the Read House and he climbed out, a group of men came up and stared at him coldly. Then he saw Mrs. Caroline Darrow, the wife of an acquaintance, coming along the street. After greeting her, he asked:

"Who are these men?"

"They are McCulloch's. General Twiggs surrendered everything to the State this morning, and we are all prisoners of war," she replied. Momentarily Lee's poise was gone. Tears clouded his eyes for the second time that day.

"Has it come so soon to this?" he asked. Mrs. Darrow noted the anguish in his tone.

He then excused himself and hurried into the hotel, where he took a room. After he had recovered his equanimity, he changed into his civilian clothes and went over to his old headquarters. He found the secessionist Committee of Public Safety now in charge.

After he had made his arrangements to start for Washington, he was told by the Texas commissioners that if he resigned and joined the Confederacy, he would receive all cooperation, but if he refused, he would not be allowed to take his personal property. Angered by what he considered an undisguised threat, he pointed out that his allegiance was still to Virginia and the Union.

He then called on his friend Charles Anderson to ask him the favor of caring for his belongings until they could be forwarded to him. Anderson was amazed to see Lee so indignant. As they walked to the storage house, Lee reminded him of their conversation with Dr. Edwards, and Anderson quoted him as saying now:

I still think . . . that my loyalty to Virginia ought to take precedence over that which is due the Federal Government. . . . If Virginia stands by the old Union, so will I. But if she secedes (though I do not believe in secession as a constitutional right, nor that there is sufficient cause for revolution), then I will still follow my native State with my sword, and if need be with my life. I know you think and feel very differently, but I can't help it. These are my principles, and I must follow them.

Nothing was done to prevent his departure. A number of officers from the Second Cavalry came to see him off at the stage depot. He was no longer reluctant to express his views, and said to one officer as they shook hands:

"When I get to Virginia I think the world will have one soldier less. I shall resign and go to planting corn."

Although many of these men would never see Lee again, and some were to meet him on opposing battlefields, they never forgot him. After the Civil War, several who had fought for the Union recalled him from those Texas days.

A captain described him as "one of the most agreeable men I ever knew; handsome, courteous as a knight, pleasant and entertaining in conversation. He was universally beloved by all the officers of his regiment."

Another officer spoke of him as "gentle and unobtrusive, yet singularly commanding," while still another remembered that "he attracted the love, admiration, and confidence of all. The little children always hailed him with glee—his sincerity, kindliness of nature, cordial manners, attracting their unreserved confidence."

And one more wrote of his "affability" and his talent for "small-talk with the ladies."

It was not only members of the garrison whom Lee impressed. Many citizens in San Antonio remembered him as long as memory served. One of these townspeople who never met him personally, and saw him only once as Lee stood on the verandah of a public building watching drill, spoke most prophetically. As she looked at Lee, noble and commanding, she said:

"There stands a great man!"

4

WHEN Lee walked into General Scott's office that blustery March day shortly after his return to Arlington, his friend Erasmus Keyes, Scott's confidential secretary, rose to greet him warmly. After they had talked a minute, Keyes said to him:

"Lee, it is reported that you concurred in Twiggs' surrender of Texas; how's that?"

Lee immediately "assumed an air of great seriousness, and calmly said: 'I am here to pay my respects to General Scott; will you be kind enough, Colonel, to show me to his office?' I opened the general's door, Lee passed in, and the two Virginians remained alone together for nearly three hours."

Although it was Scott's custom to relate to Keyes what passed during his interviews with important persons, "on this occasion he told me not a word, and he made no reference to the subject of his conversation with Colonel Lee. His manner that day when we dined alone, was painfully solemn."

Keyes recalled that Scott held "an almost idolatrous fancy for Lee, whose military genius he estimated far above that of any other officer of the army." At one time, when war with England seemed imminent, Scott said to his secretary: "It would be cheap for the United States to insure Lee's life for $5,000,000 a year!"

Scott had "selected him in his own mind as the most capable and promising officer in the service to become the principal commander in the field, and of this intention he spoke to many without reserve." But during their interview he did not directly offer the command to Lee, as has so often been maintained, for Lee has stated, and we must accept his word, that he held but *one* conversation concerning his taking command of the Federal Army, and that conversation was with Francis Preston Blair, Sr.

There is no doubt that Scott did refer to his advanced age and infirmities, and his own probable resignation, intimating that Lee would receive the command. To Lee's argument that he would not "unsheath his sword against his native State," Scott assured him that he would not be leading "an army of Northern men to *fight* against the South. On the contrary he desired to see him at the head of a Union force sufficiently powerful to keep peace and to prevent civil war, which they both equally abhorred." But as sanguine as was Lee's nature, he could not accept such reasoning. When they parted, the old General told him to think it over carefully, for to resign would be the greatest mistake of his life.

Lee regarded General Twiggs's surrender of Texas as "inexcusable," and did not hesitate to say so. For this act, Twiggs was dismissed from the army, and Colonel Sumner, commander of the First Cavalry, was promoted to brigadier general and appointed to Twiggs's post; and Lee was promoted to colonel, and put in command of the First Cavalry. President Lincoln signed his commission on March 16, and Lee accepted it when it was forwarded to him on March 28.

In spite of his grave concern over the country's condition, and the weight of the decision he must bring himself to make, Lee possessed the happy faculty of being able to set aside vexing problems and enjoy the present. He was delighted to play with his young grandson when Rooney and Charlotte came for a visit, and he enjoyed the company of their other house guests, Mrs. Barnes, Helen Peter, and Edward Lee Childe, his sister Mildred's talented son, who would one day write a biography of his uncle. He was amused by the antics of a new pup—"well but melancholy"—who carried on "perpetual combat with the wild cats. His face is much scarred & he begins to look like a veteran." He joked Mildred about her deficiencies in spelling:

"I noticed that you spelt Saturday with *two* ts (Satturday). One is considered enough in the Army, but perhaps the fashion is two."

He wrote brightly about the cat, Tom, "the delight of the house. I fear he will be ruined by indulgence," he told Mildred.

308

He is so petted by your sister & Miss Helen Peter. The latter wants to put him in ruffles but I object as I fear it will interfere with his handling the mice, a game he is much addicted to & plays very skillfully. Your sisters never array him in collars, believing that beauty unadorned is adorned the most, & that they would cloud his verdant eyes. Your brother comes up occasionally from Fort Washington to see him & Orton rides over very often from Washington.

On January 9, 1861, when the *Star of the West* attempted to slip into Charleston harbor with reinforcements for the garrison at Fort Sumter, she was fired on by Confederate shore batteries. On April 7, when P. G. T. Beauregard, commander of Confederate forces at Charleston, had word that another attempt would be made, he ordered all supplies of fresh food for the fort cut off. The next day, South Carolina's Governor Pickens received a report that United States ships were going to supply the garrison, and the State's fire-eaters, who had long been for dissolution, seethed, and harangued their followers, demanding a show of force at this latest example of "Northern aggression."

At dawn on April 12, the Confederates began the bombardment of Fort Sumter; and two days later, Major Robert Anderson surrendered after a gallant defense and no loss of life on either side. The next day, President Lincoln called for seventy-five thousand men and the Confederates, emboldened by their first *victory*, welcomed the opportunity of showing the world how easily one Southerner could take on three or four Yankees and soundly whip the Northern army in a war that would last no longer than three months.

The country now lost all semblance of sanity, and war was considered to have begun. The Virginia Convention went into secret session, and Lee called upon God to guide them to the right.

"War is a terrible alternative & should be the very, very last resort," he told a cousin.

On the seventeenth of April, he received a letter from General Scott, asking him to call at his office sometime during the following day. The same mail brought a note from his

Washington cousin, John Lee, telling him that Francis Preston Blair, Sr., highly trusted confidante of President Lincoln,
wanted him to call next morning at 1651 Pennsylvania Avenue, across from the White House.

Earlier in April, Lee had dined with his Cousin Cassius in
Alexandria. Among other guests were his brother, Smith, and
Samuel Phillips Lee, a grandson of Richard Henry Lee. Phillips was also a naval officer, and was married to the only
daughter of Francis Preston Blair, Sr. After the meal, as the
men drank their wine and smoked their cigars, the conversation turned to national affairs and Phillips announced his intention of keeping his commission. Smith said that he had decided
to resign and in the event of war, he facetiously warned his
cousin, he would plant a battery on the Virginia shore and
blow Phillips's ship out of the water. Phillips laughed and
rejoined:

"No you won't, for I will invite you on board to have a
drink!"

Others joined in the banter, most of them candidly stating
their present stands. Only Robert made no comment, and Phillips concluded from his silence that he had not yet settled the
question of his allegiance. This, at least, was the interpretation
he carried to his father-in-law who, knowing the administration's desire to retain Lee, went to see Lincoln, who authorized
him to "ascertain Lee's intentions and feelings." Blair also
talked with Secretary of War Simon Cameron, who directed
him to "sound" Lee out, and make a definite proposal.

On the morning of April 18, Lee rode across the Long
Bridge into Washington, passing the emergency quarters for
troops and horses set up on Dr. Lawson's lot, on up the avenues
of plane trees in new leaf, past the square dedicated to Lafayette, and over to the pale yellow stucco house with the haw-
thorn and crab-apple hedge. The greeting between Lee and
Blair was cordial, for Robert was already acquainted with his
fellow Virginian from Abdington. Blair is reported to have said
to him after they were seated:

"I come to you on the part of President Lincoln to ask
whether any inducement that he can offer will prevail on you to
take command of the Union Army."

310

"After listening to his remarks," Lee wrote later, "I declined the offer he made me, to take command of the army that was to be brought into the field, stating as candidly as I could, that, though opposed to secession and deprecating war, I could take no part in an invasion of the Southern States."

Blair soon saw that it was impossible to persuade Lee to change his mind, and concluded the interview in all friendliness. From Blair's house, Lee went directly to General Scott's office to tell him of the proposal and his refusal, and learn the nature of the old General's summons.

It was recalled by an aide that when Scott heard Lee's account of his interview with Blair, he looked "pained," and said to him:

"Lee, you have made the greatest mistake of your life; but I feared it would be so."

Scott is reported to have said next:

"There are times when every officer in the United States service should fully determine what course he will pursue and frankly declare it. No one should continue in government employ without being actively employed." And as Lee was about to go, he told him:

"If you propose to resign, it is proper that you do so at once; your present attitude is equivocal."

After his meeting with Scott, Lee went to see his brother, Smith, still on duty in Washington, and held with him a long and "earnest consultation," for Scott had presented a complication Robert had not considered before—the fact that he must not remain in the army without being "actively employed" and if he resigned, he must do so at once. He had hoped to be able to defer his decision until he saw what Virginia would do.

As he started for home, he came on a newsboy bawling the report of Virginia's secession. He bought a copy of the *Washington Star*, and read that the report was as yet unconfirmed. If it proved true, he knew what he must do, yet he clung to the slender thread of hope that his people might still reject secession at the polls.

The possibility of seventy-five thousand troops being put into the field any day, and Lee as a newly commissioned colonel being called on to go with them, should have spurred him

311

to immediate action; but he was so reluctant to make the final break that he was going to defer it until honor forced him to act.

The next day, he rode into Alexandria on business and saw the *Gazette* with confirmation of Virginia's secession. When he stepped into Leadbeater's Apothecary to pay his bill, the pharmacist naturally asked his opinion of Virginia's action.

"I must say that I am one of those dull creatures that cannot see the good of secession," he replied. These words were written in the ledger opposite the entry of Lee's payment, with the explanatory note: "Spoken by Colonel R. E. Lee when he paid his bill, April 19, 1861."

From his recent experience in Texas, Lee knew that state governments were apt to act rashly, and before the people could vote on the ordinance of secession, Virginia troops might seize Federal property or invade Washington. In the event of such an act, he would be called on to defend government property against the advances of his own people—something he could not in conscience do. Therefore, in the early morning hours of April 20, he wrote a brief note of resignation to the Secretary of War, and a longer letter to General Scott.

In spite of his repeated assertions that his course was determined, it is evident from his own words that up to the moment of writing his resignation, and even after he had sent it, he held grave doubts as to the wisdom of his decision and remained torn between two allegiances. He told General Scott that his resignation would have been presented earlier "but for the struggle it has cost me to separate myself from a service to which I have devoted the best years of my life, and all the ability I possessed." It was a deep attachment, one that, Mary wrote, had cost him "tears of blood" to tear himself from.

During the whole of that time—more than a quarter of a century [he told Scott], I have experienced nothing but kindness from my superiors and a most cordial friendship from my comrades. To no one, General, have I been so much indebted as to yourself for uniform kindness and consideration, and it has always been my ardent desire to merit your approbation. I shall carry to the grave grateful recollections of your kind consideration, and your name and fame shall always be dear to me. Save in defence of my native State, I never desire again to draw my sword. . . .

When his note to Simon Cameron and his letter to General Scott had been reread, he went into the parlor where Mary was anxiously waiting. She had listened to him pacing the floor upstairs, and thought she had heard him drop to his knees in prayer.

"Well, Mary, the question is settled. Here is my letter of resignation and a letter I have written to General Scott."

After she had read them, they were sealed and sent off to Washington, and Robert returned to his desk to write to Smith Lee. Once again his words are significant:

After the most anxious inquiry as to the correct course for me to pursue, I concluded to resign. . . . I wished to wait till the Ordinance of Secession should be acted upon by the people of Virginia; but war seems to have commenced, & I am liable at any time to be ordered on duty which I could not conscientiously perform. To save me from such a position & to prevent the necessity of resigning under orders, I had to act at once, and before I could see you again on the subject, as I had wished. I am now a private citizen, & have no other ambition than to remain at home. . . .

His sister, Ann Marshall, was to be tortured throughout the war by conflicting emotions. Her husband and son were strongly Union in sympathy. With them she would voice hopes for Federal victories, but after her brother took command of Confederate forces, she would dash all her former agreement by saying loyally:

"But after all, they can't whip Robert!"

To this devoted woman, he wrote next with fine perception:

Now that we are in a state of revolution, into which Virginia, after a long struggle has been drawn; & though I recognize no necessity for this state of things, & would have forborne & pleaded to the end for redress of grievances, real or supposed, yet in my own person I had to meet the question whether I should take part against my native State.

With all my devotion to the Union & the feeling of loyalty & duty of an American citizen, I have not been able to make up my mind to raise my hand against my relatives, my children, my home. . . . I know you will blame me; but you must think as kindly of me as you can, & believe that I have endeavoured to do what I thought right. . . .

But to Lieutenant Roger Jones, a close kin of Markie who chose to remain with the Union army, he wrote perhaps the most remarkable letter of all:

Sympathizing with you in the troubles that are pressing so heavily on our beloved country, I entirely agree with you in your notion of allegiance. I have been unable to make up my mind to raise my hand against my native State, my relatives, my children, my home. I have therefore resigned my commission. . . . I consider it useless to go into the reasons that influenced me. . . . I merely tell you what I have done that you may do better.

He adds greatly to the enigma of his position by stating that he agrees with Roger "entirely" in his "notions of allegiance," for but a few hours before, he had officially severed himself from that allegiance. "I merely tell you what I have done that you may do better," is the statement of a man still plagued with doubts; a man still possessed of a divided heart and mind.

There can be no question of Lee's resignation being anything but an act of emotion. He had condemned the fatuity of the South, and branded secession as revolution, over and over; but as soon as Virginia, "unmindful of her ancient fame and historic patriotism," became infected with the frenzy of the Cotton States and followed their lure, he ignored the dictates of logic and reason and heeded the elemental call of Virginia. How often had he admitted that her very air and the feel of her soil under his feet buoyed his spirits and brought him a comfort he could find nowhere else. For Virginia he was willing to condone secession by practicing individual secession.

His friends and neighbors waited anxiously to learn what he would do, for as one of them declared: "What he said upon subjects of national and civic interest were apt to lead opinions always." In view of succeeding events, it is evident that Lee had considerable influence in Virginia, which raises the question of why, when his state was debating the most vital issue of her history, he made no active attempt to hold her to the Union that held him so strongly. It is certain that if he had gone to the Richmond Convention and made known his conviction that secession was nothing but revolution, that there was no right in this fratricidal war, and had reminded Virginia of her role in the formation and inauguration of the Constitution, his temperate words would have been heard with respect and the soundness of his reasoning would have won the sober heads, which until April 1 had maintained the majority. It is more than a probability that he could have kept Virginia from her fateful step.

That he made no attempt to battle for his intellectual and moral convictions is evidence that those qualities which stirred earlier Lees to lead in patriotic action had been tempered by the more sober characteristics of his mother's people.

The day after he sent in his resignation was Sunday. In the morning, Lee rode with Custis and his daughters into Alexandria. Leaving the others to attend service in Christ Church, Custis went on to Washington to keep an appointment with his friend, Lunsford Lomax. With Ogle Tayloe and John Bankhead Magruder, Custis passed the morning at the Lomax home discussing with these young men their future course. His father had told Custis that he must consult his own judgment, reason, and conscience, and not be guided by his example, for it was a decision every man must make for himself upon principle. And he repeated to him what he had said to Roger Jones: if he had done wrong, let Custis do better.

After the service, Lee planned to stay in Alexandria and meet Judge John Robertson of Richmond, who had been sent by Governor Letcher to see if Lee would be willing to accept command of Virginia troops. Just as he stepped out of church, he was met by three of the Judge's companions, who had come to tell him that Robertson had been detained in Washington and would be unable to keep the appointment.

Lee stood for some time talking with the men in the shady

315

churchyard, and when they parted he went to see his Cousin Cassius and discuss with him the wisdom of accepting this command. In order to be alone, they took a walk beside the canal. It was Cassius' belief that Robert should wait until the ordinance of secession was ratified, but Robert was of the opinion that it would be impossible to delay his decision that long.

It is evident that he made up his mind quickly in this instance, for that evening when a messenger came to Arlington with a note of apology from Judge Robertson, and an invitation in the name of Governor Letcher for Lee to come to Richmond for consultation, he accepted without hesitation. He sent word to the Judge that he would meet him in Alexandria the next day, in time to take the train to the capital.

The following morning Lee, dressed in a black suit and a silk hat and wearing what he would in a lighter moment have described as a "sombre phiz," walked past the great Doric columns on Arlington's portico for the last time. His mood was far from jocular as he kissed his family and climbed into the carriage. He was oppressed by the knowledge that by severing his Northern allegiance he had stripped himself and his family of every material advantage, for he was convinced that the Southern cause had little chance for success. From his broad experience and his astute observation of men, events, and conditions north and south, he was well acquainted with the power and economic resources of the North, and the tenacity of her people. He did not look upon her as "a nation of *craven* shopkeepers" as the fanatics in the south did, but as a nation of shopkeepers able to turn out cannon, small arms, munitions, ships, clothing, blankets, and drugs, which the South was unable to do. He clung to no illusions concerning the length of the struggle—"it may last ten years," he predicted at the start. Nor did he count on foreign assistance through the power of "King Cotton," a delusion that ensnared all other Confederate leaders.

But to him, the most appalling thought of all was that Virginia would be the battleground, and Arlington, to which he once acknowledged that his affections and attachments were

316

more strongly tied than to any other place, would be in the very path of the invading army.

Yet, as the carriage left the shelter of the Arlington grove and started along the Alexandria post road, he knew there could be no turning back—he must look only ahead. There was nothing for him now but to place his trust in God and to repeat those immortal words of his father:

"Virginia is my country. Her will I obey, however lamentable the fate to which it may subject me."

APPENDIX

The Ancestry of Robert E. Lee

I.

THE exact date that Richard Lee of Stratford Langthorne, Essex County, England, the founder of the Lee family in Virginia, reached Virginia is unknown. However, in the official register of persons who passed through the Port of London on their way to America, for the years 1634–35, is an entry dated 5 May 1635, stating that Richard and Robert Lee, aged "22 yeres" and "33 yeres," respectively, sailed in the *Alexander*, Captain Burche, bound for the Barbadoes. Since Barbadoes was usually the first port of call for most Virginia colonists, and family tradition holds that the founding Richard Lee came with a brother, this record doubtless refers to Richard Lee of Stratford Langthorne, who was a son of Richard Lee of Nordley Regis in Shropshire.

In 1641, Richard Lee the Emigrant's name first appears in Virginia records with his appointment as clerk of the court in Jamestown. The next year, he was granted a thousand acres in Gloucester County. Later, he acquired other grants in Northumberland, Lancaster, Westmoreland, and Fairfax Counties, largely through his role as agent for the "Lord Proprietors" of Virginia's Northern Neck. By 1659, a visitor from England wrote that Lee had "a faire estate in Virginia" and that the "product of his Tobacco amounted to £2000 per annum."

By December, 1641, Lee had become clerk of the Council, and from 1643 to 1649 he served as Attorney General of Virginia. In 1649, he became Secretary of State; and in 1660, a member of the Council. He built his manor house at Dividing Creek, Northumberland County, and named it "Cobbs Hall."

Lee was described by his great-grandson, William Lee, as "a man of good stature, comely visage, an enterprising genius, a sound head, vigorous spirit and generous nature." Richard died at Cobbs Hall on March 1, 1663.

Of Richard's six sons, only his first, Richard, is of interest here, since this Richard's fourth son, Thomas, built Stratford

Hall, the birthplace of Robert E. Lee; and his fifth son, Henry, started the line at Lee Hall, from which Robert E. Lee descended.

This second Richard was a scholar. According to his grandson, while Richard was going to Oxford (which he entered at "a very early age") "he was so clever some great men offered to promote him to the highest dignities in the Church if his Father would let him stay in England; but this offer was refused, as the old Gentleman was determined to fix all his children in Virginia." Richard "spent almost his whole life in study, and usually wrote his notes in Greek, Hebrew, or Latin . . . so that he neither diminished nor improved his paternal estate. . . . He was of the Council in Virginia and also other offices of honour and profit, though they yielded little to him." Around 1674, Richard married Laetitia Corbin, the daughter of Henry Corbin of Middlesex County, and made his home at Matholic or Mt. Pleasant, a twenty-six-hundred-acre plantation in Westmoreland County. Richard died in 1714.

Richard the Scholar's fifth son, Henry, married Mary Bland, the daughter of Richard Bland of Cawsons. Their third son, another Henry, married Lucy Grymes, the daughter of Charles Grymes of Morattico Hall. Lucy Grymes was perhaps the "Low Land Beauty" to whom George Washington addressed "many lamenting verses."

The first child of Henry and Lucy Grymes was born in 1756, and named for his father, though he would become best known as "Light-Horse Harry."

In 1782, Light-Horse Harry Lee married his cousin, Matilda Lee, daughter of Philip Ludwell Lee of Stratford Hall. Only two of their children lived to grow up: Lucy Grymes and Henry. In 1790, Matilda died, and on June 18, 1793, Light-Horse Harry married Ann Hill Carter, daughter of Charles Carter of Shirley. On January 19, 1807, their fourth son, Robert Edward, was born.

II.

John Carter was the first of his family to leave his native Hertfordshire, England, and come to Virginia. Again there is no record of his arrival, but it is believed to have been in 1649. He lived first in Norfolk County, representing that county in the Assembly. When he received a grant of several thousand acres in Lancaster County, he moved and built his manor house there, calling it Corotoman after a tributary of the Rappahannock River. He then represented Lancaster County in the House of Burgesses.

Of interest here is John's eldest son, Robert, an ambitious man who acquired large land grants for his services as agent for the Lord Proprietors of the Northern Neck. He became the richest and most powerful man in Virginia, increasing his estate to some three hundred and thirty-three thousand acres and owning over a thousand slaves. "The amplitude of his possessions, and the opulence in which he was able to live, gained for him among his contemporaries the soubriquet of 'King'. . . ."

[King Carter] was conspicuously active with business affairs and public responsibilities. He was one of the early solicitors of funds for William and Mary College, a leading vestryman of Christ's church, a Member of the House of Burgesses, and for six years its Speaker, acting Governor of the Colony, in 1727, and for nearly or quite a quarter of a century, a member of the King's Council for Virginia. . . .

But it was through his descendants, through the female line established by his daughters, that lasting greatness came to King Carter, the great-great-grandfather of Robert E. Lee. Through their marriages, his five daughters became the antecessors of three signers of the Declaration of Independence, three governors of Virginia, and two Presidents of the United States, the Harrisons.

King Carter's eldest son, John, became Secretary of the Colony, an office he held so long "that the name 'Secretary' became permanently attached to him."

Secretary John inherited the family seat, Corotoman, and a large share of his father's property which he enlarged by marriage to Elizabeth Hill, the daughter of Col. Edward Hill and heiress to Shirley.

In 1750, Charles Carter, the son of Secretary John and Elizabeth Hill, married his cousin, Mary Carter of Cleve. Soon after her death in 1770, Charles married Ann Butler Moore of Chelsea, a great-granddaughter of Alexander Spotswood, Virginia's most able Colonial governor who led the Knights of the Golden Horseshoe across the Blue Ridge.

Ann Hill Carter, a daughter of Charles and Ann Butler Moore, married Light-Horse Harry Lee, and became, in 1807, the mother of Robert E. Lee.

Note: For an interesting and comprehensive study of the Virginia Lees and allied families, consult Ethel Armes, *Stratford Hall: The Great House of the Lees* (Richmond, 1936), both text and Supplementary Records, pp. 521–548.

NOTES & SOURCES
CONSULTED & QUOTED

THE largest and most important collection of primary source material on Robert E. Lee and his immediate family is the R. E. Lee Papers, housed in The Library of Congress. This not only contains most of Lee's letters to his wife, children, and other kindred for the years 1832 to 1870, but includes memoranda books kept while in Texas, letters to superior officers, and personal correspondence with friends and strangers over this same period. Here also are letters and papers of R. E. Lee's father; Mrs. R. E. Lee, and their seven children; cousins Edmund, Cassius, and Sally Lee; George Washington Parke Custis and his wife; Anna Maria Fitzhugh, Martha Custis Williams, and letters of interest to the Lees. Of great importance are the journals of the Lee daughters.

Careful reading of this material has brought to light many items of interest and importance, has corrected errors and misconceptions of long standing, and furnished letters and papers never before published.

The letters of Charles Carter Lee, eldest brother of R. E. Lee, to their half brother, Henry Lee, are a new and highly important collection of primary source material, in The Virginia State Library. These relate details of Robert's activities, establish such important dates as his engagement to Mary Custis, and reveal much that is new concerning Robert and the immediate family.

Another valuable primary source, released from restrictions, is the collection of thirty-two letters from R. E. Lee to his friend and assistant, Henry Kayser of St. Louis. These letters, written between July 26, 1838 and November 25, 1843, give details of Lee's work on the Mississippi River, his social activities, movements, opinions, and glimpses of family life. They also correct a number of errors.

Still another new and interesting collection of Lee family letters is the George Bolling Lee Papers, Virginia Historical Society, although the student is hampered by the restrictions that no part may be copied or quoted.

The Pierpont Morgan Library collection of R. E. Lee–Martha Custis Williams letters was another new and valuable source.

The Mackay Family Papers, Georgia Historical Society, proved most helpful in filling in details of Lee's lifelong friendship with this unusual family.

"The Friendship of Gen. R. E. Lee and Dr. Wm. Beaumont," by Ruth Musser and John C. Krantz, *Bulletin of the Institute of the History of Medicine*, vol. vi, May, 1938, was another new source, as was "Recollections of West Point in 1853," by An Officer's Wife, printed in *The Association of Graduates of the United States Military Academy, 1903, Bulletin No. 3*, which gave a charming picture of social life at the Academy and glimpses of Lee.

Note: All sources are listed in order of their use in each chapter. Unless otherwise identified, all letters are from the R. E. Lee Papers, The Library of Congress.

I. Beginnings, 1721–1813

1, pages 3–12.
Botanical data, firsthand observation and reference to Homer D. House *Wild Flowers* (New York, 1934). Ethel Armes, *Stratford Hall, the Great House of the Lees* (Richmond, 1936) is a valuable study of a house and the families who lived there; well documented. Letter of Ann Carter Lee to Elizabeth Collins Lee, 18 Feb., 1799, in Richard Bland Lee Papers, The Library of Congress. Letter of Ann Carter Lee to Elizabeth C. Lee, 11 Jan., 1807, Richard Bland Lee Papers. Details of Harry Lee's financial entanglements, found in the General Henry Lee Papers, The Library of Congress and The Virginia State Library. Reference also made to Thomas Boyd, *Light-Horse Harry Lee* (New York, 1931), an excellent study of R. E. Lee's father; also contains considerable information about his mother. Reference was made to R. E. Lee's biographical sketch of his father, written for the 1869 edition of the elder Lee's work, *Memoirs of the War in the Southern Department of the United States*. Harry Lee's correspondence with Nathanael Greene printed in this work. Harry Lee's eulogium on death of Patrick Henry, found in R. E. Lee Papers, The Library of Congress. Harry Lee to Madison, Monroe, Hamilton, and Washington, in Gen. Henry Lee Papers, both collections. Account of Harry Lee's love for Maria Farley, his rejection, and proposal to Ann Hill Carter, in Samuel Appleton Storrow's letter of 6 Sept., 1821, to his sister, quoted in Burton J. Hendrick, *The Lees of Virginia* (Boston, 1935).

2, pages 13–19.
Samuel Storrow to his sister, same date, in Hendrick. Letter of Maj. Henry Lee to Richard T. Brown, 24 Aug., 1833, for details of Harry Lee's part in Jefferson-Walker affair, found in The Library of Congress. Boyd's *Light-Horse Harry Lee* was referred to, as was R. E. Lee's sketch of his father. Lucy Grymes Carter quoted in Ethel Armes, *Stratford Hall*. John Askin Papers, vol. i, 1747–1795, ed. Milo M. Quaife, Burton Historical Records (Detroit, 1928), consulted for details of election capers of the time. Harry Lee's oration on death of Washington, The Library of Congress.

3, pages 19–26.
Gen. Henry Lee Papers, both collections, for his finances. Ethel Armes consulted. Ann Carter Lee to Elizabeth Collins Lee, 10 May, 1803, Richard Bland Lee Papers. Ann Carter Lee to Harry Lee, 6 July,

1806, Robert E. Lee Memorial Foundation, Inc., Stratford Hall. R. E. Lee sketch of his father for eulogium on Charles Carter's death. Ann Carter Lee to Elizabeth Lee, 2 Nov., 1806, Richard Bland Lee Papers.

4, pages 26–31.
Gen. Henry Lee Papers, Virginia State Library. Armes, *Stratford Hall.* Lee family tradition for story of little Robert and cherubs. Mary G. Powell, *History of Old Alexandria* (Richmond, 1928), a highly useful reference for a description of the old city and recollections of the many members of the Lee family who lived there. Mrs. Powell furnished anecdote of little Robert's visit to Mrs. Hodgson's. Sally Lee's recollections of the Stratford Lees, in R. E. Lee Papers. Photostat of R. E. Lee's will, Virginia State Library, furnished details of Harry Lee's property. Letter of William Henry Fitzhugh to John C. Calhoun, 7 Feb., 1824, for opinion of Mrs. Lee, in National Archives and Records. Joseph Packard, *Recollections of a Long Life* (Washington, 1902), recalled Mrs. Fitzhugh's beauty. Henry Lee, *A Correct Account of the Conduct of the Baltimore Mob* (Winchester, Va., 1814), Hamilton Owens, *Baltimore on the Chesapeake* (New York, 1941), and Thomas Boyd, *Light-Horse Harry Lee*, all consulted for account of the riot.

II. The Pursuit of Happiness, 1813–1846

1, pages 35–43.
Mary G. Powell, and Mary Lindsey, *Historic Homes and Landmarks of Alexandria, Virginia* (Alexandria, 1962) were referred to for descriptions of the old town, its homes and inhabitants. Description of Arlington in Mss. recollections of Agnes and Mildred Lee, R. E. Lee Papers. Joseph Packard furnished anecdote of Harry Lee and George Washington. R. E. Lee recalled his visit to Woodlands in letter of 1 Dec., 1866, to Martha Custis Williams, Huntington Library collection, printed in *"To Markie": The Letters of Robert E. Lee to Martha Custis Williams*, ed. Avery Craven (Cambridge, 1933). Harry Lee to his son Carter, in R. E. Lee sketch of his father in *Memoirs*. Ms. Harry Lee letters to Carter Lee, in Robert E. Lee Memorial Foundation, Inc. Recollections of Harry Lee's last days and death, told by Philip Nightingale to Charles C. Jones, Jr., who published them in *Reminiscences of the Last Days, Death, and Burial of General Henry Lee* (New York, 1870).

2, pages 43–53.
Miss Annie Minor remembered the correspondence between Ann Carter Lee and her sister, Elizabeth Randolph, and was quoted in D. S. Freeman, *R. E. Lee* (New York, 1934). Samuel Storrow wrote to his sister of Ann Kinloch Lee's bone disease and arm amputation. Letter of Ann Carter Lee to Carter Lee, 2 Feb., 1817, in C. C. Lee Papers, Virginia State Library. Harvard College records were searched for verification of Carter Lee's graduation in 1819. Edmund and Cassius

Lee's recollections of Robert's youth, in R. E. Lee Papers. Emily V. Mason, *Popular Life of Gen. Robert Edward Lee* (Baltimore, 1872), told of Robert's visits to Stratford and Shirley, and his own recollections of hunting. Miss Mason was a close friend of the family and obtained her information directly from them. Marietta Fauntleroy Turner's recollections of Robert Lee's looks, devotion to his mother and sisters, and his elders' commendations, quoted in Marietta Andrews, *Scraps of Paper* (New York, 1929), and in Armistead L. Long, *Memoirs of Robert E. Lee* (New York, 1886). Letters of William Fitzhugh, William Leary, Henry Lee, Jr., and Carter Lee, all to John C. Calhoun, are in National Archives and Records. Emily Mason printed in her work on R. E. Lee a letter from Benjamin Hallowell, who recalled Robert's diligence while attending his school. In his *Autobiography* (Philadelphia, 1883), Benjamin Hallowell wrote of the preparations for Lafayette's coming to Alexandria. Details of Lafayette's appearance taken from portrait painted while on U. S. tour. André Maurois, *Adrienne, The Life of the Marquise de La Fayette* (New York, 1961) furnished details of the Marquis' accident, and members of his party. Lafayette's letter to Harry Lee printed in Harry Lee's *Memoirs*. Sally Lee's recollections in R. E. Lee Papers.

3, pages 53–65.
John Crane and James F. Kieley, *West Point* (New York, 1947), an excellent pictorial work. Lewis Herman, *This is West Point* (New York, 1950), descriptive of the Point. R. Ernest Dupuy, *Where They Have Trod* (New York, 1940), gives an excellent picture of Colonel Thayer and his administration, the early instructors and courses, and life at the Academy at the time of Lee's cadetship. Sidney Forman, *West Point, A History of the United States Military Academy* (New York, 1950), another excellent work containing excerpts from cadet letters and diaries, and anecdotes of Benny Havens; also early history of the Academy. Fitzhugh Lee, *General Lee* (New York, 1894), also tells about Benny Havens. George Strong, *Cadet Life at West Point* (Boston, 1862), a valuable firsthand account. Reference was made to George W. Cullum, *Biographical Register of the Officers and Graduates of the U. S. Military Academy, West Point, New York* (New York, 1868), for information about Lee's classmates and instructors. L. Minor Blackford, *Mine Eyes Have Seen the Glory* (Cambridge, 1944), contains an account of a visit to Camp Adams in 1825. Dabney H. Maury, *Recollections of a Virginian in the Mexican, Indian, and Civil Wars* (New York, 1897), also pictures life at the Academy. Ann Carter Lee's letters in C. C. Lee Papers, which also contain Carter's songs, speeches, love sonnets, and other poems. Fitzhugh Lee, *General Lee*, for recollections of Carter Lee. The Mackay Papers, Georgia Historical Society, furnished letter of Jack Mackay to his mother. Joseph E. Johnston recalled Lee as a cadet, quoted in Long.

4, pages 65–73.
Sally Lee's recollections in R. E. Lee Papers. Ann Carter Lee's will in Will Book I, Fairfax County Courthouse, Virginia. Carter Lee to

Henry Lee, 6 August, 1829, in C. C. Lee Papers. R. E. Lee's will for details of his inheritance. Irenaeus N. Tucker, M.D., Mill Valley, Calif., for opinion of Ann Carter's probable disease. Gen. Charles Gratiot's order, National Archives. "Letters of Robert E. Lee to the Mackay Family," ed. by Frank B. Screven, Georgia Historical Society, contain notes on Lee's relations with the family. *The Letters of Robert Mackay to his Wife, 1795–1816*, ed. by W. C. Hartridge (Athens, Ga., 1949) has in the introduction and notes interesting details on the Mackay children, and Lee's interest in Margaret Mackay. Rogers W. Young, *Robert E. Lee and Fort Pulaski* (Washington, 1947), gives details of Lee's work at Cockspur Island. Ethel Armes referred to for details of Henry Lee, Jr.'s marriage to Anne McCarty; also description of Elizabeth McCarty. Samuel Storrow writes to his sister of Henry Lee's disgrace. Letter of Henry Lee to Richard T. Brown, 24 August, 1833, Library of Congress, gives details of his seduction of Elizabeth. Lucy Grymes Carter to Henry Lee, in Maj. Henry Lee Papers, Virginia State Library. Henry Wise, *Seven Decades of the Union* (Richmond, 1881), for firsthand recollection of Henry Lee and his relations with Jackson. Carter Lee to Henry Lee, 17 Nov., 1833, C. C. Lee Papers. Woodrow Wilson, *George Washington* (New York, 1881) for description of typical Virginian. Copies of R. E. Lee's letters to the Mackay family are in collection of the National Society of Colonial Dames of America in the State of Georgia, housed in the Georgia Historical Society. Jefferson Davis, "Robert E. Lee," in *The North American Review*, vol. 150, no. 398, Jan., 1890, for recollections of lowerclassman R. E. Lee. Erasmus D. Keyes, *Fifty Years Observation of Men and Events* (New York, 1884), contains a lowerclassman's recollections of Lee's looks and character.

5, pages 73–82.
Lee's advice on marriage found in John B. Hood, *Advance and Retreat* (New Orleans, 1880). Agnes and Mildred Lee's recollections of their mother in R. E. Lee Papers. Letters of Carter Lee to Henry Lee in Paris, 7 Oct., 1829; 28 March, 1830; 19 June, 1830; 1 Dec., 1830; 27 July, 1830; all in C. C. Lee Papers. Carter's letter of 1 Dec., 1830 establishes the fact that Robert was engaged in 1830 rather than 1831 as generally stated. Joseph Packard knew G. W. P. Custis well and, in his *Recollections of a Long Life*, describes his looks, personality, activities, and his method of painting. Letter of R. E. Lee to Margaret Mackay Elliott, dated "Saturday Night," in Fort Pulaski collection. R. E. Lee letter to Eliza Mackay, 13 April, 1831, also in Fort Pulaski.

6, pages 82–94.
Mildred Lee quoted in Carter Lee's letter to Henry Lee, April, 1831, in C. C. Lee Papers. Andrew Talcott's portrait furnished details of his appearance. George Cullum's *Biographical Register* consulted for Talcott's standing and his career. Letter of Mary Custis to Anna Maria Fitzhugh, and Mrs. Fitzhugh's reply, in Virginia Historical Society. Contemporary account of Martha Washington's wedding attire quoted

in Rupert Hughes, *George Washington, 1732–1762*, Vol. I (New York, 1926). Mildred Lee's description of the garden at Arlington in R. E. Lee Papers. Joseph Packard was a guest at R. E. Lee's wedding, and described the minister's appearance, as did many other guests. Marietta Turner, who was a bridesmaid, described the bride and Robert Lee in *Scraps of Paper*. A description of George Washington's punch bowl is found in A. L. Long's *Memoirs of Robert E. Lee;* here also is a recollection of the festivities at General John Mason's. R. E. Lee to Andrew Talcott, 13 July, 1831, in Virginia Historical Society. R. E. Lee to Eliza Mackay Stiles, 4 and 8 January, 1832, copy in Georgia Historical Society. Mackay family tradition concerning the tureen, related to the writer by Charles F. Mills, of Atherton, California, a great-grandson of Eliza Mackay. Letter of Mary Custis Lee to Eliza Mackay Stiles, 1 November, 1847, Georgia Historical Society. Lee–Talcott letters quoted from are in Virginia State Library. Description of R. E. Lee's visit to Smith Island, in letter of 22 May, 1832 to G. W. P. Custis, Duke University.

7, pages 94–102.
R. E. Lee to John Mackay, 23 Jan., 1833, original owned by Ralston B. Lattimore of Savannah. R. E. Lee to Andrew Talcott, 14 Jan., 1837, Virginia Historical Society. R. E. Lee to Mary C. Lee, 27 Nov., 1833, Huntington Library (printed *Huntington Library Quarterly* vol. 15, May, 1952, under title: "To Molly: Five Early Letters of Robert E. Lee to his Wife," by Norma B. Cuthbert). Letter of Lee to Talcott, 23 May, 1834, Virginia State Library, corrects error that Lee's head was a "massive" 23½ inches. Lee to Mackay, 28 Nov., 1833; 26 June, 1834, 18 Oct., 1834; all from copies in Georgia Historical Society. Information concerning appointment of William H. C. Bartlett to West Point professorship, supplied writer by Joseph M. O'Donnell, Chief, Archives and History Division, U. S. Military Academy.

8, pages 102–111.
Description of Mrs. Ulrich's boardinghouse in Long; also source of Lee and Mr. Schneider. Long quoted John Macomb for anecdote of Lee and Macomb riding double. Reference to Charles Dickens, *American Notes for General Circulation* (London, 1842), for description of Washington. Minnie Kendall Lowther, *Mount Vernon, Its Children, Its Romances, Its Allied Families, and Mansions* (New York, 1930), gives history of Arlington. Packard, who was a frequent guest at Arlington, described it. Lee to Mackay, 18 Feb., 1835, copy in Georgia Historical Society. Lee to George W. Cullum, 18 May, 1837, R. E. Lee Papers, Va. State Library. Lee to Talcott, 10 Feb., 1835, Virginia Historical Society. Lee to Harriet Talcott, 16 May, 1835, Va. State Library. Lee to Mary C. Lee, June, 1835, Huntington Library. Irenaeus N. Tucker, M.D., established fact that Mary Lee's illness was not a "pelvic infection." Mary C. Lee to Eliza Mackay Stiles, 23 Jan., 1836, Robert E. Lee Memorial Foundation, Inc. Stella M. Drumm, "Robert E. Lee and the Improvement of the Mississippi River," *Missouri Historical Quar-*

terly, vol. 6, 1929, and "Glimpses of the Past," also by Stella Drumm, *Missouri Historical Quarterly*, vol. 3, no. 1–2, for information about Gen. Gratiot, the threat to St. Louis, and Lee's work.

9, pages 111–127.
Lee to Talcott, 15 Aug., 1837, Virginia State Library. Thirty-two Mss. letters of R. E. Lee to Henry Kayser of St. Louis, written between 26 July, 1838 and 25 Nov., 1843, released from restrictions, give valuable details of Lee's work, activities, thoughts, and movements. These and the twenty-eight letters printed in "Glimpses of the Past" (see above) are the chief source for this period. These are in the Missouri Historical Society, St. Louis. Reference was made to John F. Darby, *Personal Recollections* (St. Louis, 1880), for firsthand recollections of Lee. Lee to Mackay, 27 June, 1838, and 19 Oct., 1838, copy in Georgia Historical Society. Lee to Mrs. Harriet Hackley, 7 Aug., 1838, Virginia Historical Society. R. E. Lee to Cassius F. Lee, 20 Aug., 1838 in Fitzhugh Lee, *General Lee*. Lee to Talcott, 3 Oct., 1838, Library of Congress. Samuel E. Chamberlain, *My Confession* (New York, 1956), gives an account of a trip on the Pennsylvania Canal and the overland journey from St. Louis. Both Lee's letters and those of his wife to Mrs. G. W. P. Custis establish the fact that only the two boys accompanied them to St. Louis, and that the artist who painted their portraits was William E. West. Information on Bernard Moore Carter found in Va. State Library. Reference made to Musser and Krantz, "The Friendship of Gen. R. E. Lee and Dr. Wm. Beaumont," *Bulletin of the Institute of Medicine*, Vol. VI, May, 1938. Ethan Allen Hitchcock, *Fifty Years in Camp and Field* (New York, 1909) recalled Lee in St. Louis; this is a valuable work by a brilliant scholar. Lee's official reports to Gen. Gratiot printed in Drumm, "Robert E. Lee and the Improvement of the Mississippi."

10, pages 128–145.
Lee to Mackay, Nov., 1839, Georgia Historical Society. Edward Carter Turner notes, Virginia State Library. Lee to Joseph E. Johnston, 26 July, 1839 in Long. Lee to Mackay, 8 Nov., 1839, Georgia Historical Society. Anecdote of Lee and his son Custis, in J. William Jones, *Personal Reminiscences, Anecdotes and Letters of General Robert E. Lee* (New York, 1874). Reference to Darby. Lee to his wife, 4 Sept., 1840, in Fitzhugh Lee. Lee to Mackay, 18 March, 1845, from original letter owned by Karl Derst of Savannah, deposited in Georgia Historical Society. Lee to Martha Custis Williams, Huntington Library. Recollections of Arlington in Agnes Lee's Mss. journal, R. E. Lee Papers. Anecdote of "Dart" and "Spec" in Robert E. Lee, Jr., *Recollections and Letters of General Lee* (New York, 1904). Henry J. Hunt quoted in Long.

11, pages 145–153.
Reference to Erasmus Keyes, *Fifty Years Observation. . . .* Description of General Scott in Fitzhugh Lee. Huntington Library collection of

R. E. Lee–"Markie" letters. Lee–Mackay, 18 March, 1849, Georgia Historical Society. Lee's letters to Henry Kayser prove that Rooney's fingers did not adhere as has been stated. Nathaniel W. Stephenson, *Texas and the Mexican War* (Yale, 1921), consulted.

III. The Halls of the Montezumas

1, pages 157–173.
Photostat of Lee's will, Virginia State Library. Lee to Gen. William N. Pendleton, concerning war, in "Personal Recollections of General Lee," by W. N. Pendleton, *Southern Magazine*, XV, 1874. Hitchcock, and U. S. Grant, *Personal Memoirs* (New York, 1887), consulted. Eliza Stiles to Catherine Mackay, Mackay Family Papers, Georgia Historical Society. J. W. Jones, *Reminiscences*. Reference to Chamberlain, who was with Wool. Lee's travels through Texas followed through his letters home. Winfield Scott, *Memoirs*, vol. 2 (New York, 1851). Jacob J. Oswandel, *Notes on the Mexican War, 1846–47–48* (Phila., 1885), gives excellent firsthand account of stop in Tampico, arrival at Vera Cruz, etc. Hitchcock was on the *Champion* and recorded the trip in his journal. Raphael Semmes, *Service Afloat and Ashore During the Mexican War* (Cincinnati, 1851), described Worth's landing. Dabney H. Maury was also present and recalled the plague of fleas. Hitchcock told of Lee's narrow escape from death. Jones told story of Lee and the old naval captain. Lee to his brother, Smith, undated letter in Fitzhugh Lee. Henry J. Hunt quoted in Long.

Note: The name of the settlement where Lee passed the night with the Monods has been a puzzle ever since J. William Jones transcribed it as "Sarassa," a settlement that never existed. A careful study of Lee's holographic letters disclosed that he made an identical capital *L* and *S*. His lower-case *v, s, r,* and *c* are also confusing. Thus, the letter written to his wife on the steamer from New Orleans to Port Lavaca seems to be headed, "On board Steamboat from New Orleans to Saracca." Considering this idiosyncrasy when reading the letter in which he names the place where the Monods lived, it reads "Lavacca." Since Lavaca once existed on the road to Gonzales, which Lee took, this must be the place, an extra *c* having crept in through haste.

As to Lee's horses: Creole is the only mare he mentions by name in existing letters from the Mexican War. She was his favorite, and he rode her in preference to the mare bought in the New Orleans market. This mare is positively identified as Grace Darling by comparing Lee's description of her in a letter to his wife, 13 Sept., 1846, with Robert E. Lee, Jr.'s description in his *Recollections*. Some misfortune befell Creole near the end or even after the war, for Grace only was brought home, giving rise to the belief that she was his sole warhorse.

2, pages 173–185.
Lee's letters home are the source for his part in battles. Semmes remembered Fitzwalter. Lee's day under a log found in Long. Both Semmes and Hitchcock, who kept journals, are the main sources be-

sides Lee's letters. Reports of Shields, Twiggs, Smith, Riley, and Scott, in Scott, vol. 2. Lee to his son, Curtis, 25 April, 1847, in J. William Jones, *Life and Letters of Robert Edward Lee, Soldier and Man* (Washington, 1906), hereafter cited as *Life*. Maury described Twiggs. Lee's crossing of the pedregal found in Jones, *Reminiscences*, Long, Hitchcock, and Scott. Hunt's recollections of the crossing quoted in Long. Joseph Johnston quoted in Long. Lee to his brother, Smith, undated, in Jones, *Life*.

3, pages 185–194.
Again, Semmes, Hitchcock, Scott, and Long. Joseph Packard told the story of Lee and the old Mexican. The trip to El Desierto was in Hitchcock's journal. Hunt quoted in Long. Lee to Markie, Huntington Library.

IV. Mounting Frustration, 1848–1855

1, pages 197–213.
R. E. Lee, Jr. for anecdotes of his father's home-coming. Lee to Smith Lee, 30 June, 1848, in R. E. Lee, Jr. This work is also a source for Lee's relations with his children. Mildred Lee's recollections of her father, R. E. Lee Papers. Lee to Mary Mercer, 9 Dec., 1848, Mercer Papers, Georgia Historical Society. Hugh Mercer to his wife, 20 March, 1849, same collection. Lee to Markie, Huntington Library. Packard quoted Lee's comment on his room in the Baltimore house. Lee and the Cuban junta in Jefferson Davis, "Robert E. Lee," *North American Review*, Jan., 1890. Lee to Jerome Bonaparte, 19 Sept., 1850, Washington and Lee University archives. Sally Nelson Robbins in *Gen. Robert Edward Lee, Soldier, Citizen and Patriot*, ed. by A. R. Brock (Richmond, 1897), for several stories of Lee and his wife. Lee to his son, Custis, 28 Dec., 1851, in Jones, *Life*. Lee to Gen. Joseph Totten, 28 May, 1852, in Henry A. White, *Robert E. Lee and the Southern Confederacy* (New York, 1897). Lee to Jerome Bonaparte, 31 July, 1852, Washington and Lee University.

2, pages 213–233.
Agnes Lee's Mss. journal. Lee to Markie, 25 May, 1854, Huntington. Information on Lee's revision of rules, and improvements while Superintendent, supplied by Joseph M. O'Donnell, who also sent a copy of Mrs. Theophile D'Ormieulx's "Recollections of West Point in 1853." R. E. Lee, Jr. for recollections. Dabney Maury is source for social life at the Point; Mrs. D'Ormieulx described Kemble's dinners and the concert season. Agnes Lee's journal was an invaluable source for family activities. Erasmus Keyes described the discussions at Mr. Kemble's. Maury recalled Jackson's visit. Jefferson Davis was consulted. Lee's remarks to Elizabeth Lindsay Lomax in her journal, published under the title, *Leaves from an Old Washington Diary* (New York, 1943). Lee to Jerome Bonaparte, 12 March, 1853, Washington and Lee. Lee to Markie, 14 March, 1855, Huntington. Lee's letterbooks while

Supt., in R. E. Lee Papers, Virginia State Library and R. E. Lee Papers, Library of Congress. Hesketh Pearson, *The Man Whistler* (New York, 1952), for Whistler's career at the Academy.

Note: Elizabeth Lindsay Lomax in her journal entry for Wednesday, Dec. 20, 1854, establishes the fact that Lee was regarded, while Superintendent, as a "marble model" by his cadets, thus correcting the error that he was considered a "marble model" when a cadet. Mrs. Lomax's source is a letter from her son, Lunsford L. Lomax, then a cadet at West Point.

V. Exile to the "Desert of Dulness," 1855–1857

1, pages 237–253.
Agnes Lee's journal is the source for the trip home. Lee to his wife, 1 July, 1855, in Jones, *Life*. Henry Adams, *The Education of Henry Adams* (Boston, 1908), for recollections of his classmate, Rooney Lee. "The Diary of Eliza (Mrs. Albert Sidney) Johnston," ed. by Charles P. Roland and Richard C. Robbins in *The Southwestern Historical Quarterly*, April, 1957. Maury was also stationed in this part of Texas, and described it fully. Lee to Eliza Mackay Stiles, 24 May, 1856, collection of Charles F. Mills, deposited in Robert E. Lee Memorial Foundation, Inc. Lee to Eliza Stiles, 14 Aug., 1856, copy in Ga. Historical.

2, pages 253–266.
Family letters in R. E. Lee Papers, the chief source for this chapter. Lee to Jerome Bonaparte, 28 Feb., 1855, Washington and Lee. Lee to Albert Sidney Johnston, 25 Oct., 1857, the Mrs. Mason Barret Collection, Manuscript Division, Tulane University, New Orleans. Lee to Anna Maria Fitzhugh, 8 Sept., 1857, Duke University. Agnes Lee's journal for account of Mr. Custis' death.

VI. Storm Clouds Gather, 1857–1861

1, pages 269–284.
Lee to Anna Maria Fitzhugh, 22 Nov., 1857, Duke University. Agnes Lee's journal for description of the drawing room. Will of G. W. P. Custis, Alexandria County Records. Lee to Custis Lee, 17 Jan., 1858, Duke. Mr. Schneider quoted in Long. Lee to Custis Lee, 15 Feb., 1858, Duke. Lee to Custis Lee, 17 March, 1858, Duke. Letter of James M. Porter to President Buchanan, 25 May, 1858, National Archives. Lee–Talcott letter, 21 Dec., 1858, Va. Historical. Excerpts from *New York Tribune*, 24 June, 1859. Erasmus Keyes for recollections of Lee at this time.

Note: Lee's letter of 20 Nov., 1858, to Anna Maria Fitzhugh (Duke), corrects the error that he refused Mrs. Fitzhugh's check for one thousand dollars. Custis Lee was stationed in San Francisco at this time, at work on the building of Fort Point guarding the Golden Gate. His letters home disclose that he and several fellow officers shared a house built by Col.

de Russy; it was surrounded by a flower garden on a slope commanding a view of the harbor and the Golden Gate.

2, pages 284–299.
Sources for the John Brown Raid: Lee's letters to his wife; Oswald Garrison Villard, *John Brown* (Boston, 1911); Samuel V. Leech, *The Raid of John Brown at Harper's Ferry, As I Saw It* (New York, 1909); Henry Kyd Douglas, *I Rode With Stonewall* (Chapel Hill, 1940). Recollections of Brown, Emerson, Alcott, Thoreau, Gerrit Smith, and others, in Franklin Benjamin Sanborn, *Recollections of Seventy Years* (Boston, 1907). Lee to Anna Maria Fitzhugh, 9 Feb., 1860, Duke. Lee to his son, Rooney, 2 June, 1860, Jones, *Reminiscences*. Lee to Custis Lee, 16 April, 1860, Duke. John S. Ford, *Rip Ford's Texas*, ed. by Stephen B. Oates (Austin, 1963). Lee's opinion of Johnston's promotion, in letter of 16 April to Custis Lee, Duke. Lee to Custis Lee, 24 Nov., 1860, Duke.

3, pages 299–307.
Lee to Custis Lee, 14 Dec., 1860, Duke. Charles Anderson, *Texas Before and on the Eve of the Rebellion* (Cincinnati, 1884). Keyes consulted for Scott's opinions. Lee to Markie, 22 Jan., 1861 Huntington Library. R. W. Johnson, *A Soldier's Recollections in Peace and War* (New York, 1887). George B. Cosby, "With General Lee in the Old Army," *Confederate Veteran*, April, 1905. Mrs. Caroline Darrow, in *Battles and Leaders of the Civil War* (New York, 1887–88). Emily Mason for recollections of Lee's admirers.

4, pages 307–317.
Erasmus Keyes. Lee to Reverdy Johnson, 25 Feb., 1868, R. E. Lee, Jr. John S. Mosby, *Memoirs* (Boston, 1917), for Lee's comment on Twiggs, and opinion of Virginia's secession. Sara Rice Pryor, *Reminiscences of Peace and War* (New York, 1904), for recollections of fire-eaters. William E. Brooks, *Lee of Virginia* (Indianapolis, 1932), gives an account of Lee dining with Cassius Lee. Lee to Simon Cameron, 20 April, 1861, to General Scott, to his sister Ann, and brother Smith, all in R. E. Lee, Jr. Lee to Lt. Roger Jones, 20 April, 1861, The Library of Congress. Constance Cary Harrison, *Recollections Grave and Gay* (Richmond, 1911), recalled how Lee's neighbors patterned their actions after his. Elizabeth L. Lomax. Letters of John Robertson to Gov. John Letcher, Va. State Library.

BIBLIOGRAPHY

Primary Sources, Manuscript

C. C. Lee Papers, Virginia State Library, Richmond

Custis and Lee Family Papers, The Library of Congress

George Bolling Lee Papers, Virginia Historical Society, Richmond

Gen. Henry Lee Papers, Virginia State Library and The Lirary of Congress

Maj. Henry Lee Papers, The Library of Congress

Richard Bland Lee Papers, The Library of Congress

Robert E. Lee Memorial Foundation, Inc., Stratford Hall, Virginia

R. E. Lee Papers, personal and official wartime letters, Duke University Library

R. E. Lee Papers, The Library of Congress

R. E. Lee Papers, personal and official wartime correspondence, Virginia Historical Society

R. E. Lee Papers, personal and official wartime letters, Virginia State Library

R. E. Lee Memoranda Books (3), kept while in U. S. Army, The Library of Congress

R. E. Lee–Jerome Bonaparte Family Letters, McCormick Library, Washington and Lee University

R. E. Lee–Henry Kayser Letters, Missouri Historical Society, St. Louis

R. E. Lee–Mackay Family Letters (typed copies), Georgia Historical Society, Savannah

R. E. Lee–Mackay Family Letters (originals), Fort Pulaski National Monument, Savannah Beach, Ga.

R. E. Lee–John Mackay Letters (originals) owned by Ralston B. Lattimore and Karl Derst of Savannah, and Lucius S. Ruder of Clearwater, Fla.

R. E. Lee–Mercer Family Letters, Mercer Papers, Georgia Historical Society

R. E. Lee–Albert Sidney Johnston Letters: Mrs. Mason Barret Collection, Tulane University Library

R. E. Lee–Talcott Family Letters, Talcott Papers, Virginia Historical Society

R. E. Lee–Talcott Family Letters, Virginia State Library

R. E. Lee Letters to Andrew Talcott (photostat copies), Virginia State Library

R. E. Lee's Letterbook while Superintendent of West Point (photostat copy), Virginia State Library

R. E. Lee's Will (photostat copy), Virginia State Library

Letters of William Henry Fitzhugh, William B. Leary, C. C. Lee, and Henry Lee, Jr., to John C. Calhoun, National Archives and Records

* * *

Primary Sources, Printed

Craven, Avery, editor, *"To Markie": The Letters of Robert E. Lee to Martha Custis Williams* (Cambridge, 1933). Originals are in the Huntington Library, San Marino, California.

Cuthbert, Norma B., "To Molly: Five Early Letters from Robert E. Lee to his Wife", *Huntington Library Quarterly*, Vol. 15; May, 1952. Originals are in the Huntington Library.

Drumm, Stella M., "Glimpses of the Past," twenty-eight letters of R. E. Lee to Henry Kayser, *Missouri Historical Society Publication*, Vol. III, Nos. 1–2, Jan.–Feb., 1936. Originals are in the Missouri Historical Society.

Jones, J. William, *Life and Letters of Robert Edward Lee, Soldier and Man* (Washington, 1906), contains a few R. E. Lee letters not to be found in manuscript.

Jones, J. William, *Personal Reminiscences, Anecdotes and Letters of General Robert E. Lee* (New York, 1874), also contains a few R. E. Lee letters not to be found in manuscript.

Lee, Fitzhugh, *General Lee* (New York, 1894), contains some R. E. Lee letters not to be found in manuscript.

Lee, Henry, *Memoirs of the War in the Southern Department of the United States* (New York, 1869), contains letters from "Light-Horse Harry" Lee to his son, Carter.

Lee, Robert E., Jr., *Recollections and Letters of General Robert E. Lee* (New York, 1924), also contains a few R. E. Lee letters not to be found in manuscript.

* * *

Printed Material Relating to R. E. Lee's Ancestry, Youth, and Career up to the Civil War

Adams, Henry, *The Education of Henry Adams* (Boston, 1908)

Anderson, Charles, *Texas Before and on the Eve of the Rebellion* (Cincinnati, 1884)

Andrews, Marietta, *Scraps of Paper* (New York, 1929)

Armes, Ethel, *Stratford Hall, the Great House of the Lees* (Richmond, 1936)

Armes, Ethel, "Stratford on the Potomac" (pamphlet, Richmond, 1928)

Blackford, L. Minor, *Mine Eyes Have Seen the Glory* (Cambridge, 1944)

Boyd, Thomas, *Light-Horse Harry Lee* (New York, 1931)

Brock, A. R., editor, *General Robert Edward Lee, Soldier, Citizen and Patriot* (Richmond, 1897)

Cosby, George B., "With General Lee in the Old Army," *Confederate Veteran*, April, 1905

Crane, John, and Kieley, James F., *West Point* (New York, 1947)

Cullum, George W., *Biographical Register of the Officers and Graduates of the United States Military Academy, West Point, New York* (New York, 1868)

Darby, John F., *Personal Recollections* (St. Louis, 1880)

Darrow, Mrs. Caroline, in *Battles and Leaders of the Civil War* (New York, 1887–88)

D'Ormieulx, Mrs. Theophile, "Recollections of West Point in 1853," in *The Association of Graduates of the United States Military Academy, 1903, Bulletin No. 3*

Drumm, Stella M., "Robert E. Lee and the Improvement of the Mississippi River," *Missouri Historical Quarterly*, Vol. 6, 1929

Dupuy, R. Ernest, *Where They Have Trod* (New York, 1940)

Fithian, Philip, *The Journal and Letters of Philip Fithian* (Williamsburg, 1957)

Ford, John S., *Rip Ford's Texas*, edited by Stephen B. Oates (Austin, 1963)

Ford, Paul Leicester, *The True George Washington* (Philadelphia, 1896)

Forman, Sidney, *West Point, A History of the United States Military Academy* (New York, 1950)

Hallowell, Benjamin, *Autobiography of Benjamin Hallowell* (Philadelphia, 1883)

Harrison, Constance Cary, *Recollections Grave and Gay* (Richmond, 1911)

Hartridge, W. C., *The Letters of Robert Mackay to his Wife, 1795–1816* (Athens, Ga., 1949)

Hendrick, Burton J., *The Lees of Virginia* (Boston, 1935)

Herman, Lewis, *This is West Point* (New York, 1950)

Hitchcock, Ethan Allen, *Fifty Years in Camp and Field* (N. Y., 1909)

Hood, John B., *Advance and Retreat* (New Orleans, 1880)

Hughes, Rupert, *George Washington, 1732–1762*, Vol. I (New York, 1926)

Hunt, Henry J., quoted in Armistead L. Long, *Memoirs of Robert E. Lee* (New York, 1880)

Jett, Dora Chin, *In Tidewater Virginia* (Richmond, 1924)

Johnson, R. W., *A Soldier's Recollections in Peace and War* (New York, 1887)

Johnston, Eliza, "The Diary of Eliza (Mrs. Albert Sidney) Johnston," edited by Charles P. Roland and Richard C. Robbins, *Southwestern Historical Quarterly*, April, 1957

Johnston, Joseph E., quoted in Armistead L. Long (q.v.)

Jones, Charles C., Jr., *Reminiscences of the Last Days, Death, and Burial of Gen. Henry Lee* (New York, 1870)

Jones, Katherine M., *The Plantation South* (Indianapolis, 1957)

Keyes, Erasmus D., *Fifty Years Observation of Men and Events* (New York, 1884)

Kimball, Marie G., *Jefferson, the Road to Glory, 1743–1776* (New York, 1943)

Lee, Cazenove G., Jr., *Lee Chronicle* (New York, 1957)

Lee, Edmund J., *Lee of Virginia, 1642–1892* (Philadelphia, 1895)

Lee, Fitzhugh, *General Lee* (New York, 1894)

Lee, Gen. Henry, *A Correct Account of the Conduct of the Baltimore Mob* (Winchester, Va., 1814)

Lee, Lucinda, *Journal of a Young Lady of Virginia*, edited by Emily Mason (Baltimore, 1871)

Lee, Robert E., Jr., *Recollections and Letters of General Robert E. Lee* (New York, 1924)

Leech, Samuel V., *The Raid of John Brown at Harper's Ferry As I Saw It* (New York, 1909)

Lindsey, Mary, *Historic Homes and Landmarks of Alexandria, Virginia* (Alexandria, 1962)

Lomax, Elizabeth Lindsay, *Leaves from an Old Washington Diary* (New York, 1943)

Long, Armistead L., *Memoirs of Robert E. Lee* (New York, 1886)

Lowther, Minnie Kendall, *Mount Vernon, Its Children, Its Romances, Its Allied Families, and Mansions* (New York, 1930)

Mason, Emily V., *Popular Life of General Robert Edward Lee* (Baltimore, 1872)

Maurois, André, *Adrienne, The Life of the Marquise de La Fayette* (New York, 1961)

Maury, Dabney H., *Recollections of a Virginian in the Mexican, Indian, and Civil Wars* (New York, 1897)

Musser, Ruth, and Krantz, John C., Jr., "The Friendship of Gen. R. E. Lee and Dr. Wm. Beaumont," *Bulletin of the Institute of the History of Medicine*, Vol. VI, May, 1938

Oswandel, Jacob J., *Notes on the Mexican War, 1846–47–48* (Philadelphia, 1885)

Owens, Hamilton, *Baltimore on the Chesapeake* (New York, 1949)

Packard, Joseph, *Recollections of a Long Life* (Washington, 1902)

Pearson, Hesketh, *The Man Whistler* (New York, 1952)

Powell, Mary G., *History of Old Alexandria* (Richmond, 1928)

Rhodes, Charles Dudley, *Robert E. Lee the West Pointer* (Richmond, 1932)

Sanborn, Franklin Benjamin, *Recollections of Seventy Years* (Boston, 1907)

Scott, Winfield, *Memoirs*, Vol. II (New York, 1864)

Semmes, Raphael, *Service Afloat and Ashore During the Mexican War* (Cincinnati, 1851)

Shackelford, George Green, "Stratford Hall, Architectural Mystery," *Northern Neck of Virginia Historical Magazine*, December, 1958

Stephenson, Nathaniel W., *Texas and the Mexican War* (Yale, 1921)

Strong, George, *Cadet Life at West Point* (Boston, 1862)

Turner, Marietta Fauntleroy, quoted in Marietta Andrews, *Scraps of Paper* (New York, 1929)

Villard, Oswald Garrison, *John Brown* (Boston, 1911)

Wilson, Woodrow, *George Washington* (New York, 1929)

Wise, Henry A., *Seven Decades of the Union* (Richmond, 1881)

Ann Carter Lee

THE MOTHER OF ROBERT E. LEE